The Death of Empedocles

SUNY series in Contemporary Continental Philosophy

Dennis J. Schmidt, editor

The Death of Empedocles

A Mourning-Play

FRIEDRICH HÖLDERLIN

A New Translation of the Three Versions and the Related Theoretical Essays with Introduction, Notes, and an Analysis by

DAVID FARRELL KRELL

SUNY PRESS

Published by
State University of New York Press, Albany

For information, contact State University of New York Press, Albany, NY
www.sunypress.edu

Production by Marilyn P. Semerad
Marketing by Fran Keneston

Library of Congress Cataloging-in-Publication Data

Hölderlin, Friedrich, 1770–1843.
[Tod des Empedokles. English]
The death of Empedocles : a mourning-play / Friedrich Hölderlin ; translated with introduction, notes, and analysis by David Farrell Krell.
p. cm. — (SUNY series in contemporary continental philosophy)
Published: Leipzig : Insel-Verlag, 1910.
Includes bibliographical references.
978-0-7914-7647-5 (alk. paper) 978-0-7914-7648-2 (pbk. : alk. paper)
1. Empedocles—Drama. I. Title.
PT2359.H2A6613 2009
832'.6—dc22

2008019674

10 9 8 7 6 5 4 3 2 1

Contents

Preface

FRIEDRICH HÖLDERLIN'S *Der Tod des Empedokles,* composed in three incomplete versions from 1798 to 1799, but never published during the poet's lifetime, is a masterpiece in fragments, a masterpiece in ruins. Hölderlin was an accomplished poet before he began his tragedy or "mourning-play," *Trauerspiel,*[1] and he had already made a name for himself through the publication of his novel *Hyperion;* yet in the three fragments or ruins of his play we have the monuments that mark the progress to his mature style. In the third version, abandoned as the year 1799 came to an end, we hear the prosody of Hölderlin's great odes and hymns, the poems written from 1800 until about 1806 for which he is best known and loved, among them, "As on a Holiday," "Bread and Wine," "The Rhine," "Celebration of Peace," Mnemosyne," and "Patmos." Portions of the Empedocles tragedy point toward Hölderlin's extraordinary translations of Sophocles' *Oedipus the Tyrant* and *Antigone,* published in 1804.

This is the first published English translation of all three versions of *The Death of Empedocles* as far as I am aware.[2] Between the second and third versions

1. The German word *Trauerspiel* may most often be taken as synonymous with *Tragödie.* Yet because mourning, *die Trauer,* constitutes such an important motif for Hölderlin's work, from his early novel *Hyperion,* through his drama *Der Tod des Empedokles,* to his late hymns, it seems best to use the English word *tragedy* only when its German cognate appears. I accept the risk of offending the English/American ear with the more literal *mourning-play* for *Trauerspiel.*

2. Michael Hamburger included translations of versions two and three in his dual-language anthology, Friedrich Hölderlin, *Poems and Fragments,* 3d ed. (London: Anvil Press Poetry, 1994), first published in 1966. See 283–386. I have also benefited from Friedrich Hölderlin, *Œuvres,* ed. Philippe Jaccottet (Paris: Pléiade, 1967), 465–559, 656–68, with translations by R. Rovini and D. Naville.

in the present volume appear four essays toward a theory of the tragic, essays in which Hölderlin tries to clarify for himself the meaning of his own "mourning-play."[3] Those essays are as difficult to read and understand as the versions of the play themselves are pellucid. Together the essays and the play demonstrate that Hölderlin was not only one of the greatest poets of the German language but also one of Germany's greatest thinkers. His importance to German Idealism and Romanticism—and, well beyond these movements or periods, to thinkers and poets of the twentieth and twenty-first centuries—is doubtless guaranteed by the late hymns. Yet *The Death of Empedocles* is a work that stands on its own, surviving on its own merits. It is not to slight the late hymns that Max Kommerell asserts that the third version of *The Death of Empedocles,* "in the sustained pace of its language," contains "the very best of Hölderlin" (MK 348). Whoever reads the mourning-play, along with the essays surrounding it, especially "The Basis of Empedocles" and "The Fatherland in Decline," will find both the play and the essays uncannily relevant for our own place and time. It will be clear to readers that the translation and explanatory notes treat Hölderlin as both poet and philosopher, a man of magnificent language and astonishing thoughts. His language stands alongside that of Goethe; his thoughts alongside those of Schelling and Hegel. Better said, both his writing and his thinking are incomparable, and one may here with justice paraphrase D. H. Lawrence on Whitman: ahead of Hölderlin—no one.

A word about the oddities of punctuation and the gaps in the text: everywhere in Hölderlin's manuscript are signs of haste, and no presentation of the text or translation of it should try too hard to hide them. Hölderlin often neglects to punctuate his lines, as though his thoughts will brook no pause; at the end of a line he very often skips punctuation altogether. In addition, when readers see gaps in the text of this English translation, they should assume that the gaps occur in Hölderlin's holograph—although nothing will substitute for checking with the various German editions. Jochen Schmidt's edition for the Deutscher Klassiker Verlag, which serves as my principal German text, resists the temptation to constitute a finalized text, and that resistance requires that the text have lacunae in it. Finally, because Hölderlin's syntax becomes increasingly complex, involuted, convoluted, and distended as the versions proceed, often stretching over many lines of verse, a line-by-line translation has very often been impossible: English wails when forced to go without its subjects, verbs, and objects all lined up in a row. I have tried above all to capture the sense of Hölderlin's lines, and also to respect his meters and

3. See Friedrich Hölderlin, *Essays and Letters on Theory,* trans. Thomas Pfau (Albany: State University of New York Press, 1988). "The Ground for Empedocles," in the present volume called "The Basis of Empedocles," appears at 50–61; "Becoming in Dissolution," in the present volume called "The Fatherland in Decline," at 96–100.

his prosody generally; I have also tried to follow him when he stretches the possibilities of the German language, drawing language itself, as it were, into uncanny territory. If, as Hölderlin once wrote, "translation is wholesome gymnastics for language" (CHV 2:538), it is also an occasion for pulled hamstrings and wrenched joints.

The four principal editions used for the translation, listed here chronologically, and with their code cited on the left, are:

StA 4 — Volume 4, Parts I and II *(Der Tod des Empedokles)* of *Hölderlin Sämtliche Werke,* ed. Friedrich Beissner. Stuttgart: Verlag W. Kohlhammer, 1952ff. This is the Große Stuttgarter Hölderlin-Ausgabe, most often referred to in the literature as StA. In 1969 Friedrich Beissner and Jochen Schmidt prepared for the Insel Verlag of Frankfurt a handy two-volume edition titled *Hölderlin Werke und Briefe.* I have not used that edition for the present volume. However, in 1973 Beissner presented the fruits of his many years of editorial labors in a small and inexpensive paperback edition of *Der Tod des Empedokles,* published by Philipp Reclam, Junior, of Stuttgart. I refer to this popular and very useful edition simply as Reclam, with page number.

FHA 12, 13, 14 — Volumes 12 and 13 (*Der Tod des Empedokles*) and volume 14 (*Entwürfe zur Poetik*) of *Friedrich Hölderlin Sämtliche Werke,* ed. Dietrich E. Sattler. Basel and Frankfurt: Stroemfeld and Roter Stern, 1988. This is the Frankfurter Historisch-Kritische Ausgabe, most often referred to in the literature as FHA. This important edition presents not only Sattler's reconstructed text (in my page references always the *later* of the two page references) but also a variorum text, that is, a text that shows each of Hölderlin's many emendations to his text—his crossings-out, his entering of parentheses and brackets, his underlinings, his replacement texts, marginal jottings, and so on. Immensely complicated, the variorum text is nevertheless invaluable for readers who have no access to the handwritten originals.

CHV 1, 2, 3 — Volumes 1, 2, and 3 of *Friedrich Hölderlin Sämtliche Werke und Briefe,* ed. Michael Knaupp. Munich: Carl Hanser Verlag, 1992.

DKV 1, 2, 3 — Volumes 1, 2, and 3 of *Friedrich Hölderlin Sämtliche Werke und Briefe in drei Bänden,* ed. Jochen Schmidt. Frankfurt: Deutscher Klassiker Verlag, 1994.

I have used the most recent edition of Hölderlin's works, Dietrich Sattler's chronological edition (the Bremer Ausgabe, published in 2004 by Luchterhand Literaturverlag, Munich, and indicated in this volume by the code BA 7, 8, with page number), primarily when questions of precise chronology arose. Readers should note the affiliation of Beissner-Schmidt and Sattler-Knaupp, such that the four major editions often fall naturally into two pairs, as it were: Friedrich Beissner and Jochen Schmidt worked together on the StA, as did Dietrich Sattler and Michael Knaupp on the FHA. One is therefore not surprised to find that Beissner and Schmidt tend to agree, as do Sattler and Knaupp. In the following notes, readers may assume that DKV and StA are in substantial agreement, and that FHA and CHV agree in their opposition to DKV and StA, unless otherwise noted. In not a few instances, however, each editor disagrees with all the others, and at those moments readers will realize how bedeviling Hölderlin's holograph can be. A look at the facsimile pages toward the end of the book will confirm their worst fears.

I have used DKV as the principal basis of my translation inasmuch as Schmidt excludes very little of Hölderlin's holograph text. Schmidt complains that Sattler's reconstructed text in FHA reduces the play by some 10% of its lines. Sattler would of course reply that he is simply following Hölderlin's instruction to delete a passage that no longer satisfied its author. However, because it is difficult to know precisely what Hölderlin would have deleted altogether from his three versions, as opposed to what he would have altered only slightly, I have decided to err on the side of inclusion rather than exclusion. Only in rare instances have I altered the text of DKV, and here once again it was for reasons of inclusiveness. In those cases I have preserved the *numbering* of the lines in DKV (so that readers will have at least one German text to which they can readily refer) by giving the added lines letters (a, b, c, and so forth) instead of numbers.

Finally, I have throughout referred to the following works of primary and secondary literature by code:

DK — Hermann Diels and Walther Kranz, ed., *Die Fragmente der Vorsokratiker,* 3 vols. 6th ed. Zürich: Weidmann, 1951. Cited by fragment number. For Empedocles, see 1:276–375.

JV 1–4 — Christoph Jamme and Frank Völkel, ed., *Hölderlin und der Deutsche Idealismus,* 4 vols. "Specula 3." Stuttgart-Bad Canstatt: Frommann-Holzboog, 2003. The bulk of the material on *The Death of Empedocles* appears in vol. 3.

KSA 1–15 Friedrich Nietzsche, *Kritische Studienausgabe der Werke,* 15 vols., ed. Giorgio Colli and Mazzino Montinari. Berlin and Munich: Walter de Gruyter and Deutscher Taschenbuch Verlag, 1980.

LV David Farrell Krell, *Lunar Voices: Of Tragedy, Poetry, Fiction, and Thought.* Chicago: University of Chicago Press, 1995. Chapters 1 and 2 focus on *The Death of Empedocles.*

MK Max Kommerell, *Geist und Buchstabe der Dichtung: Goethe, Schiller, Kleist, Hölderlin,* 6th ed. Frankfurt: V. Klostermann, 1991 [originally published in 1940].

RA *The Recalcitrant Art: Diotima's Letters to Hölderlin and Related Missives,* trans. and ed. Douglas F. Kenney and Sabine Menner-Bettscheid. Albany: State University of New York Press, 2000.

RC Roberto Calasso, *The Marriage of Cadmus and Harmony,* trans. Tim Parks. New York: Borzoi Books, Alfred A. Knopf, 1991.

TA David Farrell Krell, *The Tragic Absolute: German Idealism and the Languishing of God.* Bloomington: Indiana University Press, 2005. Chapters 7–11 deal with Hölderlin and tragedy generally, chapter 7 focusing on *The Death of Empedocles.* Much of the material in the Notes and the Analysis at the end of the present volume derive from TA.

I would like to thank Marianne Schütz and Christa Haaser of the Hölderlin-Archiv for their generous help and support, particularly for providing the facsimile pages of Hölderlin's manuscript, and Professor Lore Hühn and Dr. Roswitha Doerendahl of the Universität Freiburg for providing the Stephanus edition of Empedocles' fragments. Dennis J. Schmidt, the editor of the series in which this book appears, has been a loyal and enthusiastic fan of Hölderlin and a staunch ally of my own efforts—my deep thanks to him. My gratitude to the College of Liberal Arts and Sciences at DePaul University, and its deans, Richard J. Meister, Michael Mezey, and Charles Suchar, for their generous support of my work over the years. Thanks to my sponsoring editor at SUNY Press, Jane Bunker, to the book's production editor, Marilyn Semerad, and to David Matthew Krell, who designed both book and cover, demonstrating that the former may be judged on the basis of the latter. This is Hölderlin's book, and perhaps Empedocles' book as well, but not mine; if the book were mine I would dedicate it to my friend Ulrich Halfmann, who helped expertly with many passages and lent, as always, generous support.

To those skeptics who wonder why I have here attempted the impossible—a verse translation of Hölderlin—and who may feel that I am not fit for the task, that I have not got a poetic bone in my body, I insist that there is such a bone in me, just one, a thigh bone wrapped in endless folds of prosaic fat. I have burned that bone in joyous desperation on the altar of Hölderlin's Empedocles. As both Schelling and Hölderlin understood, there is a certain freedom in attempting the impossible.

St. Ulrich and Chicago D. F. K.

Friedrich Hölderlin: A Brief Chronology

1770 Hölderlin is born on March 20, the first son of Heinrich Friedrich Hölderlin and Johanna Christiana Heyn, in the village of Lauffen on the Neckar, in the Swabian state of Württemberg.

1772 On July 5 Hölderlin's father dies of a brain stroke at age thirty-six. On August 15 Hölderlin's sister Heinrike ("Rike") is born.

1774 Hölderlin's mother marries Johann Christian Gock, a wine merchant and diligent burgher (soon to be mayor) in nearby Nürtingen. The four-year-old Hölderlin moves with his mother and grandmother to that town. Hölderlin loves his stepfather deeply; he later refers to Gock as his "second father."

1776 Hölderlin begins to attend school in Nürtingen and also has private lessons at home. His stepbrother Carl, to whom Hölderlin will be quite close, is born on October 29.

1779 On March 13, Hölderlin's "second father," having contracted pneumonia after helping to repair flood damage in Nürtingen, dies at age thirty. The nine-year-old boy is overwhelmed by what he later calls his "tendency to mourning." He is raised now by his mother and grandmother. His mother, who plans for her son to become a country pastor, will never relinquish her control over his inheritance. Hölderlin will never achieve financial independence; Hölderlin's mother will never make of him a minister.

1780 Hölderlin begins music lessons, first on the piano, then the flute. The boy shows considerable musical talent. He attends the Latin School and continues to have private lessons. Over the next several years he studies religion—his mother is a devout Pietist—Hebrew, Latin and Greek, Dialectic and Rhetoric. He is respected and well liked by his classmates. He reads travel-adventure books with enthusiasm, developing a special love for Greek antiquity. Neither of these tastes will change. At the Latin school, in 1782, he prevents the older boys from picking on a young newcomer—F. W. J. Schelling, who is five years younger than Hölderlin. Years later, Hölderlin, Schelling, and Hegel will be roommates at the University of Tübingen.

1784 The fourteen-year-old pupil begins to attend the boarding school at Denkendorf, not far from Nürtingen. He has a scholarship that is contingent on his studying theology for purposes of ordination. The school uniform is a monk's habit, the daily routine organized around four prayer hours. The pupils' reading is strictly censored. Hölderlin writes his first serious poems. He does well in his schoolwork, is sixth in a class of twenty-nine, and works hard at the Pietist discipline of "examination of conscience." On November 12 he writes the poem "M. G." ("To My God"). Pietism pervades his early work, and yet the next November he composes "The Night," the last stanza of which reads: "Thus he rests, except that the slave of vice / Is punished by the fearful, thundering voice of conscience, / And anxiety unto death tosses and turns on the soft bedding / Where voluptuosity itself wields the lash."

1786 In October Hölderlin transfers to the boarding school at Maulbronn Monastery. He falls desperately in love with the administrator's daughter, Louise Nast, who is two years older than he. She returns his affection and he becomes more desperate. A poem dedicated to his family, "My People," contains these lines on the death of his stepfather: "When on the terrifyingly silent deathbed / My mother, senseless, lay in the dust—/ Woe! I see it there before me, the scene of wailing, / Eternally hovering before me, the darkling day of death."

1787 In spring he waxes enthusiastic over the dramas of Schiller and the poems of pseudo-Ossian, whom he compares to Homer. In April he tells his mother he will never be a pastor; she is not pleased. He returns to Maulbronn, which he dubs "Cloister Crucifix." The romance with Louise Nast continues; he befriends Louise's cousin, Immanuel Nast. By the summer he has developed symptoms of (psychosomatic?) tuberculosis. His "Lament," dedicated to Louise Nast under the code name "Stella," begins: "Stella! ah! we suffer greatly! if only we were in the grave—/ Come! come cool grave! take us both!" His study of Greek literature intensifies; he is becoming expert in the Alcaic and Asclepiadic verse forms, writes the poem "On a Meadow" in hexameters. Here for the first time he contrasts nature, which is life-giving and nurturing, to a noisome and absurd civilization—with its "walls of squalor, / Nooks and crannies of deception." Later, in his novel *Hyperion,* he will contrast "The School of Nature" with "The School of Destiny."

1788 In September he discusses with his mother the possibility of marrying Louise. His mother concurs: every country pastor needs a wife. On October 21 he enters the *Tübinger Stift,* or Protestant seminary, at the university and meets G. W. F. Hegel. Their curriculum: two years of *philosophicum,* three of *theologicum.* Like all the rest of the gifted students, these two hate the narrow-minded sectarianism and conservatism of their school. Only one of their teachers dares to peek into Kant. Within two years the students will own all three *Critiques* but will have to hide them under the boulders that line the banks of the Neckar River. In the winter of 1788–1789 Hölderlin joins a poetry circle at Tübingen with Christian Neuffer and Rudolf Magenau. "And if the rabble, a thousand strong, droned their warnings and tried / To throttle us with their thousand tongues of priestly rage / Banning all that's new, we'd laugh them off the stage, / We sons of the daughter of god, Justice."

1789 In an exchange of letters during the spring, Hölderlin and Louise Nast agree to break their engagement. The reasons: Hölderlin's lack of income and position, his moodiness and tendency to brood, his "unconquerable melancholy" caused by "frustrated ambition." Ambition to be what? Anything but a country pastor, preferably a poet. His mother disapproves of the breakup; Hölderlin begs her for money. That summer he studies flute with the virtuoso Friedrich Dulon. On July 14, the Bastille is stormed; weeks later "The Declaration of the Rights of Man" is proclaimed; on November 14 the local duke clamps down on the restive students of the *Stift.* Hölderlin knocks the hat off a schoolteacher's head out in the street because the teacher refuses to greet him properly; Hölderlin is sentenced to six hours in the university prison (doesn't every university need one?) for conduct unbecoming a student. Hölderlin hopes now to study law. "I can stand it no longer! eternally on and on / The little boy's steps, the steps of a prisoner, / Tiny steps already measured out for him / To take each day, I can stand it no longer!" And this remarkable fragment: "I hate me! it is a nauseating thing, / The heart of humankind, weak and puerile and proud, / As friendly as Tobias's puppy dog, / Then once again so spiteful! Get me out of here! I hate me!"

1790 As the duke tightens his hold on the *Stift,* the students pursue their own education outside the walls in enthusiastic meetings and wine parties. Two of Hölderlin's major research papers are produced: "History of the Fine Arts among the Greeks" and "Parallels between Solomon's Sayings and Hesiod's 'Works and Days.'" Hölderlin earns a master's degree. On October 20, the fifteen-year-old *Wunderkind* Schelling joins Hölderlin and Hegel in the *Stift.* That summer Hölderlin meets the university chancellor's delightfully spoiled daughter; he writes poems to her code name, "Lyda." He reads Leibniz, is inspired by idealism, but also F. H. Jacobi's book *On the Doctrine of Spinoza,* which explicates Spinoza's philosophy of *nature.* Jacobi's book occasions the most exciting debate in the German universities over the next few years—the debate on monotheism versus pantheism and atheism.

1791 Into Hegel's album Hölderlin writes the pantheistic motto, Ἓν καὶ πᾶν, "One and All." That spring he hikes through the Swiss Alps south of Zürich down to Lake Lucerne; on his way home he travels through that part of Swabia in the Black Forest where the Danube has its source(s). Many years later, his poems "At the Source of the Danube" and "The Ister" will recall this journey. In June he learns of Louise Nast's engagement to another, vows he will never woo again, and refers once more to his excessive "ambition." In September Hölderlin's first published poems appear, his Tübingen hymns "To the Muse," "To Freedom," "To the Goddess of Harmony," and "My Recuperation." The first review of his poems, written by an established poet, is perhaps his best: "Hölderlin's muse is an earnest muse." In November he undertakes an enthusiastic study of astronomy, which will play an important role in his poems; he is particularly entranced by Kepler's discovery of the elliptical orbit. The ellipse, having as its two foci the opposing schools of nature and destiny, will be an important metaphor in his novel *Hyperion.*

1792 Having reached age twenty-two he reflects on what it means to come of age, both in his own life (between his mother's wishes for him and his own ambition to be a poet) and in his homeland, which is struggling (as Kant had urged in his essay "What Is Enlightenment?") to reach the age of majority, to earn the right to speak out of its own mouth: *Mündigkeit.* By spring he completes his hymns "To Friendship," "To Freedom" (second version), "To Love," and "To the Genius of Youth." He begins now to sketch the novel, *Hyperion,* eventually published in two volumes, on which he will work until 1798. September in Paris is bloody, as the leaders of the Gironde fall to the guillotine; the French Revolution begins to devour its children and doubts spread among the democratically minded across Europe.

1793 In September Hölderlin meets Isaak von Sinclair, a politically engaged Jacobin; they will be lifelong friends. In the fall he visits Schiller, who becomes an important father figure to him; the famous poet arranges a tutorship for Hölderlin now that his studies in Tübingen are drawing to a close. In December Hölderlin leaves Tübingen and the chancellor's daughter behind, traveling eastward through Bamberg and Coburg to Waltershausen.

1794 In Waltershausen he tutors Fritz von Kalb, for the first six months successfully; then the boy becomes an adolescent. In April Hölderlin studies Schiller's *Anmut und Würde* ("Charm and Dignity," or "Grace and Worthiness") with enthusiasm. Fritz's mother, Charlotte von Kalb, is full of praise for the new tutor. From her, in late summer, he borrows Fichte's *Wissenschaftslehre,* or "Doctrine of Science." In early September he sends his *Fragment of Hyperion* to Schiller for publication. In October he contemplates writing a tragedy on the death of Socrates, "in accord with the ideals of Greek drama." He wants to advance beyond the Kantian boundaries (preeminently beyond Kant's proscription of "intellectual intuition") and to reestablish the rights of the Platonic εἶδος. In early November he visits Schiller in Jena, who at that moment is conversing with a stranger; the stranger ignores Hölderlin, all the while thumbing through Hölderlin's *Fragment of Hyperion.* That evening Hölderlin learns that the stranger was Goethe. When he finally does engage in a conversation with Goethe at the beginning of the following year, Hölderlin finds him "calm, with genuine majesty in his gaze, and also love. . . . One often feels that one is talking with a generous father." Hölderlin attends Fichte's lectures, visits Schiller often, meets the beautiful Sophie Mereau, and befriends the philosopher Immanuel Niethammer. Charlotte von Kalb's companion, Wilhelmine Marianne Kirms, becomes a close, perhaps intimate, friend.

1795 Hölderlin is still in Jena with his difficult charge, Fritz von Kalb. The boy's mother, Charlotte, and Hölderlin agree, however, that the tutorship should end. She continues to help Hölderlin financially during the next few months. Hölderlin borrows from Schiller's shelves Goethe's *Wilhelm Meister's Apprentice Years,* a book that moves him deeply. He works on *Hyperion.* Exchanges of letters and meetings with Schelling and Hegel lead to a common endeavor, the brief but comprehensive philosophical manifesto we now call "The Oldest Program toward a System in German Idealism." In March the publisher Cotta agrees to publish Hölderlin's *Hyperion,* although he requests that it be shortened. At the end of May Hölderlin suddenly leaves Jena for Nürtingen, perhaps because of the pressure he feels in the company of "greats" such as Schiller, Goethe, and Fichte. He writes in letters of his "fruitless efforts" in Jena, which "distracted and weakened him"; to Schiller he admits that in Jena "the boy had to deal with men"; he compares himself to a seedling that has to be protected from the brilliant sunlight of a Schiller (CHV 2:614, 655, 665). In July and December he has further philosophical conversations with Schelling, the fruit of which, to repeat, we can glimpse in the *Systemprogramm.* A friend arranges a new tutorship for Hölderlin, this time on the estate ("White Hart") of the wealthy Frankfurt banker Jacob Gontard.

1796 Hölderlin is enthusiastic about his new tutorship, expressing admiration for young Henry Gontard—and for Henry's mother, Susette. By October Hölderlin's support of the French Revolution has dwindled; he finds himself to be "in a less Revolutionary condition." In November he refuses yet another pastorate his mother would like to arrange for him; for the first time he confesses to her in some detail his decision to be a poet.

1797 Hölderlin's friend Hegel becomes a tutor in Frankfurt. The two see one another often. "I love calm intellectual human beings, because they provide such good orientation." In mid-April the first volume of *Hyperion* is published. The first copy goes to Susette Gontard, the "Diotima" of Hölderlin's novel and his poems. By summer Schiller's judgment of his young protégé has become harsher; Goethe remains puzzled by Hölderlin's intensity. Both find him and his poetry excessively earnest. Nor are things going well at White Hart; Hölderlin feels himself torn between love and hate, *zerrissen von Liebe und Hass.* Little wonder that during these months he becomes intrigued with the ancient Greek thinker of Love and Strife, Empedocles of Acragas. In August he composes a detailed plan for a tragic drama on that figure (see chapter 1, below). Actual work on the play will not begin until some fifteen or sixteen months later.

1798 February-March: much Revolutionary activity in southwestern Germany, where there are hopes to create an Alemannic Republic. Because of difficulties at White Hart and his cool reception by the "greats," Hölderlin's mood is bleak. "There are so few who believe in me." At the end of September Hölderlin is fired from his job at White Hart. Susette does not, perhaps cannot, save him. He moves to the nearby town of Bad Homburg, where his friend Sinclair resides. Here, on December 11, according to Dietrich Sattler (BA 7:7), or, according to other editors (and more likely to be the case), somewhat earlier, during October, Hölderlin begins to write *The Death of Empedocles* (see chapter 2). In mid-December he reads Diogenes Laertius's account of Empedocles.

1799 During this year, and until May 1800, he and Susette meet clandestinely; they cautiously exchange letters. These are months in which the thinker remains torn between love and strife. His poem "Achilles" treats not the cocky warrior but the forlorn lover of Briseïs who weeps on the seashore and begs his mother, Thetis, to comfort him. Hölderlin comments: "Son of gods! oh, if only I were like you, I could with intimate voice / Sing the lament of my secret suffering to one of the celestial ones." A letter to his mother in January defends the profession of poetry, "the most innocent of all occupations." Sometime in April, Hölderlin stops working on the first version of *The Death of Empedocles.* Between April and mid-June he begins a second version (see chapter 3). He plans to start a literary journal, to be called *Iduna,* to secure financial independence not only for himself but perhaps also for Susette; the publisher insists that the "greats" be involved in the project, however, and so it soon fails. During the last ten days of July he prepares a neat copy of the first 145 lines of the second version of *The Death of Empedocles* for possible publication in his proposed journal. In October and November he writes several essays on tragic poetry, trying to work out the problems of his own Empedocles play (see chapter 4). In December, after drawing up a new plan, he composes the third and final version of the mourning-play, it too incomplete (see chapters 5 and 6). A final "Sketch toward the Continuation of the Third Version" (chapter 7) is never fully elaborated; as far as we know, no more work is done on the mourning-play. In November he meets with Susette, giving her a copy of the recently published second volume of *Hyperion.* It bears the inscription, "To whom else but you?"

1800 May 8: the final secret meeting with Susette Gontard. In June Hölderlin visits friends in Stuttgart. They are struck by his evident ill health. In spite of severe health problems and depression, many poems—now in the mature style—are composed, among them, "To the Germans," "Rousseau," "Diotima: You Are Silent," "Menon's Lament for Diotima," "Stuttgart," "Bread and Wine," and "The Archipelago."

1801 In January Hölderlin begins a new tutorship in Hauptwil, Switzerland. On February 9, the Peace of Lunéville is concluded; Hölderlin composes *Friedensfeier,* "Celebration of Peace." In mid-April he terminates the tutorship; in early December he agrees to a new tutorship—in Bordeaux. He walks to Bordeaux, via Strasbourg, Lyon, and across the Auvergne. "Now I have to fear whether in the end things will go for me as they did for Tantalus of old, who became more of the gods than he could digest." Poems include "Half of Life," "At the Source of the Danube," "The Rhine," and "Germania."

1802 Hölderlin arrives during the last days of January at the residence of Consul Meyer in Bordeaux. He works on his translations of Sophocles' *Oedipus the Tyrant* and *Antigone.* In mid-May he resigns his post and walks back home, this time via Paris. At the beginning of July he arrives at Stuttgart, disheveled and disoriented; there he receives the news that Susette Gontard died two weeks earlier. Hölderlin returns to his mother's house in Nürtingen. There he works on the poem "Patmos." His mother complains that he takes too many long walks alone.

1803 Hölderlin polishes and refines his translations of Sophocles. He meets with Schelling for the last time. Both Schelling and Hegel distance themselves from their "mentally disturbed" friend.

1804 April: *The Mourning-Plays of Sophocles* is published. On June 19 Hölderlin leaves his mother's house and returns to Bad Homburg with Sinclair.

1805 February 26: Sinclair is arrested for his political views. Hölderlin too is arrested, but then released "by reason of insanity." July 9: Sinclair too is released—for lack of evidence. Hölderlin puts the final touches on his translations of Pindar's odes. Sinclair complains that Hölderlin is playing the piano "night and day."

1806 September 11: Hölderlin is committed—the most famous patient in the newly opened Autenrieth Clinic in Tübingen. He is forced to wear Professor Autenrieth's new invention—a face mask designed to prevent patients from screaming or speaking.

1807 In early May he is released into the custody of Ernst Zimmer, a Tübingen carpenter. He dwells in a tower on the Neckar, today called the "*Hölderlin Turm.*" Music is his principal occupation, although he continues to write verses. Ernst Zimmer, his wife Elisabetha, and their daughter Christiane care for the poet until his death decades later.

1843 June 7, 11 P.M.: Hölderlin dies.

General Introduction

ONE COULD ALMOST BEGIN a book on this period of Hölderlin's life (roughly, from 1797 to 1800) by saying that it was the best of times and the worst of times. That would be true in terms of both European politics, dominated by the bloody aftermath of the French Revolution, and Hölderlin's private life, his life of love, dominated by strife. Those best and worst of times in Europe and in the life of the twenty-seven-year-old struggling poet encroached on one another.

On April 16, 1797, the French army crossed the Rhine, bringing with it not only cannon fire but also the ideas that had long been firing the hopes of all young Germans. In Hölderlin's home state, Swabian Württemberg, as in the more northerly cities of Coblenz, Bonn, and Cologne, opposition to the local autocratic princes became more outspoken. Hölderlin and his circle of friends could dare to hope, and to hope realistically, that the *ancien régime* in Germany too was about to collapse. The Imperial Peace Conference in Rastatt, focusing on the conflict between Revolution and Regression (also called the Restoration), met from 1797 to 1799; Hölderlin attended the conference for ten days at the end of November 1798. There his friend Isaak von Sinclair, who was the representative of the relatively enlightened Duke of Hessen-Homburg, introduced the poet to the leaders of the south German reform movement. Although they all rejected the Reign of Terror, their revolutionary fervor and republicanism remained intense. Hölderlin returned to Frankfurt excited once again by the conflict between the forces of political and religious tyranny and the spirit of Rousseau in the German lands.

Once back home at White Hart, the estate of Susette and Jacob Gontard, where he was tutoring their son Henry, Hölderlin worked hard on the first draft of a project he had sketched out more than a year earlier and begun in earnest some weeks before. It was a tragedy or "mourning-play," *Trauerspiel,* on the death of the early Greek thinker, poet, rhetorician, and physician, Empedocles of Acragas.

Hölderlin had been tutoring young Henry Gontard since the beginning of 1796.[4] During the evenings he performed chamber music—he was a good pianist and an excellent flutist—with Henry's mother Susette and her friends. Within six months of his employment on the estate he confessed his admiration of Susette Gontard in a letter to Christian Neuffer:

> I am in a new world. I used to think I had insight into what is beautiful and good, but now when I see what all my knowledge amounts to, I have to laugh. Dear friend! there is a being in the world on whom my spirit can and will dwell for millennia, and still it will live to see how puerile all our thinking and comprehending turn out to be in the face of nature. Loveliness and loftiness, tranquillity and vitality, spirit and heart and form—they are all blessedly one in this one being. You can believe me when I say how rare it is to have even a premonition of such a thing, and then again how much more difficult it is to find it in this world. You know, of course, how I was—how completely I had disabused myself of every form of familiarity; you know how I lived without faith, how austere I was with my own heart, and therefore how wretched. Could I have become what I am now, as happy as an eagle, had this one, this very one, not appeared and transformed a life that had become pointless to me, rejuvenating, encouraging, cheering, and glorifying it in her vernal light? I have moments when all my old troubles seem entirely foolish to me, as incomprehensible to me as they would be to children.
>
> It is actually often impossible for me to think the thoughts of mortals when she is in front of me. That is why so little can be said of her.
>
> Perhaps I will be able to capture here and there in a felicitous line an aspect of her being, and then nothing would be held back from you.
>
> Yet it would have to be an hour without disturbances of any kind, an hour of celebration, were I to write of her. (CHV 2:624–25; RA 14–16)

"In the face of nature . . . spirit and heart and form . . . vernal light . . . celebration." Hölderlin's colleague on the estate, Marie Rätzer, the tutor of the three Gontard girls, confided her worries to a friend: "Frau Gontard is with Hölderlin all morning up in the pavilion and in her private quarters; the children leave them alone there, while the servants and housemaids are all over the house at their chores; and if *he* were to come home and notice it, things

4. The following materials on Hölderlin and the Gontards are taken from the factual fiction *The Recalcitrant Art: Diotima's Letters to Hölderlin and Related Missives*, ed. Douglas F. Kenney and Sabine Menner-Bettscheid (Albany: State University of New York Press, 2000), 14–34, which cites the relevant sources. In what follows I refer to this book by the code RA, with page numbers.

wouldn't go well." *He,* of course, was Hölderlin's employer, Jacob Gontard, a wealthy Frankfurt banker—and Susette's husband.

By early July 1796 the French Republic's Sambre-Maas army was advancing on Frankfurt. Jacob Gontard remained in the city under siege in order to protect his interests, while Hölderlin left with Susette and the children to greater safety in Kassel. By this time Hölderlin was composing magnificent poems to "Diotima," the priestess of love in Plato's *Symposium,* the principal female character in his novel *Hyperion,* and now the principal female human being in his life. Near Kassel, in the resort town of Bad Driburg, Hölderlin and Susette Gontard presumably confessed their love for one another. When the siege of Frankfurt ended, the family and the tutor returned to White Hart. Tensions within the Gontard household grew during the coming months, the town gossips tsk-tsked, and Hölderlin exulted—once again in a letter to Neuffer, this one dated February 16, 1797:

> Since we last wrote to one another I have circumnavigated the globe of joy. I would gladly have told you how things are with me had I been able to stand still for an instant, had I been given a chance to look back. The wave swept me forward. My entire being was so absorbed in life that it didn't have a moment to think about itself.
>
> And it is still that way! I am still entirely happy, as I was in the first moment. It is a friendship—eternal, joyful, and holy—with a being who somehow strayed into this poor, dispirited, disorderly century of ours. My sense of beauty is now secure from all disruption. For all eternity it will be oriented by this bust of the Madonna. My intellect attends her school and my riven inmost heart daily finds repose and good cheer in her all-sufficient peace. . . . My heart is full of desire. . . . I can readily imagine, dear brother, that you crave to hear me say more about my happiness, and in greater detail. Yet I dare not! I have often enough wept and berated our world, where the best thing in it cannot be named on a piece of paper one will send to a friend. I shall enclose a poem to her written toward the end of last winter.
>
> . . . I only wish I could show you her image, for then I wouldn't need any more words! She is beautiful, as angels are beautiful. A tender, intelligent face, with all of heaven's charms! Oh! I could gaze on her for a thousand years, forgetting myself and everything else: how inexhaustibly rich is the silent, undemanding soul in this image! Majesty and tenderness, gaiety and seriousness, sweet playfulness and lofty mournfulness, life and spirit—all this is united in her, in her it all becomes one divine whole. . . . "Great joy and great sorrow come to those whom the gods love." It is no art to sail a brook. Yet when our heart and destiny plunge to the seabed and then soar to the sky—that is a pilot's education. (CHV 2:649–51; RA 22–26)

The pilot's education became quite stressful during the summer of 1797. By that time the gossip was in full blossom and *he* had become aware of it. When Marie Rätzer married at White Hart on July 10, Jacob Gontard saw to it that Hölderlin was not invited to the ceremony even though Hölderlin and Marie were friends. On that same day Hölderlin wrote once again to his friend Neuffer: "I am torn asunder by love and hate" (CHV 2:658; RA 28). It was as though the two cosmic forces of which the ancient Empedocles had spoken, Φιλία καὶ Νεῖκος, Love and Strife, had invaded and possessed Hölderlin. Worse, it was as though he could never simply choose love over strife, inasmuch as strife seemed to be at home in the very sphere of love. It also seemed that those whom the gods love reap both great joy and great sorrow as their reward—again, beyond their own power to choose and the desire of others to lay blame.

The final test in Hölderlin's sentimental education came during a terrible scene at the Gontard household in the last week of September 1798. Jacob, with Susette at his side, excoriated and expelled the tutor. Susette felt forced to concur—it would be best for him to go. Hölderlin, wounded perhaps more by Susette's complicity, or apparent complacency, or abject surrender, than by Jacob's sarcasm and self-righteousness, but wounded perhaps most of all by his own indecisiveness and passivity, fled Frankfurt. With the help of his friend Sinclair he found sanctuary in nearby Bad Homburg vor der Höhe. Now that the second volume of *Hyperion* was all but complete, he planned to begin work on his mourning-play, *The Death of Empedocles,* interrupting that plan in November for the trip to the Rastatt conference.

We know that Hölderlin's first stay at Bad Homburg (1798–1800, the years of *The Death of Empedocles*) was one of retreat, rest, and recuperation—without rest, however, and without recuperation. Suddenly he was deprived of his job, of young Henry, his devoted pupil, and of "Diotima" herself. Now there were only letters to and from her, exchanged during brief clandestine meetings. Hölderlin tried to lose himself in his work. The work in question would no longer be a discourse on "aesthetic ideas," no longer a commentary on Plato's *Phaedrus,* nor would it involve Fichte's lectures at Jena.[5] Hölderlin's ambivalent

5. On "aesthetic ideas" and Plato's *Phaedrus,* see the letter to Christian Neuffer dated October 10, 1794 (CHV 2:550–51). On Hölderlin's reaction to Fichte's lectures in Jena, see Hölderlin's letters to Neuffer and to Hegel dated November 1794 and January 26, 1795, respectively (CHV 2:553 and 568–69). In the first, Hölderlin calls Fichte "the soul of Jena," and he affirms that he has "never encountered another man with such depth and energy of spirit." Several months later, to Hegel, his judgment is more critical:

> At the beginning I strongly suspected him of dogmatism, and if I may be so bold, he really was standing on the cusp of it, and perhaps still is—he

attitude toward theoretical work in general, that is, his suspicion that philosophical speculation distracted him from his genuine poetic work, had been expressed years earlier in a letter to Schiller dated September 4, 1795:

> My displeasure with myself and with what surrounds me has driven me into abstraction. I am trying to develop for myself the idea of an infinite progression in philosophy. I am trying to show that the relentless demand that must be made on every system, namely, the unification of subject and object in an absolute—in an ego or in whatever one wants to call it—is possible, albeit aesthetically, in intellectual intuition. It is possible theoretically only through an infinite approximation, as in the squaring of the circle. I am thus trying to show that in order to realize a system of thought an immortality is necessary—every bit as necessary as it is for a system of action. I believe that I can prove in this way to what extent the skeptics are right, and to what extent not. (CHV 2:595–96; TA 218–19)

The ambivalence he felt toward theoretical systems and the "infinite progression" of philosophy is most strongly manifested in a letter to Immanuel Niethammer dated February 24, 1796: Hölderlin confessed that philosophy was "once again" his "only preoccupation," as he read Kant and Reinhold and heard Fichte reverberating in his brain: "Dame Philosophy is a tyrant, and it is more the case that I put up with her compelling me than that I voluntarily submit to it" (CHV 2:614). On Christmas Eve of 1798 he expressed his doubts about the possible progress of philosophy to Isaak von Sinclair. The letter is important because it begins with a reference to Diogenes Laertius's *Lives and Opinions of the Eminent Philosophers.* Hölderlin was reading Book VIII of Diogenes, on Empedocles, and was already at work on his mourning-play. The letter goes on to invoke the tragedy of philosophical systems as such:

---

wants to take as his point of departure the *factum* of consciousness for all *theory*. Many of his assertions show this; that *factum* is just as certain and as conspicuously transcendent for him as it was for prior metaphysicians who wanted to transcend the existence of the world—his absolute ego (= Spinoza's substance) contains all reality; it is everything, and outside of it is nothing; thus there is no object for this absolute ego, for otherwise all of reality would not be in it; a consciousness without an object, however, is unthinkable, and if I myself am this object, then I am necessarily limited, if only by my being in time, hence not absolute; thus in the absolute ego no consciousness is thinkable; as absolute ego I possess no consciousness, and to the extent that I have no consciousness I am (for myself) nothing, so that the absolute ego is (for me) nothing.

> These days I have been reading in your Diogenes Laertius. I've also experienced there something that I've encountered before, namely, the fact that the transiency and mutability of human thoughts and systems strike me as well-nigh more tragic than the destinies one usually calls the only real destinies. And I believe this is natural, for if a human being in his or her ownmost and freest activity—in autonomous thought itself—depends on foreign influences, if even in such thought he or she is modified in some way by circumstance and climate, which has been shown irrefutably to be the case, where then does the human being rule supreme? It is also a good thing—indeed, it is the first condition of all life and all organization—that in heaven and on earth no force rules monarchically. Absolute monarchy cancels itself out everywhere, for it is without object; strictly speaking, there never was such a monarchy. Everything that *is* interpenetrates as soon as it becomes active. . . . (CHV 2:722–23; RA 36–38)

Finally, in a long letter dated November 12, 1798, addressed to Christian Neuffer, Hölderlin expressed both his ambivalence toward philosophy and his doubts about his own talents as a poet in the context of the mourning-play on Empedocles:

> I have been here [in Bad Homburg] for a bit more than a month. I've been working quietly on my mourning-play in the company of Sinclair, enjoying the beautiful autumn days. I was so torn apart by suffering that I have to thank the gods for the good fortune of this calm. . . . What most occupies my thoughts and my senses now is vitality in poetry [*das Lebendige in der Poesie*]. I feel so deeply how far removed I am from achieving it, even though my entire soul is wrestling to attain it, and this realization overcomes me so often that I have to weep like a child. The scenes of my drama are lacking in this or that respect, and yet I cannot twist free from the poetic errancy in which I wander. Oh, from my youth onward, the world has frightened my spirit back into itself, and I still suffer from that. There is one hospital, it is true, to which a botched poet like me can honorably flee—philosophy. Yet I cannot give up the hopes of my youth; I would rather go down with honor than alienate myself from the sweet homeland of my muses, from which mere accident has banished me. . . . I am not lacking in force, but in agility; I don't lack ideas, but nuances; I'm not missing the main tone, but all the other tones of the scale; I've got light, but not the shadows. And all for one reason: I shy away much too much from the common and the ordinary in real life. I'm nothing but a pedant, if you will. Yet, if I'm right, pedants are usually cold and loveless, whereas my heart is overly anxious to be a brother to every person and every thing under the moon. I almost think I am pedan-

> tic for no other reason than love. . . . I'm afraid that the warm life in me will catch cold in the frigid history of our times, and this fear arises from the fact that I have proved to be more sensitive than others to every destructive force that has assailed me since my youth. . . . Because I am more vulnerable than many other people I must try to win some advantage from the things that have a destructive impact on me. . . . And, just so you know everything about this moody brooding of mine, I confess to you that for the past few days my work has ground to a halt, so that I have to fall back on ratiocination. (CHV 2:710–12; TA 219)

Hölderlin's mourning-play offered him a chance to escape from the tyranny of *Philosophia,* even if—or precisely because—the play itself was a wellspring of ideas (Hölderlin often used the expression *idealisch,* "ideational," to describe its characters), and even if he interrupted work on the second version to write a series of highly philosophical studies on tragic drama. As for the ideas themselves, Hölderlin found his way to them only gradually. Among these ideas, which were the principal ones?

There is only one genuinely philosophical problem, Albert Camus tells us in the first sentence of the first section of his *Mythe de Sisyphe,* only one problem that is truly serious: *c'est le suicide.*[6] According to legend, Empedocles' death is by suicide. Of all deaths, suicide is perhaps the most terrifying to us. We others, the stunned survivors, are always left standing outside of it, forlorn and uncomprehending. (In Hölderlin's play, as we shall see, the character named Pausanias occupies this outside position.) If suicide is the only truly philosophical problem, we may be forced to conclude that philosophy should have nothing to do with conceptual understanding, knowledge, wisdom, or will. The faculties relevant to philosophy may be reduced to a struggling imagination and a mournful memory.

Centuries before Camus wrote, the poet and thinker we call Novalis, Friedrich von Hardenberg, whom Hölderlin had met together with Fichte at the house of Immanuel Niethammer in early summer of 1795, said much the same thing: "The genuine philosophical act is suicide; this is the real beginning of all philosophy; every need for philosophical disciples leads in that direction, and this act alone corresponds to all the conditions and characteristics of the transcendental attitude. . . . Detailed elaboration of this supremely interesting thought."[7] This "supremely interesting thought" leads almost everyone who takes it up back to Empedocles of Acragas, Empedocles on Mount Etna.

---

6. Albert Camus, *Le mythe de Sisyphe* (Paris: Gallimard, 1942), 15. It is no accident that Empedocles figures large in Camus' later work, *L'Homme révolté* (Paris: Gallimard, 1951), which takes its motto from Hölderlin's *Death of Empedocles.*

7. Novalis, *Werke, Tagebücher und Briefe Friedrich von Hardenbergs,* ed. Hans-Joachim Mähl and Richard Samuel, 3 vols. (Munich: Carl Hanser Verlag, 1987), 2:223.

If there is a second genuinely philosophical problem, it may have to do with the suicide of an entire city or people. One could imagine a nation in which religious and political leaders dedicate their mediocre talents to deceiving the people, indeed, to inculcating in them a kind of progressive and fatal stupor. One could imagine a city or a country in which *stupidification*—a new word for a new phenomenon?—is the principal political and social goal, a city or a country in which avarice alone competes with stupefaction for supremacy. One could imagine a place where one does not know which of the two, stupidity or avarice, has won the upper hand, that is, whether the stupidity of the nation is permeated by avarice or avarice itself has driven the nation into sheer idiocy. Empedocles apparently feels this way about Acragas; Hölderlin apparently feels this way about Württemberg. Hölderlin's character Manes, in the third version of the play, speaks of "the one" who believes himself called on to save his city from its demise—even if that demise appears to implicate the gods themselves:

> The world around him bubbles in ferment, and all
> Disruption and corruption in the mortal breast
> Is agitated, and from top to bottom; whereupon
> The lord of time, grown apprehensive of his rule,
> Looms with glowering gaze above the consternation.
> His day extinguished, lightning bolts still flash, yet
> What flames on high is inflammation, nothing more;
> What strives from down below is savage discord. (ll. 364–71)

Hölderlin's Empedocles replies to Manes:

> When brother fled from brother, when lovers passed
> Each other by in ignorance, when fathers failed
> To recognize their sons, when human words no more
> Were understood, nor human laws, that was when
> The meaning of it all assailed me and I trembled:
> It was my nation's parting god!
> I heard him, and upward to unspeaking stars
> I gazed, the place from which he had descended.
> And then I went to placate him. For us there still
> Were many radiant days. It still seemed at the very end
> We might invigorate ourselves; and thus consoled
> By memories of the Golden Age, that all-confident
> And brilliant morning full of force, the frightful melancholy
> Was lifted from me and from my people also;
> We sealed with one another free and firm bonds,
> Appealing to the living gods in supplication.

Yet often when I donned the crown of all the people's thanks,
And when the nation's soul approached me ever closer,
Crowding me alone, again the melancholy stole upon me.
For when a country is about to die, its spirit at the end
Selects but one among the many, one alone through whom
Its swan song, the final breaths of life, will sound.
I had an intimation, yet served the spirit willingly.
And now it has transpired. (ll. 421–44)

Luckily, we who live in a postmodern, postindustrial society no longer need to fret about the atavism of religious leaders and the stupidity and avarice of political leaders; we no longer need to worry about the nation's parting god and the swan song of the god's departure, the final breaths of life.

Empedocles had been an object of Hölderlin's poetic imagination before he began to write his mourning-play. A passage from the second volume of *Hyperion,* written probably in 1798 at the Gontard household, touches on the story of Empedocles' death by suicide—his plunge into the crater of Mount Etna—and seeks an explanation for that suicide. A reference by Hyperion to his lost love "Diotima" precedes and frames the allusion to Empedocles:

> I too am at the end of my rope. My own soul repels me, because I have to blame it for Diotima's death; and the thoughts of my youth, which I once held in high esteem, now mean nothing to me. For they poisoned my Diotima for me!
>
> And now tell me, is there any refuge left?—Yesterday I was up on Etna. I recalled the great Sicilian of old who, when he'd had enough of ticking off the hours, having become intimate with the soul of the world, in his bold lust for life plunged into the terrific flames. It was because—a mocker afterwards said of him—the frigid poet had to warm himself at the fire.
>
> Oh, how gladly I would precipitate such mockery over me! but one must think more highly of oneself than I do to fly unbidden to nature's heart—put it any way you like, for truly, as I am now, I have no name for these things, and all is uncertain. (DKV 2:116; TA 56–57)

An equally intense identification with Empedocles, or, rather, with the disciples and admirers of Empedocles, had already been expressed in Hölderlin's lyric poem, "Empedocles." Hölderlin first sketched it in the summer of 1797, at the time of the Frankfurt Plan, which is the first document we have concerning the Empedocles play in Hölderlin's life and work (see the first chapter of the present volume). The lyric poem, in which the theme of love is central, took final form in 1800 and was published in 1801:

EMPEDOCLES

You seek life, you search, and out of the earth
  Flows and blazes forth a godly fire to you,
    And you, in shuddering exaction,
      Cast yourself down into Etna's flames.

Thus the queen melts the pearls of her haughtiness
  In wine; let them melt! if only you had
    Not sacrificed your riches, O poet,
      In the seething chalice!

Yet you are holy to me, as is the power of earth
  That swept you away, bold victim!
    And gladly would I follow into the depths,
      If love did not hold me back, this hero.
        (DKV 1:241; TA 220)

The words "shuddering exaction," *schauderndes Verlangen,* are repeated in the first version of the mourning-play, where they have quite a different impact. For there Empedocles himself utters them sarcastically in a moment of hesitation and self-doubt, perhaps even self-contempt. Empedocles has been hearing the pleas of his favorites, Pausanias and Panthea, from the beginning of the play: these disciples and friends worry that the master's planned suicide may be an effect of melancholy or punctured pride rather than a grandiose culmination of his life and teaching, an "ideal deed." Their doubts plague Empedocles increasingly as the three versions of the play succeed on one another. And they are doubts that can only cripple action. In act 2, scene 6 of the first version, Empedocles soliloquizes: "Shuddering / Exaction! What? death alone ignites / My life now at the end, and you extend / To me the terrifying chalice, the fermenting cup, / Nature!" (DKV 2:354; FHA 12:237). Queen Cleopatra may melt her pearls in a chalice of wine, but she does so out of arrogance or haughtiness (*Übermut*). If it is neither idealism nor melancholy that induces Empedocles' resolve, is it haughty ambition that tempts him with "one full deed and at the end"? In the lyric poem, love holds the singer back; the singer's voice is therefore closer to that of Pausanias or Panthea than it is to Empedocles. Why does the love of Pausanias, or that of Panthea, fail to hold Empedocles back? If it is neither idealism nor melancholy nor haughtiness, is it a failure to love that destroys the thinker? These doubts may prevent Hölderlin from successfully completing any of the three drafts. If the historical Empedocles leaps into the crater, Hölderlin's dramatic hero remains perched on the crater's rim forever.

Hölderlin would have read about Empedocles of Acragas (the Latin Agrigentum, the modern Agrigénto, on the southwestern coast of Sicily), who lived *circa* 495–435 B.C.E., in many different sources. His principal source for the fragments of Empedocles' writings was the volume by the famous editor of Plato's works, Henricus Stephanus, entitled *Poesis philosophica, vel saltem, Reliquiae poesis philosophicae, Empedoclis, Parmenidis, Xenophanis, et al.*, published in 1573, to be discussed shortly. Horace's allusion to Empedocles in *Ars poetica* (ll. 463–66) and the more extensive treatment of him in Lucretius's *De rerum natura* (Book I, ll. 714–829) would not have escaped Hölderlin. Lucretius, who admires and emulates Empedocles, celebrates the luxuriant and dramatic Sicilian landscape that is dominated by swirling seas and volcanic Mount Etna. That landscape produces a son who seems more like a god than a mortal:

> Here is destructive Charybdis and here is Etna,
> Whose rumblings warn us of angry flames gathering
> In violence to belch forth fire once again from its gorge
> And sear the sky with lightning sparks.
> This mighty region, which seems so full of wonders
> To the nations of humankind, and is famed as quite a place
> To see, bursting with fruits and fortified with men,
> Nonetheless holds nothing more renowned than this man,
> Nor anything more holy and marvelous and well-loved.
> The poems that sprang from his divine breast
> Declare and declaim his illustrious discoveries,
> Such that he hardly seems to be of mortal lineage.[8]

However, the single most important source for Empedocles' *life* that was available to Hölderlin was surely Diogenes Laertius's *Lives and Opinions of the Eminent Philosophers.* Hölderlin did not read Diogenes until his mourning-play was under way, yet once he did read the *Lives and Opinions,* in mid-December 1798, the account of Empedocles in Book VIII left a lasting impression on him, in at least five respects.[9]

---

8. Lucretius, *De rerum natura,* trans. W. H. D. Rouse, revised by Martin Ferguson Smith, Loeb Classical Library (Cambridge, Mass.: Harvard University Press, 1992), Book I, ll. 722–33. I have altered the translation.

9. See Diogenes Laertius, *Lives of Eminent Philosophers,* 2 vols., tr. R. D. Hicks, 2 vols., Loeb Classical Library (Cambridge, Mass.: Harvard University Press), 1972), 2:366–91, which comprises Book VIII, sections 51–77, for this and the following. I shall cite this work as DL, with volume and page number. See also JV 3:354n. 5, and 356–59.

ΠΟΙΗΣΙΣ ΦΙΛΟ-
ΣΟΦΟΣ.
POESIS PHILO-
SOPHICA,
Vel ſaltem,
Reliquiæ poeſis philoſophicæ,
EMPEDOCLIS, PARMENIDIS,
XENOPHANIS, CLEANTHIS,
TIMONIS, EPICHARMI.
Adiuncta ſunt
ORPHEI illius carmina qui à ſuis ap-
pellatus fuit ὁ θεολόγος.
ITEM,
HERACLITI ET DEMO-
criti loci quidam, & eorum epiſtolæ.

ANNO M. D. LXXIII.
excudebat Henr. Stephanus.
CVM PRIVILEGIO CAES.
MAIESTATIS.

The title page of Henricus Stephanus, *Poesis philosophica*, 1573, Hölderlin's most important source for the fragments of Empedocles.

First, Diogenes reports that Empedocles was a renowned thinker, poet, and rhetorician. Important for Hölderlin, who since his early youth dreamed of being at least the first two, must have been Empedocles' association with the great masters of Greek thought and poetry prior to him: he is a disciple of Pythagoras—even if Empedocles is reputedly excommunicated from the Pythagorean Brotherhood for having betrayed one of the hermetic doctrines (an important detail for the second of the three versions of Hölderlin's play); Empedocles is also a student of Parmenides, the thinker of "the well-rounded sphere of truth" (DK B1, l. 29). The one, well-rounded sphere will prove to be important for Empedocles' own cosmology: into the Parmenidean sphere Empedocles will inject the opposing forces of Love and Strife, Φιλία καὶ Νεῖκος. Like his predecessors, Empedocles is a poet who composes in hexameters. He is an admirer of Xenophanes of Colophon, the acerbic critic of Homer and Hesiod and the poet of a Zeus whose power resides in his "unmoving thought" (DK B25–26). Empedocles is, furthermore, a rival of Zeno, the inventor of dialectic—inasmuch as Empedocles is the creator of rhetoric. If Empedocles is a master rhetorician, however, he is also a bard: the epithet ὁμηρικός is the superlative encomium for any Greek poet, and that is the word Diogenes uses to describe the Sicilian sage. He elaborates on this Homeric quality when he writes that Empedocles is μεταφορητικός, "well-versed in poetic devices," and even "powerful in versification to an uncanny degree," καὶ δεινὸς περὶ τὴν φράσιν. Indeed, Empedocles' skills extend to all the sciences and arts: according to several of Diogenes' sources, he composes both tragedies and philosophical discourses, is both rhetorician and physician, dramaturge and thaumaturge, an expert in all the φάρμακα and all the incantations that influence body and mind.

Second, Diogenes reports some controversy surrounding Empedocles' politics. He notes that after the death of Empedocles' father, Meton, signs appeared that a tyranny was about to install itself in Acragas; Empedocles "convinced the citizens to cease their hostilities and to respect their equality as citizens" (DL 8:72). Empedocles is therefore a radical democrat, thinking only of the welfare of the common people. When in the first version of *The Death of Empedocles* the citizens of Agrigent beg Empedocles to become their "Numa," that is, to be for them what the legendary Numa Pompilius was for preclassical Rome, a king who settles civil strife and rules justly through laws rather than edicts, Empedocles tells them that the time of kingship has irrevocably passed. Indeed, the Empedocles who calls on the citizens to throw off the fetters of tyranny, especially the tyranny of their priests, also frees his own slaves. Yet a shadow is cast over Empedocles' democratic tendencies. Diogenes reports that, according to some, the poet and rhetorician was actually arrogant and self-seeking, or at least utterly self-centered, ἀλαζόνα καὶ φίλαυτον, and that he was a recluse who in reality did not care a bit for his people. Empedocles sacrifices himself on the altar not of his nation but of his solitude. And Hölderlin? Like the ancient Empedocles, Hölderlin is a staunch democrat and a believer in the republican form of government, even if affairs in Paris and by now in Germany as well are bloody. Yet he is also a man whose solitude grows deeper daily.

Third, Diogenes reports at least something of Empedocles' central teaching in Περὶ φύσεως, "On Nature," namely, the doctrine of the four elements, earth, air, fire, and water. Empedocles calls them the four roots, or rhizomes, ῥιζώματα. When Hölderlin sends a portion of the second version of his play to his stepbrother Carl, he underlines the four elements in the passage, as though to enhance Carl's education in early Greek philosophy (DKV 2:1098). The four Empedoclean elements are subject to the forces of mixture and separation (μίξις, διάλλαξις), which, as we mentioned, Empedocles more often calls the forces of love and strife (φιλία, νεῖκος). The mere mention of love and strife as universal forces reminds us of Hölderlin's love of nature, as also of Diotima; indeed, the two loves are inextricably—if inexplicably—linked. Hers is, as Hölderlin reports to Neuffer, "the face of nature." Yet these loves are crossed by destiny and permeated by strife.

Fourth, love is a force that the Greeks generally, and Empedocles in particular, associate with Aphrodite. The love (and the strife?) that this goddess instigates in both mortals and immortals plays a role in Empedocles' second book, the Καθαρμοί, or *Purifications*, which Diogenes also mentions. Hölderlin was struck by a reference Diogenes makes twice to a certain woman whom Empedocles the physician reportedly healed. Several such cases may have existed, but the name *Pantheia* is associated with one of them. Pantheia, which Hölderlin will write as *Panthea,* herself a poetess and a companion of Pindar, is in turn associated with a certain Pausanias, who is said to have been the favorite or the beloved (ἐρώμενος) of Empedocles. Pantheia, a victim of the plague, was given up for dead by her father and by all the citizens of Acragas. For thirty days her body had been without respiration or pulse, even though it was still preserved intact. Empedocles the doctor and pharmacologist, and perhaps the thaumaturge as well, reputedly discovered a source of warmth in her belly. Somehow, perhaps through the administration of an elixir, he managed to preserve her life. After having been restored to health, Pantheia became a disciple, albeit only briefly, inasmuch as she is particularly associated with Empedocles at the time of his death. During the sacrifice offered for her recuperation, her doctor and savior reportedly took his life by leaping into the crater of Etna. During the night, Diogenes reports, the crowd heard the voice of a woman or a god cry out, 'Εμπεδοκλέα! Nietzsche, who drew up numerous plans for an Empedocles drama, suspected that this woman who disclosed to the philosopher the meaning of nature in fact joined Empedocles in death;

whether Hölderlin ever entertained the idea of such a *Liebestod* we do not know, but it did not become a part of his play.[10]

Fifth, and finally, the various accounts of Empedocles' death Diogenes Laertius offered must have intrigued Hölderlin. Four years earlier, in October of 1794, Hölderlin had planned to write a tragedy on the death of Socrates. It may be that Plato's *Phaedo* was still in his mind as he was thinking about the Sicilian magus. For, as we shall see, Plato plays an interesting—though utterly anachronistic—role in Hölderlin's play. At all events, the undying fame of the ancient philosophers does not intrigue Hölderlin as much as their free death, their "full" or "ideal" deed at the end of their lives. That mortal deed cloaks them in the mantle of immortality, or at least suggests something of the exceptional and excessive. Yet to say such a thing is to broach the possibility of hubris. Diogenes twice refers to Empedocles' mantic pretensions and places these words in Empedocles' mouth: "As for me, I walk among you as immortal god, no longer a mortal," ἐγὼ δ' ὑμῖν θεὸς ἄμβροτος, οὐκέτι θνητός πωλεῦμαι (DK B112). This is perhaps an extreme form of the statement Hölderlin makes to Neuffer, "It is actually often impossible for me to think the thoughts of mortals. . . ." Empedocles' is the ultimate hubris, one must say, the most nefarious and unspeakable *nefas* that one can imagine—unless his self-willed death outstrips the claim to divinity and is itself the ultimate hubris. At all events, Diogenes delights in the multiple reports concerning Empedocles' death: a fraud perpetrated by the crafty thaumaturge and desperate dramaturge, who sets the scene for the launching of his own legend, who plays the τραγικός up to the very end and yet in that end is finally unmasked, or at least unshod—inasmuch as the crater spews the philosopher's bronzed sandal back onto the rim; or, on the contrary, the authentic hierophant, γεγόνι θεός, "become god," having mixed his flesh and blood with the roots of fire, water vapor, volcanic gases, and liquefied earth in Etna.

Hölderlin first mentioned the exact title of his play, *Der Tod des Empedokles,* in a letter to Schiller in late summer of 1799, after the first two versions had been completed; from the outset, however, he had intended to tell the story of the *death* of Empedocles. Indeed, as he moved from the second version to the third, Hölderlin eliminated virtually all the material having to do with the city of Agrigent and its political and religious turmoil: in version three Empedocles is poised for the leap right from the start. As we know, however, he never takes that final step. Hölderlin never brings him to that pass. Why not?

---

10. See, however, ll. 261–66 and 462–69 of the third version of the play. For Nietzsche's proposed drama on Empedocles, see D. F. Krell, *Postponements: Woman, Sensuality, and Death in Nietzsche* (Bloomington: Indiana University Press, 1986), chapter 2.

Before responding to this question—and if the earlier remarks on the restraining force of love are not already a reply that is because this entire volume is in response to the question—we have to return to the matter of Hölderlin's sources, especially his source for the Empedoclean fragments in the collection by Henricus Stephanus.[11] In Stephanus's anthology Hölderlin would have found much of the material that derives from Diogenes Laertius, Aristotle, Plutarch, Sextus Empiricus, Athenaeus, Galen, Clement of Alexandria, Porphyry, and others. Missing from the Stephanus collection, however, are the important fragments from Simplicius, from which so much of our information about Empedocles' first book, "On Nature," derives. As mentioned earlier, from the sources available to him Hölderlin would have been well informed about Empedocles' doctrines of the four roots (earth, air, water, and the fiery ether or upper air), of the one sphere, and of the two opposing forces, love and strife. Perhaps the most important aspect of these two forces is that the one never banishes the other entirely from the sphere. Two fragments of Empedocles suggest the consequences of this. The first, from Simplicius, which Hölderlin perhaps did not know, encourages us to examine the "witnesses" of Empedocles' words:

> Observe the sun, bright to look at and everywhere ardent, which permeates all with its warmth and its glistening rays; observe the rain, which evokes everything dark and cool and causes the earth to release all that is firm and grounding. And in quarrel everything stirs and assumes contrary forms and is discordant, whereas in love these things unite and languish for one another [ποθεῖται]. For from this all else springs, everything that

11. Hölderlin had other sources available to him, such as Georg Christoph Hamberger, *Zuverlässige Nachrichten von den vornehmsten Schriftstellern vom Anfange der Welt bis 1500,* 1756, Jacob Brucker, *Historia critica philosophiae,* 6 vols., 1742, and Ralph Cudworth, *Systema intellectuale huius mundi,* 1680. Yet the volume by Henricus Stephanus seems to have been the most important source, and it will be discussed in detail in what follows (with references to page numbers in the body of my text). The Stephanus text, which is extremely rare, is also difficult to decipher. I have located a number of its fragments in Diels-Kranz, however, and I list these here in order that we may have some sense of the fragments that Hölderlin actually read. I cite the DK fragments in the order they appear in Stephanus, with the page number of Stephanus's text in parentheses: among the fragments in Stephanus are DK B100 (12, 17), B21 (18), B3 (20), B8 (22), B111, B112 (23), B117, B136, B137 (24), B122, B115 (25), B76, B81, B67 (26), B145, B146, B114, B4 (27), B38, B133, B147, B132 (28), B118, B125, B124, B119, B128 (29), B139, B33 (30), B90, B1, B156, B157 (31). This list is not complete, but may serve as a starting point. On this question of Hölderlin's sources for Empedocles, see JV 3:346n. 35 and DKV 2:1097.

> was, is, and shall be, trees and men as well as women and animals and birds and water-nourished fish, and gods too, long-lived and richest in honors. (DK B21)

The word ποθεῖται is formed from πόθος, which means mourning and grief. Love itself, it seems, involves mourning, languor, and languishment, as both Hölderlin and Schelling had always suspected. Languishment, while not obviously born of strife, arises as the shadow side of love. The second fragment, which Hölderlin was more likely to have known, comes from Plutarch, who refers to those human beings who are beset by "the languor of love," or *Liebessehnsucht,* as Diels-Kranz translate πόθος: "Languor of love steals upon him, which through vision awakens a memory" (DK B64). To repeat, while mourning and languishment are not strife as such, they are surely reminiscent of the Νεῖκος that is never entirely overcome by Φιλία within the sphere. Although Aphrodite is the beneficent source of unity among mortals, "the life-dispensing Aphrodite," "the all-harmonizing Aphrodite," she hammers into mortals the "nails of love" (DK B 151, B71, B87); she is the goddess who thickens the plot in the way fig juice thickens milk (DK B33); she herself is the goddess of sundered or riven meadows, σχιστοὺς λειμῶνας Ἀφροδίτης, and "of shadowy parts," γυναικοφυῆ σκιεροῖς γυίοις (DK B61, B66). (Note that the word for "meadows" in B66 is precisely that which Empedocles calls the fields of Ἄτη, that is, "the fields of doom" [see B121]: the meadow metaphor itself implies that love and strife flourish side-by-side, at least on this earth.) Just as the earth enables us to perceive earth, and water grants us the feel of water, and ether shows us ether, so does love enable us to perceive love, whereas strife gives us a view of "wretched strife" (DK B109). And yet we would never be able to contrast the two within the sphere if either were to vanish. If we ask what accounts for the *alternation* of love and strife, Empedocles' reply is "a broadly sworn oath," a kind of cosmic contract that enforces the change of epochs "when time has run its course," τελειομένοιο χρόνοιο (DK B30). This sort of time is surely different from mere succession, the time from which, as we shall see, Empedocles yearns to escape. The undeniable yet enigmatic relationship between temporal succession in any given human lifetime and historical-epochal time must have disquieted both Empedocles and Hölderlin. An even more severe problem for them both, however, is the fact the alternation of eons is never complete; that is to say, neither love nor strife is ever wholly vanquished in the cycle. That this is so for love undergirds all our hopes for the return of a Golden Age, no matter how discordant our present. That this is so for strife is more troubling—for what would give strife greater pleasure than breaking its contract with both love and epochal time, insisting on controlling the elements within the sphere even after the time has come to give love a chance?

What could be more natural for Νεῖκος? Another fragment recorded by Simplicius—to which Hölderlin may not have had access—will bring this difficulty to light in a particularly stark way. But let us turn our attention for a moment to the sphere, the Parmenidean sphere that seems so snuggly, in which both love and strife pursue their respective unifying and disintegrating functions. For this threesome—*love* and *strife* within the *sphere*—presents a classic example of the ancient and modern quarrel between monism (the *one* sphere) and dualism (the *two opposing* forces). Ancient *and* modern quarrel, one must say, and perhaps a modern version will serve as the best way to introduce the problem.

Sigmund Freud, in a late work on the question of limited or infinite analysis, complains that he has been unable to convince most of his associates of the *dualism* that he sees at work in the human psyche, namely, the duality of psychic forces, one of them serving to unify and build, the other to disrupt and destroy.[12] Yet he is consoled, he says, by the fact that he has happened upon an early Greek thinker who shares his exquisite dualism—indeed, one who projects that dualism onto the entire universe. Here is a very long (yet abridged) quotation from section six of his 1937 article "On Finite and Infinite Analysis":

> Empedocles of Acragas, born circa 495 B.C.E., enters on the scene as one of the most magnificent and remarkable figures in the cultural history of Greece. His many-sided personality engaged in activities that went in the most varied directions; he was a researcher and thinker, a prophet and thaumaturge [*Magier*], a politician, philanthropist, and physician who was well-informed about nature; he is said to have freed the city of Selinunt of malaria, for which his contemporaries honored him as a god. His spirit seems to have united within itself the most acute oppositions; precise and sober in his physical and physiological investigations, he nevertheless did not shy from obscure mysticism; he constructed cosmic speculations of astonishingly phantasmatic boldness. . . . Yet our interest turns to that particular doctrine of Empedocles which comes so close to the psychoanalytic theory of drives that the two would be identical were it not for the difference that the theory of the Greek is a cosmic phantasm. . . . The philosopher teaches that there are two principles underlying all occurrences in cosmic as well as in psychic life, two principles in eternal conflict with one another. He calls them φιλία—*love*—and

12. For the following see Freud, "Die endliche und die unendliche Analyse," in Sigmund Freud, *Studienausgabe Ergänzungsband, Schriften zur Behandlungstechnik* (Frankurt am Main: Fischer Taschenbuch Verlag, 1982), 384–86.

> νεῖκος—*strife*. One of these powers . . . strives to compress the primordial particles of the four elements into a unity, the other, by contrast, tries to cancel all these intermixtures and to isolate the elements from one another. He conceives of the cosmic process as a continuous, never-ending alternation of periods in which the one or the other of the two fundamental forces is victorious, so that at one time love, but at another time strife imposes its will and rules the world, at which point the other, defeated party rises up and wrestles its opponent to the ground.
>
> The two fundamental principles of Empedocles—φιλία and νεῖκος—both in name and in function are the same as our two fundamental drives *Eros* and *destruction*. The one endeavors to bind everything at hand into ever-greater unities, the other to dissolve these unities and to annihilate the configurations that they have brought into being. . . . We no longer think of the mixture and separation of material substances, but on the fusion and separation of drive components. We have also in a certain way provided biological support for the principle of "strife" by tracing our destructive drive back to the death drive, namely, the compulsion of living creatures to revert to lifelessness. Naturally, that does not mean to deny that an analogous drive already existed earlier on; it does not mean to assert that such a drive first came into being with the appearance of life. And no one can predict in what sort of guise the kernel of truth contained in the doctrine of Empedocles will show itself to later investigators.

What might have soured Freud's consolation, which rests on the supposition that even if his contemporaries will not accept his dualism of drives, *Eros* and the *death drive*, Empedocles of Acragas might well have, is the thought that the Empedoclean dualism may revert to a monism. If the principles of love and strife are engaged in strife within the sphere, wrestling one another to the ground, then strife haunts the sphere during both periods. In Freud's world, this might mean that the Eros on which therapy counts—the drive to unify and to resist destruction—may itself be invariably contaminated by the destructive drive. The resulting tragic monism would draw psychoanalysis into its turbulence. But let us return now to Empedocles' own monistic Parmenidean inheritance, that is to say, his inheritance of the one sphere in which the two forces strive against one another—*strife* being the name of *one* (the *monos*) of the two contending powers.

That Empedocles is a disciple of Parmenides becomes clear when we hear his words concerning the one sphere, words reminiscent of the well-rounded sphere of truth to which Parmenides refers. Empedocles describes the sphere as being "perfectly round, everywhere equal and endless, filled with enormous pride over the solitude that rings it round" (DK B28). Empedocles' Parmenidean strain also shows itself in his denial of birth and death for humankind: "There is birth of particular beings among mortals just as little as there is an end in accursed death; rather, there is only mixture and exchange, 'birth' being but the name human beings commonly use for this" (DK B8). Of course, human beings are not the only living beings that undergo mixture and exchange instead of birth and death. Empedocles' denial of human exceptionality and superiority is radical. In more than one place he insists that consciousness and the power to make ethical decisions—what Aristotle was to call φρόνησις—is a matter of Good Fortune, Τύχη, and in any case belongs to many orders of living things besides humankind: "For you must know that everything has consciousness [φρόνησιν ἔχειν] and participates in thinking [καὶ νώματος αἶσαν]" (DK B110; cf. 103). As we read the Καθαρμοί, however, it becomes apparent that Empedocles himself has committed some dreadful crime against the unity of life and the collective consciousness, whether wittingly or not. Fragment DK B115, which Hölderlin knew, reads:

> It is a proclamation of Necessity, a decree of the gods, ancient, prevailing since time immemorial and sealed with broad oaths: when one has besmirched his own members with the blood of murder and thus has incurred guilt, and when one has furthermore sworn an oath to some one among the daimons, who are allotted a very long life, they must wander remote from the blessed for three times ten thousand years, whereby in the course of time they assume the shapes of all sorts of mortal creatures, treading one weary path after another. For the power of the air chases them to the sea, the sea spews them onto the land, the earth hounds them to the beams of the blazing, inexhaustible sun, and the sun pursues them into the vortex of the air. Each takes him from the others, but they all hate him. Among these I too now belong [τῶν καὶ ἐγὼ νῦν εἰμι], a fugitive from gods and a vagabond [φυγὰς θεόθεν καὶ ἀλήτης], because I put my faith in raging strife [νείκεϊ μαινομένωι πίσυνος].

Empedocles knows strife not simply as one of the two cosmic forces; he knows it as his own life story and as his fate. Hölderlin also had access to the following three fragments, the first from Diogenes Laertius, the second and third from Clement of Alexandria (via Stephanus). First, the famous brief biography of Empedocles' former lives: "For I have already been, once upon a time, boy, girl, plant, bird, and mute fish diving in the briny sea" (DK B117; Stephanus 24). Second, Empedocles' account of one of his many births on the plains of doom: "I wept and howled as I looked about the unfamiliar place" (DK B118; Stephanus 29). Finally, third, the outcome of these multiple births here on earth: "From how vast a height and from what great happiness I have been cast down!" (DK B119; Stephanus 29). The "plains of doom," cited in DK B121, although not in Stephanus, Hölderlin knew in any case, inasmuch as he alludes to them in *Hype-*

rion (CHV 1:616: *das Feld des Fluchs,* "the accursed field"); the Greek says that these are the meadows of Ἄτη, which is the universal term in Greek tragedy for infatuation and doom—in short, a tragic destiny. Hölderlin also knew of perhaps the most mournful of Empedocles' exclamations (DK B124; Stephanus 29):

> ὢ πόποι, ὢ δειλὸν θνητῶν γένος, ὢ δυσάνολβον, τοίων ἔκ τ' ἐρίδων
> ἔκ τε στοναχῶν ἐγένεσθε.

> Oh, woe! oh, you wretched race of humankind, oh, you lamentable race:
> you have sprung from such quarrels and sobs!

If one sin banishes mortals from the companionship of gods and thus terminates the Golden Age, casting mortals down onto the plains of doom, that sin is cannibalism—if indeed one has learned the lesson that all living things participate to some degree in consciousness and thought and that all living things are akin. For that lesson tells us that a delicious piping hot Arby's is equivalent to the flesh of one's flesh. It means that we all belong to the House of Atreus, one of the original houses of tragedy—recall how Cassandra can smell the blood in the walls of Agamemnon's palace and can see the slaughtered children of Thyestes at their ghostly play. Fragment DK B137, to which Hölderlin will allude in his play, is perhaps the most drastic of all the fragments in Empedocles' *Purifications*:

> And the father seizes his own son, whose shape has been altered, slaughters him—and adduces a prayer to his deed, the wretched fool! Anyone who wants to sacrifice a being that pleads for its life is quite mad; the father is deaf to his son's cries, and after he has slaughtered him he prepares an evil feast in his home. In the same way, the son grapples with his father and the children with their mother, tearing the life out of them and swallowing down their own flesh.

"Woe is me!" cries Empedocles (DK B139, Stephanus 30), "that the inescapable day did not see me annihilated before the thought occurred to me that my lips should commit the horrid crime of devouring flesh!" It is as Roberto Calasso, thinking of the Greeks but writing in our own time, says: "The primordial crime is the action that makes something in existence disappear: the act of eating. Guilt is thus obligatory and inextinguishable" (RC 311). Not even vegetarianism suffices. At every human banquet a place is set for Strife. The problem, as we will later hear Jacques Derrida say, is how to "eat well," and it will not be solved by a short course on dietetics.

No matter how dire the fragments from *Purifications* may be, however, the poetry and thought of Empedocles of Acragas are utterly seductive. Neither

Hölderlin nor any other ancient or modern thinker or poet can resist them altogether. Some would say that there is magic in them, as befits the words of a magus or thaumaturge.[13] Fragment B17 may serve as an example:

> Fire and water and earth and air up above;
> Off to the side, Strife; the whole well harmonized,
> And in the center, Love, equal in breadth and in height;
> Look at her with your mind's eye, do not be abashed.
> You know her, she surges in the limbs of mortals;
> Thanks to her they think of love and do unifying deeds,
> Calling out her name: O Delight! Aphrodite!
> As she spins there among the other elements,
> No mortal male [θνητὸς ἀνήρ] can recognize her.
> But you must follow my footsteps, the footfall of my words.
> They will not disappoint you.

No disappointment, to be sure. But now to the final fragment from Simplicius that exposes the difficulty of trying to compel strife to submit to alternation, to join the ring dance with love. Fragment B35 tells us that even as love is uniting the limbs of mortals strife perdures as a remnant within the sphere—ἐνέμιμνε is his word. Always and ever at least some degree of invidious isolation and insidious enmity prevails in the sphere, "to the extent that strife lingers still, hovering in suspense," ὅσσ' ἔτι Νεῖκος ἔρυκε μετάρσιον, "insofar as strife still remains, hovering back behind." This is the enigma about which Aristotle is circling when in *Metaphysics* I, 4 he complains of a "contradiction" in the Empedoclean cosmos. How could Hölderlin, himself mad for unifying deeds but also the victim of strife "off to the side," strife "hovering in suspense," have resisted the Empedoclean seduction? And yet if the one sphere is divided against itself in love and strife, and if the self-division of the sphere as such derives from strife, then the rule of strife in the sphere arguably never ends. Strife, even when "off to the side," "remaining back behind," "hovering in suspense," contaminates the sphere to the point where love cannot be identified as such: *love has no identity apart from the petulant strivings of languor and the sometimes noisy, sometimes silent strife of mourn-*

13. One of the very few extant copies of Stephanus's 1573 collection—the one that came into my hands from the library of the University of Tübingen—was long ago defaced by a scholar who still wrote in Latin, defaced perhaps soon after its publication. Alongside a fragment from Diogenes Laertius (DK B111) that tells of Empedocles' repute as a thaumaturge, a man who like Dracula controls the very winds, the scholar wrote into the margin, in the blackest of black inks, *Magica.* Whether he was condemning or approving, the defacer was certainly intrigued, even spellbound.

ful languishment. This would be a radicalization of what the young Hölderlin was thinking in his essay "Judgment and Being," namely, separation: if identity does not equal absolute being (CHV 2:50), if I am set into opposition even with myself, and not simply after the manner of Fichtean positings, then am I not forever a fugitive and a drifter? Does not the soul "wander and flee," φεύγει καὶ πλανᾶται, a victim of strife on the "plains of doom"?

One cannot help but think of a line Georg Trakl wrote a century or more after Hölderlin, Trakl being the poet who picked up the lyre when it slipped from Hölderlin's hands: *Es ist die Seele ein Fremdes auf Erden,* "A foreign thing is the soul on earth." The earth? That is the place where no experienced psychoanalyst would ever phantasize about a love without strife; it is where, according to Heidegger, there is strife with the world. Indeed, strife and striving characterize the very *worlding* of the world, which juts from the earth only to sink back into it. To say these things is surely to leap too far too fast. Let us for the moment conclude simply that strife and love may not be the equal partners that Empedocles wishes them to be, and that their dissymmetry might be grounds for a mourning-play.

ONE

The Frankfurt Plan

COMPOSED IN AUGUST 1797, the Frankfurt Plan is the first detailed sketch toward Hölderlin's mourning-play. A full year and more intervened before he could begin work on the play itself, however; the year 1798 was largely occupied with the second volume of his novel *Hyperion.* Late in that volume, as we have seen in the General Introduction, Hölderlin envisages Empedocles, "the great Sicilian," who is "intimate with the soul of the world" and possessed of a "bold lust for life," ultimately weary of "ticking off the hours." The Frankfurt Plan is all about Empedocles' chagrin in the grip of the hours, his despair over the time of succession, which is time spent on the plains of doom.

In the very first paragraph of the plan, Hölderlin notes those aspects of the ancient philosopher's character that fascinate him: Empedocles' desire for an intense rapport with nature, for union with the cosmos, and his contempt for all limited and one-sided human projects. Above all, and most generally, Empedocles is troubled by "the time of succession." No doubt, Empedocles' frustration with successive time is Hölderlin's frustration with Kant. If for Kant there are three modi of time, namely, (1) the persistence or perdurance of time as such (*Beharrlichkeit*), (2) time as a sequence and succession of instants (*Folge, Nacheinander*), and (3) time as the possible simultaneity of events in an instant (*Zugleichsein*), the irony is that in human experience the middle mode swallows the other two. At first, to be sure, persistence and perdurance appear to carry the day, so that the metaphysics of substance and subsistence can itself proceed unperturbed. In the "Schematism" of the second edition of *The Critique of Pure Reason* (B 183), Kant notes parenthetically: "(Time does not run out; rather, within it the existence of the mutable runs its course. Thus within experience what corresponds to time, which is itself immutable and durable, is that which is immutable in existence, i.e., substance, and in substance alone can the succession and simultaneity of appearances be determined in accord with time)" (ibid.). Yet the time that never runs out is precisely that of the succession of the manifold of appearances, and no rabbit in the hat of substance metaphysics—no a priori synthesis or unity of apperception or even free play of the imagination—will entirely banish the mocking persistence of the *Nacheinander*, the one-damn-thing-after-another to which human beings are subjected. No wonder they never seem to be able to get it together. Matthew Arnold, in his play *Empedocles on Etna* (act 2, l. 69), believed that the challenge Empedocles faced could be encapsulated in the words, "To see if we will poise our life at last."

Hölderlin belongs to that first generation of thinkers after Kant who dream of an *intellectual intuition* that will revive and rejuvenate the metaphysical rabbit. Yet Hölderlin eventually comes to identify the sole possible intellectual intuition as an *aesthetic* intuition beyond the grasp of both theoretical and practical reason. Furthermore, he understands aesthetic intuition to be insight into *tragic unification.* But that is a long and intricate story. Enough for the moment if we recognize in the oxymoron of time as persistent succession or unchanging mutability the secret appeal of the passionate, rebellious Empedocles of Acragas for so many moderns. For that oxymoron points to another more ancient one—lovehate—which says that in one and the same sphere harmony and disharmony, by turns, hold the elements together and tear them apart. The tragedy of Empedocles, which, according to the Frankfurt Plan, at first may be seen as arising from family quarrels and political disputes, ultimately will have to do with the thinker's "inmost essence." Once the "accidental occasions" have been stripped away, the tragedy of Empedocles will be seen as arising from time itself. For successive time is also the temporality that enjoins "the great man's death."

THE FRANKFURT PLAN

EMPEDOCLES
A MOURNING-PLAY IN FIVE ACTS

ACT 1

Empedocles, by temperament and through his philosophy long since destined to despise his culture, to scorn all neatly circumscribed affairs, every interest directed to sundry objects; an enemy to the death of all one-sided existence, and therefore also in actually beautiful relations unsatisfied, restive, suffering, simply because they are special relations, ones that fulfill him utterly only when they are felt in magnificent accord with all living things; simply because he cannot live in them and love them intimately, with omnipresent heart, like a god, and freely and expansively, like a god; simply because as soon as his heart and his thought embrace anything at hand he finds himself bound to the law of succession—

Empedocles takes particular offense at something that occurs during a festival of the Agrigentians; his wife, who had hoped to attain some influence as a result of the festival and who had gently persuaded him to participate in it, now scolds him sarcastically and in a way to which he is particularly sensitive; that offense and the resulting domestic quarrel give him occasion to follow his own secret inclination to leave his city and his home and betake himself to a lonely region of Mount Etna.

SCENE 1

Several pupils of Empedocles with some members of the general populace. The pupils want to convince the others that they too should join the school of Empedocles. Another of Empedocles' pupils, his favorite, comes to join them;* he forbids the other pupils to engage in any sort of proselytizing and orders them all to leave, since the master is accustomed to devote these hours to private meditation in his garden.

SCENE 2

Empedocles' monologue
His prayer to nature

* Leave now, all of you! he cries to the others as he enters.

Scene 3

Empedocles with his wife and children.*

The wife's gentle complaints concerning Empedocles' morose mood. Empedocles' heartfelt apologies. The wife's request that he be there at the great festival, which may perhaps cheer him up.

Scene 4

The festival of the Agrigentians.** Empedocles takes offense.

Scene 5

The domestic quarrel. Empedocles' departure,† without his saying what his intention is, or where he is going.

Act 2

Empedocles' pupils visit him on Etna, first of all his favorite, who truly moves him and almost draws him out of his loneliness of heart; then the others, who arouse in him yet again his indignation in the face of human neediness, so that he solemnly bids them all adieu; in the end he advises even his favorite to leave him.

Scene 1

Empedocles on Etna

Monologue. Empedocles' more decisive devotion to nature.

Scene 2

Empedocles and his favorite

---

* One of the little ones calls down from the house Father! Father! Can't you hear me? Thereupon, the mother comes down to fetch him in to breakfast, and the web of their conversation is now spun.

** A merchant, a physician, a priest, a general, a young man, an old woman.

† He says that he is taking his wife and children with him, he bears them in his heart, it's only that they cannot keep him there. It's only that the horizon crowds him too close; he says he has to leave in order to attain to the heights, so that from a remote distance he may look upon them as upon everything else that lives there, and smile upon it all.

Scene 3

Empedocles and his pupils

Scene 4

Empedocles and his favorite

Act 3

Empedocles' wife and children visit him on Etna. To their tender pleas his wife adds the news that the Agrigentians plan to erect a statue of him that very day. Honor and love, the only ties that bind us to actuality, bring him back. His pupils, overjoyed, come to his house. His favorite rushes to embrace him. Empedocles looks on as his statue is erected. He publicly thanks the people, who respond with applause and cheers.

Act 4

Those who envy him learn from several of his pupils about the harsh remarks he made concerning the people of Agrigent while his pupils were visiting him on Etna. The envious ones use those remarks to rile up the people against him; the crowd then actually topples his statue and drives him out of the city. His resolve now ripens—the resolve that has been dawning in him for some time now—to unite with infinite nature by means of a voluntary death. With this plan in mind he takes his second more profound more painful departure from his wife and children and returns to Mount Etna. He avoids his young friend because he feels certain that his friend would not be fooled by the consolations Empedocles had used to placate his wife, and that his friend would have surmised his genuine intentions.

Act 5

Empedocles prepares himself for his death. The accidental occasions of his resolve fall away altogether for him, and he now regards that resolve as a necessity proceeding from his inmost essence. In the brief scenes that he has here and there with the people who dwell in the region, he finds on all sides confirmation of his way of thinking, his resolve. His favorite arrives on Etna once again, having guessed the truth; yet the young man is so completely overwhelmed by his master's spirit and by the magnificent animatedness of the master's inmost heart that he blindly obeys his command and departs. Soon after that Empedocles casts himself into the searing flames of Etna. His favorite, wandering disconsolate and distracted through the region, soon finds an iron shoe, his master's shoe, which the volcano has catapulted from its abysses; he recognizes it, shows it to Empedocles' family and to his disciples among the populace; he gathers with these disciples at the volcano's edge in order to express their sorrow and to celebrate the great man's death.

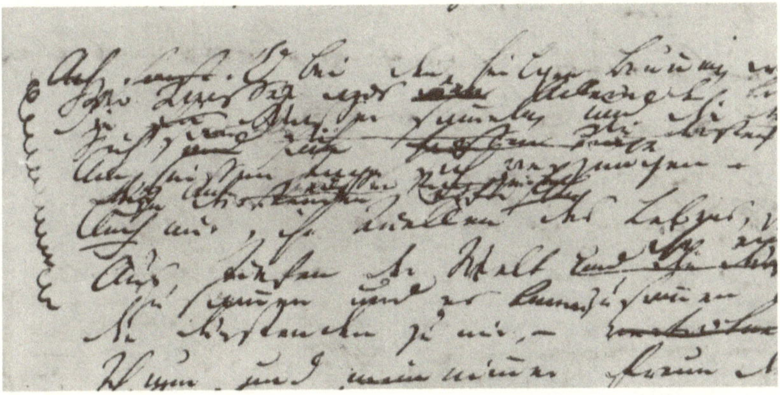

TWO

The Death of Empedocles

First Version

HÖLDERLIN BEGAN TO WRITE the first version of his mourning-play late in 1798, more than a year after completing the Frankfurt Plan. Dietrich Sattler (BA 7:7) dates the beginning of the first version at December 11, 1798; mid-October seems to be the more likely date. At all events, by April 18, 1799, Hölderlin ceased work on this first and longest version and was already contemplating a second draft. Nothing in the first version retains the Frankfurt Plan's call for a family quarrel. Indeed, Empedocles' wife and children disappear altogether from the first version. By contrast, the political dispute plays an important—although ever-diminishing—role in the sequence of the three versions. This first version consists of two acts, act 1 having nine scenes, act 2, eight; the first act, which presents the political conflict, takes place in the city of Agrigent, the second, which has more to do with Empedocles' conflict with his gods, on the slopes of Mount Etna. The principal dramatic event of this version is Empedocles' banishment from the city in act 1, and, in act 2, his decision to abandon his disciples, including his favorite, the faithful Pausanias, and to end his life in the crater of Etna.

More specifically, Empedocles is caught up in two conflicts in this first version of the play. First, he is a victim of the envious and invidious machinations of the priest, Hermocrates, and the archon, Critias, against him. Second, he is driven by the feeling that the gods of his youth, that is, the gods of nature, of sky and earth, have abandoned him—perhaps through his own fault. Thus the second conflict points to the first, because the priest and the archon charge that Empedocles has blasphemed—that he has proclaimed himself a god and thus has insulted the gods of the city and the countryside. Without doubt the play has a strongly political dimension, reflected in the lines that try to relate the philosopher's suicide to the theme of national rejuvenation: "On human life the grand desire is / Bestowed that it rejuvenate itself. / And from the purifying death that they / Themselves will choose, upon a time propitious, / Will rise, Achilles from the Styx, the nations" (ll. 1497–1501). Yet the fickle crowd, which blindly follows Hermocrates in first banishing Empedocles and then begging him to return to the city, hardly serves as a worthy foil for Empedocles' conflict. The first conflict therefore cedes to the second. The development of Empedocles' character in this first version rests on the extent to which the philosopher lends credence to, and thus falls prey to, Hermocrates' accusations and his own self-doubts. Hölderlin's marginal notations throughout the manuscript insist that it is important for Empedocles—if he is to rejoin his gods through a voluntary death—to make his suicide an essentially *affirmative* act, an act of love rather than strife. His is to be an ideal deed, "one full deed and at the end." What threatens this deed is Empedocles' wrath against the priest and his remorse—perhaps even rancor—over his own doubts. As Delia will lament toward the end, Empedocles seems all-too-anxious to plunge into the crater, as though swallowed up in guilt and thus in betrayal of life and the earth. Life is Zeus the father, and earth is Demeter the mother, "the compassionate friend of the human soul" (MK 343). Does one rejoin the gods of either sky or earth by vaporizing oneself out of feelings of worthlessness? A mortal would have to exercise the greatest caution before deciding such a question. Here one cannot afford to make a mistake, precisely because mistakes in this case are eminently possible. One of the principal questions of the play is Empedocles' hubris, or *nefas,* that is, his having uttered the unspeakable, namely, that he is no longer a mortal but a god. What attenuates this question is the fact that Empedocles is clearly an exceptional human being, one who, as it were, tantalizes the gods only because they have bestowed such lavish gifts on him. Would not feelings of worthlessness be a delusion and the desire to rejoin the gods through suicide the ultimate delusion?

As the versions proceed, the female characters, Rhea (later, in scene 9 of act 1, called Delia) and Panthea, have less and less a role in the play. Yet this is not to say that they pertain to those inessential "accidents" that Hölderlin resolved to remove from the plot. Indeed, their speeches contain some of the best poetry in the play. Moreover, Delia's challenge to Empedocles' planned suicide is decisive for all three versions. Max Kommerell notes that Panthea's and Delia's words in the first version are taken up by the Egyptian priest, Manes, in the third; the implication is that Hölderlin places some of his most important ideas in the mouths of these women, who continue the tradition of "Diotima" in Hölderlin's early work, *Hyperion,* and anticipate the figure of the wise old man in the third version of the play (see TA 324–30). What all these characters entertain is the possibility that Empedocles' suicide may be the result of profound melancholia, and not at all of an affirmative resolve.

Another essential aspect of the play, one that clearly causes Hölderlin difficulty, is the relationship between Empedocles and his "favorite," Pausanias. We recall that the lyric poem "Empedocles" appears to have as its narrative or poetic "voice" someone very much like Pausanias, that is, someone who is held back from the crater's edge by love. A poem first sketched in November 1799, "Winter," concludes with the following lines:

> And among the friendly tutelary spirits dwells
> With him still one that gladly blesses, and even if
> All the others that nourish us, those goodly forces,
> Became our enemies, love would still love. (BA 8:50)

The role of love in a mourning-play is problematic if only because, as Hölderlin says in a letter, the elevated diction of tragedy makes it sound as though the lovers are always squabbling. So it is with Empedocles and Pausanias in act 2. The deeper problem, however, is how one can justify—especially in dramatic terms, that is, on the stage—Empedocles' rejection of Pausanias's love. The refusal of Empedocles to abide with Pausanias and Panthea intensifies the problem indicated earlier, namely, the problem of an entirely affirmative relation to one's own death, especially death by suicide. Can such an affirmative relation countenance—or is it in fact contradicted by—the refusal to love? Does one rejoin the gods of nature by turning one's back on love?

Finally, the last scene of act 2, in which Pausanias, Panthea, and Delia speculate on the reason for Empedocles' disappearance, leaves us with a sense that the philosopher's "one full deed and at the end" is problematic in the extreme, that in fact it cannot be carried out. As we know, Hölderlin fails to bring that deed onto the stage. One is left with Delia's words to Pausanias ringing in one's ears: the death of a hero may inspire certain souls, but it merely lacerates others.

> Ha! magnificent soul! the death of this great man seems
> To elevate your soul; me it only tears apart. What
> Remains of all this, tell me, what here still has life? (ll. 1996–1998)

In terms of the formal aspects of the play, Hölderlin begins by writing prose; only gradually does he slip into the rhythm of iambic pentameter. The present translation tries to respect the iambs once they get established, but in order to remain close to the meaning of the German text it does not aim for any specific number of feet in a line. All footnotes in the text are Hölderlin's; in the holograph they are marginalia introduced at various places on the page. They are in each case perceptive remarks that might well serve as keys to an interpretation of the play. Throughout the volume, the gaps in the text are Hölderlin's; material in brackets has been added by editors for the sake of clarity.

The Death of Empedocles
First Version

[Act 1, Scene 1]
Panthea, Rhea

PANTHEA
This is his garden! There in the veiled
penumbra, near the bubbling spring, he stood
not long ago, as I passed by—you
have never seen him?

RHEA
O Panthea!
It was only yesterday I came with my
father to Sicily. Yet once when
I was but a child I saw
him in a chariot race
at the games in Olympia.
There was much talk about him then,
and always his name has stayed with me.

PANTHEA
You have to see him now! now!
They say the plants gaze up at
him as he walks by, and the waters 'neath the earth
strive upward to the surface when his staff grazes the ground!
And all that may be true!
and when in a storm he looks at the sky
the clouds part and reveal the shimmering
cheerful day.—Yet
what does any of that say? you must see the man himself!
if only for a moment! and then flee! I myself avoid him
a terrifying, all-transforming essence is in him
——

RHEA
How does he live with others? I grasp nothing
of this man;
Does he have his bootless days, as we all do,
When one feels stale and insignificant?
And is there also human suffering for him?

PANTHEA
Ah! when last I saw him there within
The shadow of his trees, he surely felt
His own deep sorrow—the godly one
In wondrous languishing, sadly searching
As though he had lost much, looks down
To earth, then up into the twilight of
The grove, as though into blue remoteness
His life had fled from him, and the humility of
His royal countenance seized
My troubled heart—you too must go under,
You magnificent star! and it won't be long!
This I could sense—

RHEA
Have you ever
Spoken to him, Panthea?

PANTHEA
Oh, that you remind me of it! Not long ago I
lay stricken unto death. Already the bright day
was darkening before me and the world faltered
like a soulless phantom in its course around the sun.
My father, although a sworn enemy
of the man, called him on that desperate day,
appealed to the one who was intimate with nature,
and when the splendid man reached out to me
and bade me drink his elixir, my struggling life
fused in magic reconciliation, and as though
restored to sweet and sensuous
childhood I fell into a trance for many days,
and scarcely did I need to draw a breath—how
now in newborn joy my essence for the first time
unfolded to a world I'd long renounced,
my eye disclosed the day in youthful curiosity,
and there he stood, Empedocles! how godlike
and how present to me! beneath his smiling eyes
my life blossomed forth again! ah,
like a fleecy morning cloud my heart
soared upward to that sweet light and I was
its tender reflection.

RHEA
O Panthea!

PANTHEA
The sounds that surged from his breast! in each syllable
of his, every melody sang out to me! and
the spirit in his words!—at his feet
I'd sit, for hours at a time, as his pupil
his child, gazing out into the ether that is all his own
and, clambering joyously to his own heaven's
height, my senses fairly wandered.

RHEA
What would he say, love, if he but knew!

PANTHEA
He doesn't know. He needs nothing, traverses
His own world; reposing gently like a god
He walks among his flowers; the very breeze
Forbears disturbing this most fortunate one,
and from out of himself there waxes
In ever-enhancing enjoyment an enthusiasm
Within, until from the night of his creative rapture
The thought, like a spark, leaps,
And cheerfully the spirit of deeds that are
To come crowd his soul, and the world,
The leavening life of humankind, and the larger
Natural world about him radiate—here he feels like
A god within his element; his joy intones
A canticle of heaven; he then steps forth
To face his people, on days when jostling crowds
In vacillating tumult crave
A man more powerful than they,
That is when he rules, the splendid pilot, and
He helps them; and when they finally grow
Accustomed to this eternal stranger, when they
Would fain accommodate themselves to him,
He's gone—into its shade the silent plant world
Will draw him, where he finds himself more readily,
And its enigmatic life is present to him
In all its multifarious force.

RHEA
Woman! listen to you! how do you know all this?

PANTHEA
I follow traces that he leaves—what, beyond him,
Is there for me to follow? ah! and if I've grasped him,
What's that? To be him, that is life, and
We others are the dream of life.—
His friend Pausanias has also told me much
About him—the young man sees him
Day in, day out, and Jove's eagle is
Not prouder than Pausanias—this I do believe!

RHEA
I find no fault, dear love, in what you say,
And yet my soul mourns wondrously
About all this; I want to be like you,
And then again I don't. Do all of you on
The island act like this? We too take
Our pleasure in great men, and one of them
Is now the very sun to every Athenian woman,
Sophocles! to him among all mortals first of all
The most resplendent nature of young womanhood
Appeared and granted him a pure memorial of itself
Within his soul—
          every woman wishes she could be a thought of this
Amazing man, and every one of us would gladly save
The ever lovely beauty of her youth before it wilts
Depositing that beauty in the poet's soul
And each inquires and riddles as to which of the city's
Young women that tender earnest heroine may be
Who hovered there before his soul, the one he calls
Antigone; and all grows bright
About our brows when this friend of gods
On cheerful festive days enters the theater;
Yet our delight is free from trouble
And never does our loving heart lose itself
As yours does, captive to a painful worship—
You sacrifice yourself—I do believe he possesses
Too much of grandeur, you cannot live at peace,
This boundless one you love so boundlessly,

And how will this help him? you yourself, you sensed
His downgoing, good child, and you intend
To go into decline with him?

PANTHEA

Play not upon
My pride, and fear for him, not me!
I am not he; when he goes down
His downgoing cannot be mine,
For great is also the death of the great
what is coming to confront this man,
Believe me, will confront but him alone,
And if he were to sin against all gods, and
Invite their wrath upon him, and if I
Should want to sin as he had done,
To draw the selfsame lot in suffering, that
Would be as though a stranger tried to interrupt
A lovers' quarrel—What have you to do with us,
The gods would say; you fool, you never could
Insult us in the way he can.

RHEA

You are perhaps
More like him than you think; how else
Could you delight in him?

PANTHEA

Dear heart!
I do not know myself why I belong
To him—if only you could see him!—
I thought he might be coming out,

you would have seen him then as he
Passed by—a thing to wish for! is it not so?
Though I should wean myself of wishes, for it seems
As though importunate prayers do not please
The gods, and they are right in this!
No longer will I pray this way—yet hope
I must, you good gods, for I know
Nothing other than him—
I'd rather pray like other people, Dispense,

Please, rain and sunshine—if I only could!
O eternal mystery, what we are
And what we seek, we cannot find; and what
We find, that we are not—yet what is
The hour, Rhea?

RHEA
Your father's now approaching.
I do not know, should we stay or go—

PANTHEA
What did you say? my father? come! away!

[SCENE 2]
Critias the Archon, Hermocrates the Priest

HERMOCRATES
Who is that walking there?

CRITIAS
My daughter, I believe
And Rhea, daughter of my houseguest, who
Arrived just yesterday at my home.

HERMOCRATES
Is this by chance? or are they too seeking him
Believing, as the people do, that he's been taken up?

CRITIAS
That marvelous report has surely not yet reached
My daughter's ears. And yet she worships him,
She's like the rest of them; I would that he were gone—
To forests, deserts, or across the sea
Or down below, beneath the earth—wherever his
Unbounded thought may drive him.

HERMOCRATES
But no! they must be made to see him once again,
So that their frenzied lunacy departs from them.

CRITIAS
Where is he, then?

HERMOCRATES

Not far from here. There
He sits in darkness, soulless. For it has so befallen that
The gods have robbed him of his force, ever since
The day the man, besotted, to be sure, in front of all
The people recklessly proclaimed himself a god.*

CRITIAS

The people are besotted, as is he himself.
For they know nothing of the law nor of emergency
And they respect no judge; their ways are like
The foam upon the blindly surging surf
That floods our peaceful shores,
And every day is spent in wild feasting;
A feast to outdo all the feasts, the modest holidays
Of our good gods have of a sudden
All gone missing; concealing everything,
This necromancer obscures both sky and earth
In storms he's brewed for us. And now, surveying all
Without a care, his spirit entertains itself
Within his silent halls.

HERMOCRATES

Almighty was
The soul of such a man in your domain.

CRITIAS

I tell you: they know nothing else than him
Desire that all should come from him,
And he should be their god, should be their king.
I too stood stupefied by him, profoundly so
When he preserved from death my daughter.
What do you make of him, Hermocrates?

---

* For us, such a thing is more a sin against the intellect; for the ancients, it was, when seen from the side of intelligence, more excusable, because it was more comprehensible to them. It was not a *faux pas* in their view; it was a crime. They did not excuse it, however, because their delicate sense of freedom could not bear such a proclamation. Precisely because they respected it and understood it better, they feared it all the more—this arrogance of genius. For us, this is not something dangerous, because we cannot even be touched by it.

HERMOCRATES
The gods once loved him overmuch.
Yet he is not the first whom soon enough
They thrust into the senseless night,
Cast down from heights of their familiarity
Because he proved forgetful of the difference
In his extravagant delight, feeling for
Himself alone; so it went with him, he is
Now punished, in arid wastes abandoned—although
The final hour for him has not yet come;
Whoever has for so long been their darling
Will not long bear the insult to his soul,
I fear; his drowsy spirit will spark to flame
Anew to work out its revenge,
And, half-roused, a fearsome dreamer speaks
In him as once it spoke in those enthusiasts of old
Who wandered throughout Asia bearing reeds for staffs,
Whose word was how the gods first came to be.
For then the wide world, replete with life,
Becomes lost property to him,
And monstrous cravings stir within
His breast; no matter where it leaps,
The scorching flame will clear the path ahead.
All law and art, all custom, every holy word
And all that once did ripen here for him in time
All these are sore disrupted, and joy and peace our man
Can never let prevail again among the things that live.
And he will never be the tranquil one again.

CRITIAS
Old man! you do envisage nameless things
Your word is true and when it is fulfilled
Then woe to you, dear Sicily, as lovely as
You are with all your groves and temples.

HERMOCRATES
The gods' own words will strike him down before
His ploys begin. Call the people to assembly, that I
May show to them the face of him
Of whom they say he's soared unto
The ether. They shall be witness to
The curse I'll lay upon him

And to his banishment in barren wasteland,
That there, never to return again,
He'll pay, and dearly, for that evil hour he
Made himself a god.

CRITIAS

Our people, though, are weak.
What if the bold one masters them,
Do you not fear for me and you and all your gods?

HERMOCRATES

The priest's harsh word will shatter his bold sense of self.

CRITIAS

And will they banish thence the man they once did love,
Must he then suffer, made wretched by your holy curse,
Be banished from his gladdening gardens
And from the town that was his home?

HERMOCRATES

But who would dare to entertain a mortal in their land
When he is branded by a well-deserved curse?

CRITIAS

Yet what if you should seem to be blaspheming
To those who once revered him as a god?

HERMOCRATES

The tumult of the crowd will wane as soon as they
Espy him with their eyes again, the one they dreamed
Was taken up into the gods' high dwelling!
Already they have made a turn, and for the better,
For yesterday they gathered, drifting hereabout
In mourning, wandering, saying much
Of him, as I was walking this same path.
At which I said today I would
Conduct them to him; meanwhile they
Should tarry in their homes, quiet each and all.
And that is why I asked you now to come
With me, that we might see if they
Obeyed me. You find no one here. So, come.

CRITIAS

Hermocrates!

HERMOCRATES
What is it?

CRITIAS
I see him there
In flesh and blood.

HERMOCRATES
Then let us go, Critias!
That he may not ensnare us in his talk.

[SCENE 3]

EMPEDOCLES
Into my stillness you came softly wandering,
You found me out in my dark grotto,
You, my friend! you came as I had hoped
And from afar, above the earth; I rightly sensed
Your sweet recurrence, lovely day
And my familiar friends, you energetic
Forces in the heights! and you are close
To me again as once before, you blessed ones,
You never-erring sturdy trees within my grove!
You grew so steadily and daily drank
From heaven's source, you humble ones
With light and sparks of life well sated
The ether pollinating all your blossoms.

O intimate nature! I have you now before
My eyes, do you still know your friend, the one
You deeply loved, do you know me now no more?
The priest who brought you living song
Like sacrificial blood that's gladly shed?

Oh, by the sacred founts, where quietly
The waters gather, where those who thirst
On summer days rejuvenate! in me
In me, you founts of life, you once flowed all
Together from the world's depths;
The parched then came to me—desiccated now
Am I, no more do mortals take their joy

In me—am I all alone? and is it now night
Up here, the daylight notwithstanding? woe!
An eye that saw more lofty things than mortal eye
Is now struck blind, I grope about me—
Where are you, O my gods? woe, do you now leave
Me like a beggar? and this breast that loves
And is attuned to you, why do you now repel it?
Why bind in narrow shameful bonds
The one born free, who on his own is
His own and no one else's? Am I condemned
To suffer this; is my anemic soul in timid Tartarus
In thrall to ancient works and ancient days?
I recognize my self; I will it! I'll have air
About me, ha! and daylight—begone!
By my pride! the dust of this poor path
I will not stoop to kiss, where once upon a time
I walked in dazzling dreams—that's gone now!
I was beloved, beloved of you, my gods
Ah, intimately, as you live with one another
So you lived in me, and no! that was
No dream; in this heart of mine I felt you
I saw you I knew you I worked with you

O Phantom!

That's gone now
And you alone, conceal it not! you have
Yourself to blame, you wretched Tantalus
The sacred precincts you've besmirched,
With haughty pride revoked the covenant,
Pernicious one! for when the genial spirits of the world
Loved you, forgot themselves in you, you remembered
Yourself alone, believed, you unregenerate fool,
That all beneficence had sold itself to you,
That these celestial ones would serve you slavishly!
Among you is there nowhere an avenger
Must I alone pronounce contempt and curse upon
My soul? Is no one there to snatch from my poor head
The Delphic crown, no one better suited
Than I myself to shave my head, as
Befits a balding seer—

[Scene 4]
Empedocles, Pausanias

Pausanias
O all
You powers of heaven, what's this?

Empedocles
Begone!
Who sent you here? the work I have to do,
Would you now ruin it for me? I'll tell you everything
In case you do not know; then bring all you may do
Into accord—Pausanias! Oh, seek not
The man to whom your heart once clung,
He is no more, and go, my gentle youth!
Your countenance enflames my sense,
And be it blessing, be it curse, with you
Each is much too much for me. But as you will!

Pausanias
What's happened? Long have I abided
With you, was thankful to the daylight
When from afar I saw you, and now I find
You noble man! alas! like the oak Zeus struck
From crown to sole you have been shattered.
Were you alone? I did not hear a spoken word,
And yet uncanny sounds of death reverberate in me.

Empedocles
It was the voice of one who thought himself beyond
The mortal, because a generous nature
Had given him too much.

Pausanias
To be like you,
Familiar as you are with all the godly things in this
Our world, can never be too much.

Empedocles
So said I,
My dear boy, when the holy magic
Had not yet quit my spirit, and when they

Still loved me, me who in return loved
Intensely all the tutelary spirits of the world,
O light of sky!—it was not men
Who taught me this—for long ago, when
My longing heart fell short and missed
The living whole, I turned to you,
I hung on you, I clung to you as plants will cling,
In pious joy, long and long, as though blind.
For mortals scarcely recognize the pure
Yet when
        the spirit in me bloomed, as did you yourself,
And when I knew you, I cried out, You are alive
And as you wander cheerfully among the mortals,
And as your heavenly youth so nobly radiates
From you and floods all things with its own light,
That all may don the colors of your spirit,
For me as well this life became a poem.
Your soul was in me; openly my heart,
Like yours, gave itself unto the earnest earth
The suffering one, and oft in holy night
I swore to – ˘ her, unto death
To love with fearless faith the fateful one
And not to scorn a single one of all her mysteries.
The winds then wafted otherwise within my grove,
And mountain springs were gurgling tenderly,
And on the flowers' mild yet fiery breaths
O earth! came gently to me your more reposeful life,
All your joys, earth! not as you grant them smilingly
To weaker ones, but splendid, as they are,
All ardent, all true, ripening in labor and in love,—
You gave them all to me, and oft when
Perched on mountain heights remote
I gazed and mused on life's divine delirium,
Too deeply moved by all your alterations,
And intimating my own destiny, then
The ether breathed to me, as it does to you,
A salve upon my love-torn breast,
And magically in his vast depths dissolved
The riddles nesting in me—

PAUSANIAS

                    You blessed one!

EMPEDOCLES
I was! oh, if only I could say the way it was
And call it by its name—the changes and the charges of
Your splendid tutelary forces, whose comrade I then was,
O nature! could I but one more time revive it in my soul
That in my mute and mortifying breast
Your sounds might chime again!
Am I still that? O life! and if they were to whelm me,
All your winged melodies, and if I were now to hear
Your ancient consonance, grand nature!
Alas! abandoned by it all, did I not live
With this our holy earth and with this light,
With you from whom the soul may never roam,
O father ether! and with all that lives
On all-gathering, all-present Mount Olympus?—
[Now I weep as one ostracized,]
And nowhere can I stay, alas, and you
As well are taken from me,—don't say a word!
For love expires as soon as gods have flown,
You know that well; so leave me now, I am
No longer what I was, have nothing more in you.

PAUSANIAS
You still are that man, as truly as you ever were.
And let me say, incomprehensible it is
To me, the way you would annihilate yourself.
I well believe it's true, your soul sinks in sleep
At times in you, when it has had enough
Exposure to the world, just as the earth,
Which you do love, oft occludes herself in deep repose.
Yet do you call her dead when she but rests?

EMPEDOCLES
How sweetly now you toil to grant me consolation!

PAUSANIAS
You mock my inexperience and think because
I did not know your happiness as intimately
As you did, now that you're in pain
I'm talking nonsense. Did I not see you
Performing deeds, when our savage state attained
Its shape and its direction from you; in its power

I felt your spirit and your spirit's world, when oft
A word from you upon a salutary moment
Gave me a life for many years, so that
A new and a propitious time began
From that point on for the boy; as with caged deer,
When from afar the forest calls they think of home,
Thus my heart would often throb when you invoked
The gladness of the ancient primal world, and
Did you not limn the lines of times to come
For me, the way an artist's knowing glance can add
The missing piece and make the painting whole?
Does not the destiny of humankind reveal itself entirely
To you? And know you not the forces of this nature,
That you who are in league with them as mortal never was
Can, when you will, steer them all in silent mastery?

EMPEDOCLES
Enough! you do not know how every word
You're saying stings and tortures me.

PAUSANIAS
So must you then in melancholy hate all things that are?

EMPEDOCLES
Oh, honor what you do not understand!

PAUSANIAS
Why
Conceal it from me, why make your suffering
A riddle to me? believe me, nothing is more painful.

EMPEDOCLES
And nothing causes greater pain, Pausanias,
Than riddling on our suffering. Do you not see?
Alas! I'd rather you knew naught of me
And all my mourning. No! I should
Not utter it aloud, holy nature!*

---

* His sin is the original sin, and therefore is absolutely nothing abstract, just as little as supreme joy is something abstract; it is merely that this has to be presented in a genetically vital way.

Gentle virgin, fleeing every rough approach!
I spurned you, declared myself alone
Your lord and master, arrogant
Barbarian that I am! I held you fast to your simplicity,
You pure powers, ever youthful!
And you who raised me joyously, and with delight
Did nourish me, you who always came back
To me, you good ones, I did not respect your soul!
Oh, yes, I knew it all, had fully learned
The life of nature; how should it have
Remained as sacred as it once was; the gods had
Become mere menials to me, I alone
Was god, and spoke it out in haughty insolence—
Oh, believe me, would I never had
Been born!

PAUSANIAS

What? By dint of a mere word?
How can you, who are so bold, waiver so?

EMPEDOCLES

By dint of a mere word? yes. And may
The gods annihilate me, as they once
Did love me.

PAUSANIAS

Others do not speak as you do.

EMPEDOCLES

The others! how could they?

PAUSANIAS

Indeed,
You marvelous man! So intensely loving,
Envisaging the everlasting world
And all its tutelaries, all its forces, never anyone
Like you, and therefore you spoke that bold word,
Even you, alone, and thus you also feel
So strongly how with one proud syllable you tore
Yourself away, abandoning the hearts of all the gods
And now most lovingly you'll sacrifice yourself to them,
O Empedocles!—

EMPEDOCLES
Behold! what's this?
Hermocrates the priest, and with him
A crowd of people, and Critias the archon—
What do they want of me?

PAUSANIAS
They have long
Been in pursuit, to find out where you were.

[SCENE 5]
Empedocles, Pausanias,
Hermocrates, Critias, a crowd from Agrigent

HERMOCRATES
Here is the man of whom you say
That living he has risen to Olympus.

CRITIAS
And he looks mournful, like a mortal.

EMPEDOCLES
You wretched mockers! do you take pleasure
When someone suffers whom you once thought great?
And do you take him to be easy booty,
The strong one, once he's weakened?
His fruit has fallen ripe upon the earth; it tempts you;
Believe me, not all ripens for the likes of you.

AN AGRIGENTIAN
What does he mean by that?

EMPEDOCLES
I beg you, go
And tend to your affairs; do not meddle
In what is mine—

HERMOCRATES
Yet just one word
A priest may surely speak to you?

EMPEDOCLES

Woe!
You pristine gods! you living ones! Must this
Conniving hypocrite infect my mourning with
His poison? Go! Often I protected you,
And so it's meet that you should shield me
You know that this is true, I've told you so,
I know you and your arrant lot.
And long it was quite riddlesome to me,
How nature in her daily rounds put up with you.
Alas! for even as a boy my pious heart
Avoided you who soil all you touch;
My pious heart, intensely loving, clove
To sun and ether, all the messengers
Of our grand nature intimated from afar.
For surely even then I felt it, I feared
That you would bend my heart's free love
Of gods to some obnoxious servitude,
That I would treat all things as you treat them,

Begone! I cannot bear to face a man who
Abuses holy things as stock in trade.
His gaze is false and chill and dead,
And so are all his gods. Why stand there
Thunderstruck? Get you gone!

CRITIAS

Not until
The sacred curse has marked your brow
You arrogant blasphemer!

HERMOCRATES

Be at peace,
My friend! I warned you that his melancholy now
Would surely seize him.—The man jeers
At me, you heard him, citizens
Of Agrigent! though I will not exchange
Harsh words with him in savage quarrel. It does not suit
An aged man like me. Yet you yourselves
Should ask him, who is he?

EMPEDOCLES

Oh, leave me,—
You surely see it profits none to prod
A wounded heart. Grant me the chance
To wander quietly the path I tread
Along the sacred silent route of death.
The sacrificial beast will be released from yoke
And plow, no more the driver's lash to suffer
Preserve me too this way; do not deprive me of
My suffering with all your pestilential talk,
For holiness is here; release my breast from the
Calamity you are; my pain pertains to gods.

FIRST AGRIGENTIAN

What is this, then, Hermocrates, why says
The man such unfamiliar things?

SECOND AGRIGENTIAN

He says that we should go; he's clearly skittish.

HERMOCRATES

Well, what do you suppose? his senses have grown dull
Because he claimed to be a god before your very eyes.
Yet since you never take my word for true,
Inquire of him yourselves. Let him tell you.

THIRD AGRIGENTIAN

We do believe you.

PAUSANIAS

You do believe him, all of you?
You shameless ones!—Your Jupiter
Has failed to please today, his countenance is gloomy;
Your idol grants you now no sanctuary
And so you're ready to believe the priest? Your idol stands
Stock still and mourns, his spirit taciturn; in times
Devoid of heroes all the youths will yearn
For him when he's no longer here; and you,
You slither all about him, hissing,
Dare you do that? have your senses grown so coarse
That this man's eye does not admonish you?
And now that he's grown gentle, cowards dare

Approach him—O sacred nature! In your cycles
How put up with vipers such as these?—
And now you gape at me and fathom not
A single word of what I say; you'll have
To ask the priest. For he knows everything.

HERMOCRATES
Oh, listen how now in our faces, yours and mine,
The upstart scolds. Ah, but then why shouldn't he, he's
Allowed, his master dares do all, you see.
Whoever lures the people says whatever thing
He likes; I know that well, and yet I do not strive
Against it for my part, since up to now
The gods endure it. Tolerating much, they remain
Quite still until the savage boldness reaches its
Crescendo. But then blasphemers one and all
Are snatched away to darkness and abyss.

THIRD AGRIGENTIAN
O citizens! I'll tell you what. With these two
In times to come I'll have nothing more to do.

FIRST AGRIGENTIAN
Say,
How did it come about that this one fooled us so?

SECOND AGRIGENTIAN
They simply have to go, the pupil and his master.

HERMOCRATES
The time has come!—I plead with you, O fearsome ones!
You gods of vengeance!—Zeus conducts the clouds
Poseidon tames the briny waves,
But you who tread so softly, to you alone
Is given lordship over all that lies concealed
And where a self-empowering wight
Emerges from the cradle, there you are,
And as he waxes strong in sacrilege you
Abide with him, silently espying, hearkening to
The depths within his breast, until a careless,
Insouciant word betrays to you the gods' own enemy—
Him too, yes, you knew him, the sly and secretive

Seducer, he who robbed the people of their sense
And flaunted all the laws of this our fatherland,
And never did he heed the ancient gods of Agrigent,
And all their priests he disrespected,
Yet he was not invisible to you, you terrifying ones!
He kept it hushed, of course, his monstrous dark intent;
But he is finished now. Despicable one!
Did you imagine they would dance a jig when you
Of late and in their face announced yourself a god?
You would have ruled in Agrigent,
A tyrant solitary and omnipotent;
And you alone would have possessed
These good people, this fair land. Yet they
Were silent, shocked; they simply stood there;
And you grew pale, it crippled you,
The evil canker in your darkling halls,
For there you fled, escaping light of day.
And now you'd like to come and shower me
With all your grief, blasphemer of the gods?

FIRST AGRIGENTIAN
Well, now it's clear! he must be put to death.

CRITIAS
I told you so; I never trusted
The dreamer.

EMPEDOCLES
O raving ones!

HERMOCRATES
You speak
Once more and do not sense that you and we
Share nothing any longer; a stranger now,
You are unknown to all that lives.
The source that slakes our thirst is not
For you, nor is the fire that serves us well;
Whatever cheers a mortal's heart
The gods of vengeance now will snatch from you
For you is not the cheering light up here above
Nor green of earth nor any of her fruits,

And breeze no longer grants to you her blessings
Whenever in your heart you thirst and beg for cooling
In vain is all of that for you, you'll not partake again
Of what belongs to us; for you belong to the
Avengers, yes, the holy gods of death alone.
And woe to him from this day forth who
In his soul receives a friendly word from you,
To him who greets you, offering his hand,
To him who gives you drink at noon
Invites you to his table's entertainments,
To him who, when at night you knock upon his door,
Might grant you sleep beneath his roof,
And when you die, whoever sets a flame upon
Your funeral pyre—woe to him and you! begone!
No longer will the nations' gods endure,
Where temples are, the man who spurns them all.

THE CROWD
Let him be gone! Let not his curse besmirch us!

PAUSANIAS
Oh, come with me! you will not go alone. There is
One still who honors you, although it is forbidden,
Dear friend! you know the blessing of a friend
Is mightier than any priest's most baneful curse.
Oh, come with me to foreign shores! there too
We'll find the light of heaven, and I will pray that it
May shine companionably in your soul.
In proud and cheerful Greece, across the sea,
The hills grow green, and pleasing shade we'll find
Beneath the maple trees for you, and zephyrs mild
To cool the wanderer's breast; and when you are
Exhausted on those dog days on our far paths
We'll pause, and with these hands I'll draw you drink
From fountains fresh, and I'll go foraging for food,
And twigs I'll weave to shade your head,
And moss and leaves I'll gather for your bed,
And while you're sleeping I'll keep watch for you;
And if it needs must come to pass, I'll kindle there
The flame upon your pyre, the flame that they forbid,
These shameless ones!

EMPEDOCLES

O faithful heart!—For me,
You citizens, I ask for nothing; let all be as you say!
I beg you to reflect for this boy's sake alone.
Oh, do not turn your faces from me!
Am I not he about whom you once lovingly
Assembled? You yourselves would shrink
From reaching out and touching me,
Unseemly then it was for you to jostle friends.
You sent to me your sons, and they gave me
Their hands, those amiable ones, and perched
Upon your shoulders came your little ones
And with your arms you raised them up to me—
Am I not still that one? know you not the man
Of whom you said you could as beggars go
From land to land with him, if he elected you,
And if there were a chance in hell you'd follow him
To Tartarus below, far, far down below?
You children! you yearned to give me everything
And often petulant you forced me to receive from you;
It was the thing that fueled and fed your lives.
Then I returned the favor, giving you of mine,
And you felt I was giving more and better.
Now I am to leave you; deny me not
This one request: safeguard this youth!
He never did you harm; he merely loves me
As you yourselves did love; and tell me now,
Is he not noble, is he not beautiful! and it's true,
In days to come you'll need him, believe me!
I've told you many times: it would be night
And bitter cold on earth, calamity would gnaw
Upon the soul, were not the good gods
From time to time to send such youths
To vitalize the wilting life of humankind.
You should keep hale, I told you then,
These genial tutelaries—protect him now
And call not woe upon him! promise me!

THIRD AGRIGENTIAN

Begone! We'll hear no more of all
You say.

HERMOCRATES
The boy will walk the path that he himself
Has chosen, pay the price for willful insolence;
He goes with you, the curse on you inculpates him.

EMPEDOCLES
Yet you are silent, Critias! Do not try to hide it,
You too are struck; you knew the boy, did you not,
And streams of sacrificial blood will never purge
Your sin? I beg you, tell them, my good man!
They are as though intoxicated, speak a soothing word
So that their senses may return to these poor men!

SECOND AGRIGENTIAN
He still berates us? Dwell on your own curse,
Stop talking now and go! Otherwise we'll lay
Our hands on you!

CRITIAS
Well said,
Citizens!

EMPEDOCLES
So!—you'd like to lay your hands
On me? How's that? Foaming at the mouth
And salivating for my life, you wretched
Harpies? can you then not wait until
My spirit's flown to desecrate the corpse?
Come on! tear the flesh and share the prey
And let your priest beg blessings on your meal,
His family friends, avenger gods, he has invited!—
You balk, you unregenerate! do you know me?
And shall I spoil the nasty prank you have contrived?
By your gray hairs, man! you should return
Your dust to dust; to be the Furies' footman
You are not man enough. Behold!
You stand there in your ignominy, yet would try
To master me? Of course, it is a paltry piece
Of work to hunt and kill a bleeding beast!
I mourned; this man knew that, thus waxed
The coward's courage; now he seizes me
And sinks the people's fangs into my heart.

Oh, who, who will save the savaged prey, who
Will offer sanctuary, sparing one who homeless
Drifts scarred and shamed past strangers' houses, begs
The gods within the grove to harbor him—come, my son!
Yes, they have hurt me; yet I'd have blotted it
From memory—but they've hurt you? ha!
Then all this nameless lot should go to hell!
And may they die* a creeping death, and for their dirge
The priestly raven's song! Because the wolves
Assemble there where corpses are, let one find
Its way to them, to gorge itself on blood
And gore, thereby to purify
Our Sicily of them. Arid looms
[The land where once the purple grape
Did flourish for a better people, and golden fruit
In shady grove, and noble grain; and one day
A stranger will inquire as he treads upon the ashes of
Your temples whether once upon a time back then
Your city stood there? now go! You'll find me
In one hour nevermore.—]
(as they exit)

Critias!

To you I'll say but one word more.

PAUSANIAS
(after Critias has returned)

Then let
Me meanwhile go and bid my aged father fond
Farewell.

EMPEDOCLES

But why, you gods? What did
The young man do to you? Go then,
Poor boy! I'll wait outside the city, on the path
To Syracuse; we'll wander there together.
(Pausanias exits on the other side)

---

* No curse! he has to love unto infinity; then he dies, in order not to have to live without love and without his tutelary spirit. He has to *consume,* as it were, all the rest of that conciliatory force that perhaps could have restored to him his prior blessed felicitous life—had these things not transpired.

[SCENE 6]
Empedocles, Critias

CRITIAS
What is it?

EMPEDOCLES
So you too persecute me?

CRITIAS
Why ask
Me that?

EMPEDOCLES
I know full well!
You'd dearly love to hate me, yet hate me you do not:
You merely fear; yet you had naught to fear.

CRITIAS
It's over. What can you want now?

EMPEDOCLES
You
Yourself did not concoct this scheme; the priest
Compelled you by the force of his own will;
Do not accuse yourself. If only you had said
A true word for the boy; you faltered there
Before the people.

CRITIAS
Did you have nothing else
To say to me? superfluous chatter
Was ever your first love.

EMPEDOCLES
Oh, speak softly
I saved your daughter's life.

CRITIAS
You did do that.

EMPEDOCLES

You bristle and you feel ashamed
To speak with one our fatherland has cursed;
This I do believe of you. Imagine that it is
My shade now talking, returned
In honor from the blessed Land of Peace—

CRITIAS

I'd not have come in answer to your call,
Had not the people wished to know
What else you had to say.

EMPEDOCLES

The thing I have to say to you means nothing
To the people.

CRITIAS

What is it then?

EMPEDOCLES

You must depart from Sicily; I tell you this
For her, your daughter's, sake.

CRITIAS

Think about
Yourself and have no care for others.

EMPEDOCLES

Do you
Not know her? is it beyond your ken to know
How very much it's better for a city full of fools
To perish than for one outstanding one to fail?

CRITIAS

You think because you'll not be here no good
Can happen in our land?

EMPEDOCLES

Do you not know her?
And do you tamper like a blind man with the gift
The gods bestowed on you? and that bright light
Within your walls illuminates in vain?

I tell you openly: captive to a nation such as this
A pious life will find no rest; with all
Her beauty, hers will be a lonely life;
She'll die deprived of joy; for never will
This tender earnest daughter of the gods take
Barbarians to heart, believe me when
I speak! Departing spirits tell the truth.
So do not marvel at my counsel!

CRITIAS

What should
I say to that?

EMPEDOCLES

Depart with her, go to
A consecrated land, to Elis or to Delos,
Where dwell the folk for whom she pines so lovingly
And where, all silently assembled, images of heroes
Stand free within the laurel wood. There she'll rest;
Among the silent idols will
Her gentle sense be nurtured to
Her tender satisfaction; there amid the noble shades
Her pain will nod, the pain that she has locked away
Within her reverent breast. When on that day
The handsome youths of Hellas gather at the feast,
And strangers throng about her, greeting one another,
And life, on all sides joyous, full of hope,
Surrounds her silent heart, a cloud of gold,
The dawn will also stir to joy
This pious maid who loves to dream;
Among the best of youths whose hymns
And wreathes were won in fair contest she will
Choose one, that he may lead her from the shadows
That all too soon became her sole companions.
If it should please you, obey me.

CRITIAS
Have you in your distress so many
Golden words to spare?

EMPEDOCLES

You must not mock!
Departing spirits happily rejuvenate once more.

The look of dying men is but the fading of
The light which, once joyous in its force,
Shone all about you. Let it be extinguished
In equanimity; if I have cursed you, may your child
Receive my blessing, if blessings I may give.

CRITIAS
Let that be, don't treat me like a boy!

EMPEDOCLES
Then promise me, and do what I've advised,
Abandon this poor land. If you refuse
That lonely girl may beg until an eagle swoop
And snatch her from the rabble to
Ethereal heights. I can think of nothing better.

CRITIAS
Oh, tell me then, have we not done you
Justice?

EMPEDOCLES
Why are you asking now? I have
Forgiven you. But will you now obey?

CRITIAS
So quick
My choice can never be.

EMPEDOCLES
Choose well, then;
She should not stay where she will perish;
And tell her to remember him who once was
Beloved of all the gods. Will you do that?

CRITIAS
Why do you ask? I shall. And now
Set out upon your way, you wretched man!
(He exits)

[Scene 7]

Empedocles

Yes!
I shall go my way, Critias,
And do you know where to? I'm ashamed
To say that I've delayed to the extreme.
How often, often I was warned! I should
Have gone back then. But now the need is great!
What was I waiting for, and for so long,
Till fortune, spirit, and my youth had passed
And nothing but absurdity remained, and misery.
O silent ones! you good gods! the mortals' too
Impatient word goes rushing out ahead
And will not let the hour of accomplishment
Mature unhurried. Many things have gone
Their way; it will be easier now. He clings
To everything, this old fool! when in former days
He was without a thought, a quiet boy
Who played upon this good green earth, he
Was freer then than he is now; oh, to have
To part!—not even my fair cottage have
They left me—this too I lose, O gods!

[Scene 8]

[Empedocles], three of Empedocles' slaves

First Slave

You're leaving, lord?

Empedocles

Indeed, I'm leaving, my good – ⏑ –
So fetch me please my travel gear, as much
As I myself can carry; take it for me
Out there into the street—for this will be
Your final act of servitude!

Second Slave

O gods!

EMPEDOCLES

You always were
So happy in my company, familiar to me
From sweet youth on, the days when we grew up
Together in this house, my father's house,
Now mine, and always foreign to my breast
Has been the master's icy word.
The fate of cruel slavery you've never had to feel.
This I believe of you, you'd gladly follow me
Wherever I must go. Yet I cannot allow
The priest's fell curse to cause you pain.
You know him, do you not? The world's opened up
For you and me, my children; now each of us
Must seek his own best fortune—

THIRD SLAVE

Oh, no!
We will not leave you, cannot leave you.

SECOND SLAVE

The love you bear toward us—the priest knows nothing of it.
Forbid the others though he may, he can't command us.

FIRST SLAVE

If we belong to you, then let us stay
With you! It's much more than a day or two
That we have been united, you told us that yourself.

EMPEDOCLES

O gods! no child have I, I live
Alone with just these three, and yet I cleave
To this unprepossessing place as though entranced,
Am I somnambulant, struggling as in dreams
To move my legs? Things cannot be otherwise for us,
Good friends! No more to speak of it I beg you now,
And let us act as though we are no more ourselves.
I'll grudge the priest his pleasure
In cursing everyone who loves me—
You will not go with me, I tell you now.
Go in the house and take the best things you can find
And don't delay; then flee, for if you don't
The new lords of the house will capture you
And you'll be servants to a milksop.

SECOND SLAVE
With these hard words you send us on our way?

EMPEDOCLES
For your and my sakes—emancipated friends!
With manly force you must direct your lives;
And may the gods console and honor you;
You will begin to live from this dear moment forth.
Some people now are passing by. No more malingering!
But do what I have said.

FIRST SLAVE
Lord of my heart! Preserve your life,
Do not go down!

THIRD SLAVE
But tell us, will we not
Set eyes on you again?

EMPEDOCLES
Oh, do not ask; it is
In vain.
(He gestures forcefully for them to leave)

SECOND SLAVE
(while departing)
Alas! a beggar now, he'll drift from place to place,
And will his life be always insecure?

EMPEDOCLES
(gazes after them silently)
Farewell! I've been too brusque
In sending you away; farewell, my faithful friends!
And you, paternal house, where I grew up and blossomed!—
Beloved trees! always you were consecrated by
The joyous hymns that I intoned, I, the friend of gods,
Reposeful friends of my repose! now you must die
And give the breezes back your life, for now
The vulgar folk will dawdle in your shade
And where I walked felicitous they'll mock;
Woe! you gods! I'm exiled, and did
The soulless priest, the priest without vocation, imitate

What you have done to me, celestial ones? You left
Me stranded here, for I belittled you, beloved ones!
And he deprives me now of my dear homeland;
His curse reverberates. Did I lay it on
My wretched self, the rabble but reflecting it?
Alas the one who once lived intimate with you,
The blessed ones, and called the world his in joy;
He has no place to lay his head in sleep,
Nor in himself a site of sweet repose.
So, whither now, you mortal paths? You are many;
But where's the shortest one for me? oh, where?
The quickest route, for if I should delay, then shame befall.
Ha! my gods! in years gone by, in stadiums
I steered my chariot, ignored the smoking wheel; so now
I'll race my way back home to you, true hazard now for me.
(He exits)

[Scene 9]

Panthea, Delia [formerly Rhea]

Delia

Becalm yourself, dear child!
And cease all wailing! lest we be heard.
Here's the house; I'll go in. He may still be there
And you will get to see him once again.
But meanwhile do keep quiet—do I really dare
Go in there?

Panthea

Oh, do so, do so, Delia dear.
I'll pray meanwhile for calm, so that
My heart won't fail when in this bitter hour
Of fate I look upon the lofty man.

Delia

O Panthea!

Panthea

(alone, after some moments of silence)

I cannot!—ah, it would even be
A sin were I to muster equanimity.
And so then, he is cursed? I cannot grasp it, and you,

You dark enigma, may well deracinate my senses!
And how will he be taking all of this?
(a pause; then, in fright, to Delia, who returns)
What's happened?

DELIA
Alas! can all be dead
And barren?

PANTHEA
Gone?

DELIA
I fear it. All the doors
Gape open, but no one's to be seen inside.
I called, I heard the echo of my voice, but only that
Throughout the house; I couldn't stay a moment longer—
Alas! she stands there mute and pale, as though
She doesn't know me, poor girl. Don't you recognize
Me anymore? I'll bear this with you, dear heart!

PANTHEA
Now! You must come!

DELIA
Where to?

PANTHEA
Where to? alas,
That, that I do not know, of course, you gentle gods!
Woe! no hope! and do you shine on me
So uselessly, O golden light above? He
Is gone; this lonely one can find no reason why
Her eyes should still perceive the light.
It cannot be, no! the deed is far
Too insolent, too hideous, and all of you
Have done it. Must I still live, surrounded by
This crowd, and acquiesce? oh, woe and weeping!
To all that's happened lamentation is my sole reply!

DELIA
Oh! then weep! For crying does more good
Than silence or mere chatter.

PANTHEA

Delia!
Just over there he would go walking! And his garden
Meant so much to me, as it was his. Ah, oft
When life would treat me badly, and I,
Unfit for company, despairing of all others,
Would roam our hills, I'd look this way and see
The crowns of those green trees, and think,
There is someone still! My soul took wing
On thoughts of him—alas! how cruelly they've
Destroyed my icon, tossed it in the street,
I never would have thought it possible.

DELIA

So now a splendid man
Has fallen.

PANTHEA

Is this all that you can say? O Delia
He came to us, a new sun in the sky
That shone and drew unripened life
Most amiably on golden ribbons to himself,
And long had Sicily anticipated him.
There never ruled on this fair isle
A mortal such as he; the people knew that he
Was one who dwelled with all the tutelary spirits of
The world, confederate with them, replete of soul!
You took them all into your heart, woe! must you now
On that account be stigmatized and drift from land to land
With poison in your breast, their endowment to you?
You did this to him! oh, let me not
You judges wise! escape unscathed.
I honor him, and if this be unknown to you
Then I must throw it in your face,
That I as well may be ejected from the city,
And if it was my raving father put him under curse
Ha! then let him lay that curse on me.

DELIA

O Panthea, it terrifies me when you thus
Exaggerate your keen. Is he that way as well,
Does he too nourish his proud spirit on pain,
And when he suffers most does he lash out?

I won't believe it's so, for if it is, I am afraid.
What might he then resolve to do?

PANTHEA

Would you
Cause *me* anguish? Yet what have I just said?
I won't go on—yes, patient will I be,
You gods! will never strive in vain
Again for what you've taken from me,
And what you deign to give, that I will accept.
You holy man! if I can find you nowhere, then
At least I'll smile to know that once in times gone by
You were here. I'll find repose, for if my senses be
Deranged his image will escape me;
My only wish is that the day's alarms
Won't chase away the shade that is my brother,
The shade that guides me where I softly go.

DELIA

You dreamer, dear to me! he's still alive, you know.

PANTHEA

Alive? but yes, of course! he lives! he walks across
Vast fields at night and all day long. His roof
Is joined by tempest clouds, upon the soil he finds
His bed of rest. Rude winds assail his hair
And raindrops weep their tears upon
His face; his clothes dry out again
Beneath the burning sun; at hot midday
He trudges on the shadeless sands.
Familiar paths he does not take; in cliffs,
With those who live by seizing booty,
Estranged, like him, and ever suspect,
That's where he hides, his curse they do not know
They offer him what meager food they've cooked,
To fuel his limbs for further wandering.
Thus he lives! woe! and even that's unsure!

DELIA

Yes! It is terrible, Panthea.

PANTHEA

Terrible, you say?
You poor girl, perhaps it won't be long you will

Console me on the day they come to tell
The news and share the talk
That he lies dead upon the road.
The gods will doubtless look on unconcernedly;
For they kept still when shame was heaped upon his head
And he was driven from his home in squalor.
O you! how will you end? already you are weary,
You thrash upon the ground, proud eagle!
You paint your path with blood, and if one
Among the craven hunters finds you crushed
Upon the rocks he'll dash your dying head
And people say that you were once the favorite of Jove?

DELIA
Alas, you sweet and lovely soul! do not go on
This way! no more such talk! If you but knew
The care that seizes me for you! I'll drop upon
My knees and plead with you if that will help.
Becalm yourself. For we must leave now.
Yet many things may change, Panthea.
The people may regret their deed. You know
How much they loved him once. Come! I'll go
To see your father, and you shall help in this
As well. Perhaps we'll win him over.

PANTHEA
Oh, we shall! we'll do it, you good gods!

ACT 2*

A Region of Mount Etna
A Farmer's Cottage

[SCENE 1]

Empedocles, Pausanias

EMPEDOCLES
How are you faring?

---

* Here the sufferings and humiliations to which he is exposed must be presented in such a way that it is impossible for him ever to return, so that his resolution to go to the gods appears to be more forced upon him than voluntarily chosen. Also so that his reconciliation with the Agrigentians presents itself as supreme generosity.

PAUSANIAS
Oh, how good it is
To hear you say a word, dear friend—
Up here the curse is not enforced, our native land
Lies far behind, upon these heights
Don't you agree? we're free to breathe
And we can look the day right in the eye
And hold our heads up high; care won't rob us of
Our sleep, and it could even be that human hands
Will serve us all the foods we crave.
You need assistance, friend! the holy mountain
Will receive us, paternal as he is; he'll grant
His rest to guests who are displaced from home.
If you agree, we will reside awhile here in
This cottage—should I call to them, in case
They should refuse to grant us refuge?

EMPEDOCLES
Do try—already they are coming out.

[SCENE 2]
Empedocles, Pausanias, a farmer

FARMER
What are you looking for? The road
Is down below.

PAUSANIAS
We beg you, grant us refuge in
Your home; do not be shocked by our appearance,
My good man. Our path is hard and often one
Who suffers seems to others suspect—may
The gods relate to you what sort we are.

FARMER
It's clear you've fallen on hard times of late;
That I surely do believe. And yet the city's not
Far off; surely there you've got a friend, and he
Will take you in. Stay with him; you'll find
More comfort there than with a stranger.

PAUSANIAS

Alas,
A friend and host would sooner be ashamed of us
Were we to come to him in our misfortune;
It wouldn't be without good payment for
A stranger, were he to meet our meager needs.

FARMER
Where have you come from?

PAUSANIAS

What need to know?
We'll pay with gold, you'll be our host.

FARMER
Though gold may open many doors,
This door of mine it will not budge.

PAUSANIAS

What do you mean?
But give us bread and wine; we'll pay what you demand.

FARMER
You'll find these things much better elsewhere.

PAUSANIAS
Oh, that is harsh! Perhaps you'll grant me then
A strip of gauze to bind
The bleeding feet of my dear friend;
The stony paths have wounded him—
Just look at him! He's Sicily's good spirit,
Worth more than princes are! and there he stands
Before your door, blanched with care,
And begging cottage shade and humble bread,
And you refuse him? you'll leave him stranded
Exhausted, thirsty, here outside
On this hot day, when even hardy beasts
Seek out a cave where solar fire does not blaze.

FARMER
I recognize you. Woe! accursed ones
Of Agrigent. I sensed it from the start.
Begone!

PAUSANIAS

O Thunderer! we will not go!—
This farmer must assure me of your safety, holy friend!
While I go out and search for food. Against
This tree you'll take your rest—and listen, you!
If harm befalls this man, from any hand at all,
I'll steal upon you in the night and burn you out
Before you wake, your straw house all in flames!
Think it over!

[SCENE 3]
Empedocles, Pausanias

EMPEDOCLES

Dispel your cares, my son!

PAUSANIAS

How can you tell me that? your life is worth
My loving care! and this one thinks
It nothing injuring a man on whom a curse
Was laid, the malediction on us both;
And his desire could goad him on
To kill that man, if only for his cloak;
It seems to him unfitting such a man should
Go free among the living. Aren't you
Aware of that?

EMPEDOCLES

Oh, yes, I am aware.

PAUSANIAS

You say
It with a smile? O Empedocles!

EMPEDOCLES

Faithful heart,
I've wounded you. I never would
Have done so.

PAUSANIAS

It's only my impatience.

EMPEDOCLES
Becalm yourself! for my sake, calm. Soon
All this will pass.

PAUSANIAS
Say you so?

EMPEDOCLES
You will
Observe.

PAUSANIAS
How is it now with you? should I go out
Into the fields in search of food? if you're not hungry
I'd rather stay with you, dear friend, or maybe we
Should first head into the hills, seeking there
A place for us to stay.

EMPEDOCLES
Look over there! mirroring
The light, a spring; it is our very own. Take
Your hollow gourd and fetch a draft
To freshen my parched soul.

PAUSANIAS
(at the spring)
Clear and cool
It gushes forth from our dark earth, my father!

EMPEDOCLES
First you drink. Then draw again and bring me some.

PAUSANIAS
*(as he hands him the drink)**
The gods will bless it for you.

EMPEDOCLES
I drink to you!
You ancient friends of mine! to you, my gods!

---

* from now on Empedocles must appear as a higher form of essence, altogether restored to his prior love and power.

And to my recurrence, nature! Already it
Is otherwise. O you goodly ones! you shall
Precede, and when I come you will be there.
all must bloom before
It grows and ripens!—be still, my son! and heed
We'll speak no more of all that has transpired.

PAUSANIAS
You are transformed and now your eye
Is glistening as in victory. I do not understand.

EMPEDOCLES
We'll want to be like boys again, together all
The day, with endless talk in company. It won't
Be hard to find some shade, we are at home,
Where faithful, long-familiar friends without a care
Can share congenial conversation—
My favorite! we have, like little boys
Who share a bunch of grapes, in lovely moments
So often eaten to our hearts' content
And, yes, you had to join me in this place
That of our solemn celebrations not a single one
Would suffer our neglect, be lost to us;
Indeed, you had to pay a heavy price in pains,
And yet I too must pay them recompense.*

PAUSANIAS
Oh, tell me all, that I like you
Find joy.

EMPEDOCLES
Have you not seen? They are recurring
The lovely times of my entire life again today
And something greater still is yet to come;
Then upward, son, upward to the very peak
Of ancient holy Etna, that is where we'll go
For gods have greater presence on the heights
With my own eyes this very day I shall survey
The streams and islands and the sea.

* (further elaboration of the joy that his unfortunate resolve gives him).

And may the sunlight, hovering golden over all
These waters, deign to bless me in departure,
The splendid youthful light of day, which in
My youth I loved. Then all about us both
Eternal stars will scintillate in silence as
The glowing magma surges from volcanic depths
And tenderly the all-impelling spirit of the ether will
Arrive and touch us. Oh, then!

PAUSANIAS

You terrify me
With these words, I do not comprehend you.
Your look gives cheer, your speech is splendid,
And yet I'd rather see you mourning.
Alas! humiliation burns within your ardent breast,
You've suffered it and deem yourself a nothing
Though you are much.

EMPEDOCLES

O gods! he too now in the end
Denies me my tranquillity; he rowels my mind
With unconsidered speech. If that's your will,
Then leave. By death and life! this is not
The hour for words expended on
My suffering and my self.
That's all been laid to rest; I'll hear no more.
Begone! it's not the sort of pain that smiles
And duly feeds her hungry brood
With mournful flowing breast—these are adder bites
And I am not the first whose heart the gods
Have struck with poisonous avengers;
Have I deserved this? I can easily forgive
Your ill-timed reminders; it is but
The priest who haunts your eye, and in your ear
The rabble's mocking cry still rings,
Fraternal keen that kept us company
As we abandoned our beloved city.
Ha! I say—by all the gods who see me here
They'd not have dared do this to me
Were I my former self. What? humiliation!
That any day of all my days should now

Betray me to these cowards—silence! let it all
Be buried deep below, *so* deep that deeper still
No mortal matter ever was interred.

PAUSANIAS
Alas! I've carelessly disquieted his cheerful heart
That lordly heart, and now his cares are greater than
They were before.

EMPEDOCLES
Let your lament now cease
And do not plague me further; in time all is
Annealed for gods and mortals both
Soon I'll be reconciled, nay, already I am.

PAUSANIAS
Can this be?—can the dismal melancholy
Be healed, and do you feel no longer isolated
No longer poor, you lofty man, and do you think
That human deeds are innocent, mere hearth flames,
For this is what you taught me once; is it true once more?
Behold! then I will bless this crystal fount
At which your brand new life commenced for you
And on the morrow happily we'll clamber down to
The sea; to safer shores the tide will carry us;
What matter all the toils and perils of our trip,
Our spirit's cheerful, our spirit's gods exhilarated!

EMPEDOCLES
Pausanias! do not forget this one lesson,
No mortal ever finds a thing that's free of cost.
And only one thing helps.—O my heroic lad!
Do not go pale, observe my former happiness,
Beyond all thought, for it restores
The youthfulness of gods to me, even as I wilt;
My cheeks are full of roses; things cannot be so vile.
Go, my son ⏑ – ! I cannot betray my mind
And my desire entirely to you—this
Is not for you—so do not try to own it,
And leave it here for me, as I leave yours to you.
What is it now?

PAUSANIAS

A crowd of people! climbing up
Toward us.

EMPEDOCLES

And do you recognize them?

PAUSANIAS

I can't
Believe my eyes!

EMPEDOCLES

What? shall I go mad
Again? what? shall I go down in senseless woe
And grief, down to where I would go peacefully?
They are Agrigentians.

PAUSANIAS

Impossible!

EMPEDOCLES

Is this
A dream? my exalted rival, yes, the priest,
Along with all his ilk! I spit on them! I can't
Be healed of wounds I carried from my fight
With them; is there no force of greater worth
To challenge me? it's vile to have to wrestle those
Who are unworthy; and precisely now?
In this my holy hour, in which
Our all-forgiving nature sets the tone,
Prepares the soul, that it be in accord!
Again this crew descends on me
And mixes in its raving senseless hue and cry
With my sweet swan song. Well, let them come!
I'll make them pay! I sheltered far too long
These wretched people, sham beggars in the guise
Of children, now I've had enough!
Have you not all forgiven me for being good
To you? Nor can I forgive myself.
Advance, you piteous specimens, if you must.
In wrath as well I can proceed unto my gods.

PAUSANIAS
Oh, how will all this end?

[SCENE 4]
Empedocles, Pausanias,
Hermocrates, Critias, the people

HERMOCRATES
Of naught take fright!
Don't let the voices of the men upset you, the ones
Who banished you. For they forgive you.

EMPEDOCLES
You shameless ones! is this all you know to do?
What do you want of me? you know me!
You are the ones who branded me. Yet do
The lifeless people want their persecution to be felt?
And have they not humiliated him enough,
The one whom once they feared? they seek him out
Again to take their minds' refreshment in his pain?

HERMOCRATES
You've paid the price for all your crimes; enough
Of suffering, I can see it in your countenance;
Be well again and do return to us; you'll be received
By these good folk in their dear homeland once again.

EMPEDOCLES
Lo and behold! my great good fortune's now proclaimed
Aloud, and by this pious dove of peace: day after day
I am condemned to witness your revolting dance
Your fuss and foppery, in which like restless shades
Deprived of sepulcher, distracted and distraught,
You dash this way and that, a wondrously defective
Throng in dire need, you god-abandoned ones,
With your absurdly beggared arts,
To be in your vicinity is such an honor. Ha!
If I had nothing better in the offing I would live
Deprived of tongue, savage in the mountain wilds,
In rainstorm and in scorching sun, forced to share

My food with animals, before I would
Return to your blind mummery.

HERMOCRATES
So this is how you thank us?

EMPEDOCLES
Oh, say that once
Again while gazing upward if you can, upward
To this light which gazes down upon all things!
Are not Helios's beams lightning bolts to hypocrites?
why did you not stay far
Away, why insist on insolence, appearing now
Before my eyes and forcing me to say my final word
That it might take you by the hand to Acheron;
What have you done? what did I ever do to you?
You were admonished; for many days your hands
Were chained by fear, and long your rancor
Lay festering in its bonds, held prisoner by
My spirit. Could you find no rest, and did
My life inspire such grief in you? for more
Than thirst and hunger does the nobler gall
The baser; could you find no calm? you had
To risk attacking me, you shapeless heap of misery?
You must have thought I'd be like you if only
With your own shame you painted my entire face,
That was a stupid thought, my man!
Were you to pour your poison in a cup
And hand it up to me you'd never share in
My beloved spirit; it would purge you with
The purged blood that you had desecrated.
In vain. We travel separate roads. Die
Your vulgar death, it's only fitting, with
The feelings of a soulless knave; to me
Another lot has fallen; another path
You gods once prophesied when I was born
For you were present then—
Your work is done, priest, and your brambles
Will not entangle my great joy. You surely grasp that!

HERMOCRATES
I cannot understand the lunatic at all.

CRITIAS
Enough, Hermocrates! you'll only drive into
A rage the one who's been humiliated.

PAUSANIAS
Yet tell me why you bring along a cloying priest,
You fools, when you mean to do some good?
And why choose – ⌣ – ⌣ as conciliator
The god-abandoned one who cannot love;
For quarrel and for death are he and all his kind sown
Upon the fields of life, and never for the sake of peace!
You see now, this is so; why not then years ago!
So many things in Agrigent would never have
Befallen. You've done so much, Hermocrates;
Your whole life long you've banished pleasures
By making mortals anxious.
So many child heroes, helpless in their cribs,
You've suffocated; like a flowering field
Youthful, forceful nature slumped and died
Beneath your scythe. Much I saw myself
And much more I have heard. When a nation is to die
The Furies send one man alone who through
Deception lures the vital human beings to
Commit the evil deed he has devised.
And in the end, his skills well honed,
The sly asphyxiator, holier than thou,
Attacks his man. It works heartrendingly well
Because the godlike man will fall before the meanest.
My Empedocles!—you shall go your way,
The way you've chosen. I cannot stop you,
My blood evaporates in my scorched veins.
Yet this man who has shamed you, this fell
Corruptor, when you've abandoned me I'll seek him out,
I'll find him though he hide behind the holy altars,
His hiding will not help him, he'll have to face me,
I know his very element.
I'll drag him to the fetid swamp—and if he begs
And whimpers for his life I'll show the sort
Of mercy to his hoary head that he has shown
To others. Down he'll go!
(to Hermocrates)
You hear me? I'll keep my word!

FIRST CITIZEN
No need to wait, Pausanias!

HERMOCRATES
Oh, fellow citizens!

SECOND CITIZEN
Still wagging that long tongue? you! it's you
Who's ruined us, you robbed us of our very senses
With your gab; you stole from us the love of
A demigod! He is no longer that. He does
Not know us anymore; alas! he looked upon us once
With gentle eyes, this kinglike man; the way he spurns
Us now defeats my heart.

THIRD CITIZEN
Woe! if only we
Were living still in Saturn's age, like those
Of old, thriving under friendly heights,
And each found joy within his house and
Was satisfied. Why did you call upon our heads his
Inexorable curse, the curse he's laid on us,
Alas! he had to do it;
And now our sons will say
When they've grown up that we're the ones
Who killed the man the gods once sent.

SECOND CITIZEN
He weeps!—oh, greater still, more loving than
Before, the man now seems to me. And you
Still strive against him, standing there
As though you cannot see; you do not fall upon
Your knees before him? On the ground, man!

FIRST CITIZEN
And still
You play false idol? you'd dearly like to carry on
With all your treachery? Prostrate yourself before me!
I'll plant my foot upon the nape of your frail neck,
Until you tell us that you've finally lied your way
Down to the very verge of Tartarus!

THIRD CITIZEN
Do you not know what you have done? Better
To desecrate a temple than to do what you have done, ha!
We worshiped him, and we were right to do so;
With him we would have been as free as gods are free,
But then along you came, unwelcome as a plague,
Your evil spirit dwelled among us;
Deprived of heart and word and all the joy he had
Bestowed on us, we fell in loathsome tumult.
Ha! shame! for shame! like lunatics
We raved when you condemned to death
This best beloved man. It cannot be undone;
Were you to die deaths sevenfold you never could
Undo what you have done to him and us.

EMPEDOCLES
The sun inclines to westward now,
And I must travel farther on, my children.
Let the priest be! too long now we've
Been quarreling. What's happened
Will all pass; in times to come we'll let
Our fellows live in peace.

PAUSANIAS
Is all then equal in its worth?

THIRD CITIZEN
Oh, love us once again!

SECOND CITIZEN
Do come and live
In Agrigent. A Roman friend has told us that
Their Numa is what made them great.
So, come, divine man! Be our Numa.
A long time now we have been thinking
That you should be our king. Do! Accept!
I'll be the first to hail you, and we all want it.

EMPEDOCLES
The time of kings has passed forever.

THE CITIZENS
(terrified)
Who are you, man?

PAUSANIAS
Thus are crowns declined,
You citizens.

FIRST CITIZEN
I cannot grasp the words
That you have said, Empedocles.

EMPEDOCLES
Does she
Protect within the nest her brood forever,
The eagle? Were they still blind she'd let
The fledglings slumber 'neath her wing, the poor
Unfeathered ones, their dim life lived in twilight.
Yet once they've seen the light of day
And once their pinions have grown strong,
She flings them from their cradle, so that they
Will undertake their own flight. Shame on you,
That you should still want kings.
You are too old; your fathers' times
Were different. You can't be helped
If you won't help yourselves.

CRITIAS
Forgive! by all the heavenly gods! you are
A great man, a man we have betrayed!

EMPEDOCLES
It was
An evil day that came our way, Archon.

FIRST CITIZEN
Forgive, and come with us! For you the sun
Of your dear homeland shines more brightly
Than it does elsewhere, and if you will not wield
The scepter you deserve, we still
Have many gifts and honors for you.
For wreaths we have green leaves and winning names.

For statues, never-aging bronze.
Oh, come! our young folk,
The pure, who never did insult you,
Will serve you—if you'll just dwell in our
Vicinity that will be enough; we must forbear if you
Decide you will avoid us, lingering in your garden all
Alone until you have forgotten what we did to you.

EMPEDOCLES
Oh, not again! you light of my dear homeland, you
Who raised me, you gardens of my youth and joy
Once more I am to dwell on you in thought,
You days of honor, when I lived a pure
Unspoiled life with these my people.
We're reconciled, good friends!—leave me now,
It would be best if you would never look again upon
The face of him you have rebuked; remember him,
The man you loved; your minds, now clarified,
Will never more be led astray.
Let my image live with you in youth that never ends
And may your hymns of joy, the promised hymns,
Ring out more brilliantly when I am far away—
Oh, let us part, lest foolishness and dotage still
Divide us; it seems we have been warned;
We shall be one who at the fitting time, by dint
Of their own power, chose the hour of their parting.

THIRD CITIZEN
You leave us here befuddled?

EMPEDOCLES
You offered me
A crown, you good men! for that, receive from me
Whatever's holy in me. I've long been saving it.
In brilliant nights, when overhead the universe
Disclosed itself, and when the holy air
Of night, with all its stars, as one spirit
Surrounded me with joyous thoughts, then
I often felt in me a burgeoning vitality;
At break of day I found the words
To tell you, earnest words, long held back.
And full of happiness I called, impetuous for

The golden clouds of morn to rise out of the Orient
And celebrate their feast anew, at which my lonely song,
With you in festive chorus, would sound. But then
My heart would always close again, hoping for
Its own time, a time within me that should ripen.
This day is my autumnal day, the fruit is falling,
Falling by itself.

PAUSANIAS

Oh, had he only spoken sooner in this way,
Perhaps these evil things would never have befallen him.

EMPEDOCLES

I do not leave you stripped of counsel, my
Dear friends! Fear nothing! The children of the earth
Will always shrink from all that's new and strange;
To stay at home, be left alone, is everything
The life of plants and carefree animals desires.
Restricted in what is their own, they care only for
Survival; farther down the path of life
Their senses do not take them. Yet in the end
The anxious ones will be exposed and, dying, each
Return to its own element, that it may find
Rejuvenation, as though luxuriating in a bath's
Refreshment. On human life the grand desire is
Bestowed that it rejuvenate itself.
And from the purifying death that they
Themselves will choose, upon a time propitious,
Will rise, Achilles from the Styx, the nations.
Oh, give yourselves to nature, before she takes you!—
For you have thirsted long for things unfamiliar, and
As though imprisoned in a sickly body the spirit
Of Agrigent is yearning now to slough off the old ways.
So, dare it! your inheritance, what you've earned and learned,
The narratives of all your fathers' voices teaching you,
All law and custom, names of all the ancient gods,
Forget these things courageously; like newborn babes
Your eyes will open to the godliness of nature,
And then your spirit will take flame from
The light of heaven, sweet breath of life
Will then suffuse your breast anew,
And forests full of golden fruits will sway beneath

The wind, and springs will jet from rocks, when
The world's life, her spirit of peace, embraces you;
She'll nurse your soul and calm you with a blessed lullaby;
And from the velvet twilight of delight
The green of earth will glisten once again
And mountains seas clouds and stars,
The noble forces, all heroic brothers bound to you,
Will then appear before your eyes, that like a warrior
Your breast will clamor mightily for deeds, and you
Will dwell within your own grand world, shake hands
With one another, give the word and share the good.
Oh then dear friends—partake of deeds and fame,
Like faithful Dioscuri; each will be the equal of
The others—like slender statues in repose your
New life will come to rest on well-conceived
Arrangements, letting law tie confederate bonds.
You tutelary spirits of our all-transforming nature! then,
Oh then, you'll summon all unto your cheerful side, you
Who take your joy in heights and depths,
However toil and luck and sun and rain may
Befall the heart of mortals in their narrow quarters,
You will invite from all the far-flung corners of the world
The liberated peoples to the celebrated festival,
Hospitable! pious! for mortals then will donate lovingly
Their very best; no form of servitude
Will cramp and crush the breast—

PAUSANIAS

O father!

EMPEDOCLES

O earth, again you will receive the heart's full nomination,
And like the flowers shooting from the dark recesses in you
The glowing faces of the grateful then will spring smilingly
From hearts that are abundant in their life.
And

Then, crowned with wreaths of love, the fount will
Flow, rushing downward, swelling full of blessings to
The stream, and with the echo of its quaking banks

The sound will wax most worthy of you, father ocean;
Encomia will rise again from free delight.
The human genius then will feel affinities celestial
O sun god! with you, will feel them anew
And what it shapes will be both yours and all its own,
With pleasure and with courage, full of life, deeds
Will come as easily to it as rays to you,
And splendid things will die in mute and mournful breast
No more. It often slumbers like a noble grain of seed,
The mortal heart encased in its dead husk, until
Its time has come; the breath of ether there
Surrounds it ever lovingly,

                                        and soaring with the eagles
Their eye imbibes the morning light; yet there are
No blessings for the dreamers, precious little of
The nectar that the gods of nature offer every day
Will go to nurture creatures caught in slumber.
Until they tire of toil in coiling bonds, until
The breast in cold estrangement feels like
Niobe fettered to her mountain, till the spirit feels
More full of force than all the sagas tell, and life,
Remembering now its origins, goes out in search
Of living beauty, and happily unfolds upon
The presence of the pure, then
A new day sparks the sky, ah! and otherwise than
Before, — — nature, and astonished,
Incredulous, as, after an age deprived of hope,
In holy union each beloved clings to love, a love
One thought was dead, thus clings the heart
To

                                                that they are this!
The ones we so long did without, the living,
The goodly gods,

                                declining with the star of life!
Farewell! It was a mortal's word, the word of one

Who lovingly still hesitates an hour between you and
His gods, who now have called him.
The day on which we part, our spirit augurs all,
And they tell true who never will recur.

CRITIAS
But whither will you go? Oh, by Olympus, by the living,
The gods you finally revealed to this old man,
To this blind man before you, do not abandon us.
For only if you should abide will the people prosper,
A new soul permeating branch and fruit.

EMPEDOCLES
Let others speak on my behalf when I am far away,
The flowers of the sky, the blossoms of the stars
And all those stars on earth, the myriad germinations;
Divinely present nature
Needs no speech; no, never will she leave you to
Your own devices, if but once she has drawn near.
For inextinguishable is the moment that is hers;
And with her, victorious throughout the ages,
Bestowing blessings from above, fire celestial.
And when the glorious days of Saturn come,
The new, more manly days,
Then think of times gone by, and live a life warmed by
The genius of your fathers' sayings once again!
To celebrate with you will come, as though invited by
The canticle of vernal light, the all-forgotten world
Of heroes rising from the realm of shades,
And with the golden clouds of mourning may
Your memories be gathered, joyful ones! about you.—

PAUSANIAS
And you? and you? alas, I will not call it by its name
Before these people here, who are most fortunate,

That never may they guess what is about to happen,
No! – ⌣ – you cannot do it.

EMPEDOCLES
Such wishes! You're all children, you still would like
To know what's comprehensible, what's right; you are

Mistaken! you speak, my foolish friends! to a power that
Is greater than you are, though clearly it's no use to do so
And as the stars roll on unstoppable, thus life rolls
Along the path to its accomplishment.
You do not hear the voice of gods? whereas I, before
I learned, through listening, the language of my parents,
With my initial breath, in my primordial vision,
Already I was hearkening to that voice, and always
I thought it higher than the human word.
Upward! they called out to me and every breeze
Incited mightily the agonizing longing in me,
And if I wanted still to tarry here a moment more, it
Would be as though the growing boy, already in
His awkward years, still played the games of childhood.
Ha! soulless as a knave I drifted hereabout
In night and shame before you and my gods.

I've lived; as from the crowns of trees
The pollen sprinkles downward and the golden fruit
And flower and grain pour forth from darksome earth,
Thus came from toil and need my joy to me,
And heaven's friendly forces then descended;
In your depths, nature, gathered silently
The sources of your heights, and your joys
All came to rest within my breast
They were but one delight whenever I
Reflected on this wondrous life, and then with all
My heart I prayed and begged the gods for this alone:
As soon as I could not sustain my holy happiness
In youthful strength, beyond all tumult,
And when like all the former favorites of heaven
My spirit's plenitude became my folly,
To send a warning, dispatching swiftly to
My heart an unexpected envoy as
A sign the time of cleansing now
Had come, that when the hour was right I
Might save myself in new and youthful vigor
That in the midst of human beings this friend of gods
Would not become a plaything, oaf, and nuisance.

They kept their promise; mightily I have
Been warned, just once, it was enough.

For if I failed to understand I'd be
A common sort of steed that honors not the spur—
And waits upon the goading whip instead.
Do not therefore demand the swift return of him
Who once did love you, though a stranger in
Your midst, born to live a brief life
Oh, do not ask that this man put at risk
His holiness, his very soul, for mortals!
A lovely parting has been granted us today
And in the end I still could give to you my
Love's best, my very heart, with all my heart.
Therefore and forever, no! why should I abide with you?

FIRST CITIZEN
We need your counsel.

EMPEDOCLES
Then ask of this young man! and do not be ashamed.
From spirits that are fresh emerge the wisest things,
Provided that one asks about important things in earnest.
Remember that a freshet granted to the priestess,
The ancient Pythia, the sayings of the gods.
And young men are themselves your gods.—
My favorite! I'm glad to step aside; may you
Survive me; I was the morning mist,
Adrift and transitory! and while
I blossomed all alone, the world slumbered;
Yet you, you have been born to brilliant daylight.

PAUSANIAS
Oh! I must be still!

CRITIAS
Do not convince yourself,
O best of men, and us with you. For me, all
Is darkness to my eyes and I cannot
Descry what you are undertaking, cannot say, Stay!
Postpone it for a day. The moment often comes
And seizes us amazingly; thus we pass on,

As fleeting ones caught up in fleeting moments.
Our pleasure of an hour often feels as though
We'd planned it over time, and yet it's but
The hour itself that dazzles us, and we see only *it*
In everything that's past. Forgive me!
I would not spurn the spirit of the mightier man,
No, not today; I see it well, and I must let you be,
Can look on merely, even if within my soul
The cares are mounting,—

THIRD CITIZEN

No! oh, no!—
He shall not go to foreign lands, he shall not cross
The sea to Hellas' shores nor to the coast of Egypt,
To brothers who have long not seen him,
Oh, beg him to abide! I sensed it,
For this man radiates some things that make
Me tremble for my life, sacred, terrifying things,
And all grows luminous in me and then goes dim again,
More now than in my former days—you see and serve
A fate that is your own, a fate that is magnificent,
And gladly do you bear it, your thoughts are lordly.
Yet also think on those who love you,
The pure, and also on the others, those
Who failed you, the rueful ones. You, generous man,
Have given us so much; what will life be like without you?
Oh, bestow on us the presence of your self
For just a little longer, kindly man!

EMPEDOCLES

Oh, sweet ingratitude! I surely gave enough
For you to live on.
[I've told you. You're allowed to live
As long as you draw breath; not I. The one
Through whom the spirit speaks must part betimes.
Divine as nature is, she oft reveals herself
Divinely through humanity, and only thus does
Our ever-probing race come to know of her again.]*
This mortal, he whose heart she's filled with sheer

---

* stronger! prouder! his last supreme flight

Delight, has faithfully announced her;
Oh, let her now destroy the vessel so
That it may never serve some other use
And turn divinity into mere human work.
Allow the most felicitous of human beings
To die before they fall to self-aggrandizement,
Frivolity, and shame; let free humanity, upon
The fitting hour, offer loving sacrifice unto the gods,
For whom time's early harvest is the best. This is mine.
And well I know my lot. And for the longest time
Upon the youthful day I've prophesied it to myself
Do honor me in this. And if tomorrow you
Should fail to find me, then say: he was not to wane
By ticking off the days, he was not to be a slave
To care and illness,

unseen he went
His way, no human hand interred him,
No eye has seen his ashes,
For nothing else was fitting for the man
Before whose face, upon that holy day, and at
The mortally propitious hour, divinity dropped the veil—*
For him whom light and earth did love, for him
Whose proper spirit the spirit of the world awakened,
Where spirits are, to which in dying I return.

CRITIAS
Woe! he is implacable, and one's own heart
Would feel ashamed to say another word to him.

EMPEDOCLES
Come, give me your hands, Critias!
And all of you, your hands.—You, my best
Beloved, stay awhile with me, you ever-faithful youth,
Accompany your friend until the evening. Do not mourn!
For holy is my end, and even now—O air!
You, air, embrace this newborn
When upward he traverses unseen paths;
I catch your scent as does the mariner who nears

* (Principal passage)

The forest blossoms of the mother isle,
A memory transfigures now his weathered face,
Abiding with his first delights once more!
And, oh, oblivion! conciliating queen!—
My soul is full of blessings, friends!
Now go and greet the city that's our home
And all its fields! On that fair day when you
Go out into the sacred grove to bring
A feast to all the gods of nature,
And when with friendly birdsong you are
Received on cheerful heights, then wafting
a strain of me in that song,
Your friend's word sounding, veiled in loving chorus
By our harmonious world—this, you loving ones, this you
Will hear, it is more splendid thus. What I have said
While tarrying here is of little worth,
Yet may a ray of light illuminate your path
And guide you downward to the silent source, that it
May bless you as it permeates the twilit clouds.
And may you then remember me!

CRITIAS

Blessed one!
You've overcome me, holy man!
I'll honor what befalls you, and
I'll not give it a name. Did it have
To be this way? It happened all
Too fast. While you were dwelling still
In Agrigent, and ruling there discreetly, we paid
No heed. You're taken from us now; we had
No chance to think. Joy comes and goes, does not
Belong to mortals as their own, and spirit hastens out
Along its path before the world can ask a question.
Alas, then, can we ever even say you dwelt upon a time
Among us?

[SCENE 5]

Empedocles, Pausanias

PAUSANIAS
It is accomplished; now send me too
From hence! It should be easy for you!

EMPEDOCLES

Not so!

PAUSANIAS

I know full well, I should not speak this way
To you, the holy stranger; yet I would not
Restrain the heart within my breast.
You've spoiled that heart, you've drawn it to yourself—
And is it to the likes of me, I thought when I
Was just a boy, this splendid man
Inclines; can he be truly drawn to me
In friendly conversation, though by then
The man's words were long-familiar to me;
It's all gone now! gone! O Empedocles!
And still I call you by your name, still I grip
The faithful hand of him who flees.
Behold! I am still here, it's me and me alone,
As though you could not leave me, loving one!
You spirit of my happy youth, did you embrace me then
In vain, have I in vain unfolded all
This heart of mine in hopes of victory
And grandest expectations? I know you
No more; it is a dream. I don't believe it.

EMPEDOCLES

Did you not understand?

PAUSANIAS

My heart I understand,
For true and proud it beats and burns for yours.

EMPEDOCLES

So grant what honors most my own heart.

PAUSANIAS

Is honor found in death alone?

EMPEDOCLES

You've heard it,
And your own soul testifies to me; for me
There are no others.

PAUSANIAS

Alas! is it then true?

EMPEDOCLES

What do
You take me for?

PAUSANIAS
(intensely)

O son of Urania!
How can you ask?

EMPEDOCLES
(with love)

Yet am I a knave, shall I
Survive the day of my dishonor?

PAUSANIAS

No!
By your enchanting spirit, man, I would not
I could not spurn you, even if love's neediness
Compelled me now to do so, my beloved! then, die
If this must be, die and thus bear witness.

EMPEDOCLES

I knew
You'd not deprive me of your joy the moment when
You had to let me go, courageous one!
For where is sorrow? wreathing round
Your head are dawn's vermilion clouds, and once
Again your eye bestows on me its energetic rays.
And I, I kiss sweet promises upon
Your lips, and say you will be mighty, you
Will shine, your youthful flame will spark
To soul and flame everything that's mortal
That with you it may rise to holy ether.
O yes! best beloved! it's not in vain I've lived
With you; beneath a soothing sky so many joys
Have bloomed for us alone, and from
Our first victorious and golden moment;
And often will my silent grove

And empty halls remind you of these joys
When you pass by in springtime, and
The spirit that once joined us, you and me, will
Surround you; thank it then, thank it now!
O son! Son of my soul!

PAUSANIAS

Father! my thanksgiving
Will come as soon as all the bitterness
Is lifted from me.

EMPEDOCLES

Yet that thanks too
Is lovelier, which, like parting joy, itself
Will tarry in the parting.

PAUSANIAS

Oh, must then joy depart? I do not grasp it.
And you? what would it help you

EMPEDOCLES

Compelled by mortals I am not; in full force I
Go down, and fearlessly; I tread the path
I have elected; this is my felicity
And my prerogative.

PAUSANIAS

Let that go, do not say aloud
To me such terrifying things! You still breathe, and still
You hear your dear friend's words, and still
The stirring blood of life is pulsing from your heart;
You stand, you gaze, the world about is bright,
Your eye is clear as you encounter all the gods.
The sky reposes there on your free brow, and
More joyously than all the radiant joys of humankind
Your tutelary spirit, splendid friend, illuminates the earth!
And all of this should pass away?

EMPEDOCLES

Pass away?
But it's enduring, like the stream the frost
Has fettered. Silly boy! does the holy spirit of life
Nod off to sleep and hold its purity transfixed
At any place where you might hope to bind it?
The spirit is possessed of joy forever, it
Will never tremble in imprisonment
Or languish hopeless where it lies,
a world's delights
It must pass through, and does not ever end.—
O Jupiter Emancipator!—now go inside,
Prepare a meal, so that the field's fruits I
May savor once again, and the grape's full force;
May my parting hence be glad with thanks;
And to the gracious muses too, who loved me, we
Shall sing a hymn of praise—do it now, my son!

PAUSANIAS

Your words are wondrous masters over me, for I
Must yield to you, I must obey, I want to
And yet I do not want to.

[SCENE 6]

EMPEDOCLES

(alone)

Ha! Jupiter Emancipator! closer now
And closer still my hour advances, and from
The chasms comes the trusty messenger of this
My night, the evening wind, the harbinger of love
To me. It will happen! It has ripened! O heart,
Now beat and stir your waves, the spirit up
Above you scintillates like stars;
And all the while the homeless clouds
Of heaven, ever-fleeing, drift on by.
How am I? I stand astonished, as though
My life were starting over, for all is different now,
And for the very first time, I am, I am—and is that why
So often in the past, in times of deep repose,
You ineffectual man, a languor overcame you?

Is that why life was so carefree for you, so
That you would find the joys of overcoming all
In one full deed and at the end?
I'm coming. Dying? it's only into darkness,
One step; and still you'd love to see, O eye of mine!
You've served your time with me, most serviceable eye!
And now must night awhile surround
My head in shadow. Yet joyous leap
The flames from an intrepid breast. Shuddering
Exaction! What? death alone ignites
My life now at the end, and you extend
To me the terrifying chalice, the fermenting cup,
Nature! that he who sings you drink a draft of it,
His spirit's ultimate enthusiasms!
I am at peace with it; I seek now nothing further than
The site of my own sacrifice. I am well.
O Iris, rainbow over plunging chutes of water,
When jets of silvery mist leap up
My joy will be the way you are.

[Scene 7]
Panthea, Delia

Panthea

no! I'm not astonished that
He yearns to join his gods; what did
He ever get from mortals?
His foolish nation fed his lofty sense,
Their insignificant lives
Despoiled his heart

So abscond with him, you who gave him all and then
Gave him to us, oh, take him now away, nature!
More transitory are the ones you love,
I realize this now; they soon wax great,
And no one knows how they have come
To be that way, but then, alas!
These fortunates will vanish soon enough!

DELIA

I find it is
More fortunate to tarry happily with human beings.
May that incomprehensible man forgive me.

PANTHEA

O Delia! our pride alone prevents
Our comprehending him! though certainly
It would have been a mighty testimony to the power
Of human ploys and plans had the proud man

DELIA

And yet the world's so beautiful.*

PANTHEA

Beautiful
Indeed it is, more beautiful today than ever.
A bold one never should depart without receiving gifts.
Does he still gaze upon you, O heavenly light above?
And do you look upon him now, as I perhaps
May never do again? Delia! that is the way
Our brother heroes meet intensely, eye to eye,
Before they leave their common meal for slumber
Yet will they not all meet again at break of day?
Oh, words! of course my heart is trembling, as is yours
You sweet child! and gladly would I have
Things otherwise, yet I'm ashamed of this.
It's he who's doing it! is it not holy thus?

DELIA

Who is that stranger, the young man coming down
The mountain!

PANTHEA

Pausanias. Alas must we
Now meet again this way, my fatherless friend?

---

* Too stark an opposition

[SCENE 8]
Pausanias, Panthea, Delia

PAUSANIAS
Is Empedocles then here? O Panthea,
You honor him; you've climbed the mountain
To see once more that earnest wanderer
Who walks his path to darkness!

PANTHEA
Where is he?

PAUSANIAS
I do not know. He bade me go, and
When I returned again I did not see him.
I called to him in all the rocky clefts but could
Not find him. Surely, he'll return. He promised as
A friend to me to linger until nightfall.
Oh, if only he would come! our best beloved hour
Is ever on the wing, flying faster than an arrow.
I shall be full of joy, shall be with him again,
And so will you, Panthea! and she as well,
This noble stranger, who will see him
Only once, as in a splendid dream. His end
Alarms you both; every eye can see it coming
Yet no one calls it by its name; I do believe
The two of you will not recall it when you see
The living man again in all his flourishing.
For in the face of such a man will vanish marvelously
The sum of things that mortals take as mournful, frightful;
Before the man's felicitous eye everything is light.

DELIA
How is it that you love him, yet you begged in vain?
You pleaded with him long enough, entreated
This grave man, that he might stay and dwell
With humankind a little longer.

PAUSANIAS
Could I do much?
He grips my very soul when he replies to me
Proclaiming what he wills. Oh, that is it!

That he can only give us joy when he denies himself,
His heart beats counter to itself, profoundly so,
Whereas he is at one whenever he is on his own,
This endlessly mysterious man. It is
No vain persuasion, do believe me,
When he empowers his own life. For oft
When he was in his own remote and silent world,
And proudly self-sufficient, I saw him in
A darkling intimation; my soul brimmed
And stirred, though I could not feel a thing.
The presence of the pure one made me anxious,
He was untouchable; yet once the word fell
Decisive from his lips it was as though
The sky resounded joyously
In him and me alike; and raising no objections I
Was seized yet never felt more free.
Ah! even if he went astray, all the more
Profoundly I would recognize him, inexhaustibly true,
And if he dies his genius will leap out of his ashes
More brilliant then than ever to my eyes.

DELIA
Ha! magnificent soul! the death of this great man seems
To elevate your soul; me it only tears apart. What
Remains of all this, tell me, what here still has life?
Calamity consumes the neophyte, the blossom,
Before we've time to think, and once the mortal eye
Has opened to the world, a world that is so strange to
The child in man, scarcely has he warmed to it,
Grown happily familiar with it, when a chilling fate
Rebukes him, although he's just been born; and
Contented in their joy not even best beloveds can
Remain, alas! and soon the very best will cross
The line and join the party of the gods of death;
The best go gladly hence and make us feel
Ashamed that we remain among the mortals.
I once was told that gods think otherwise
Than mortals. Each takes things in earnest which
The other thinks a trifle. Divinely serious
Is spirit, virtue, but mere whimsy seems to gods
Those never-ending human machinations.

Alas! more like gods than mortals
Your friend appears to think.*

PAUSANIAS
Oh, by the blessed ones! do not condemn
The splendid man whose honor has become
His misery, the one who has to die because he
Too beautifully lived.
                                    what can the son of gods do?
For infinitely all the infinite are struck.
Alas! a nobler countenance was never more
Outrageously insulted! I was forced
To see it,

* (because Empedocles has such low esteem for temporality)

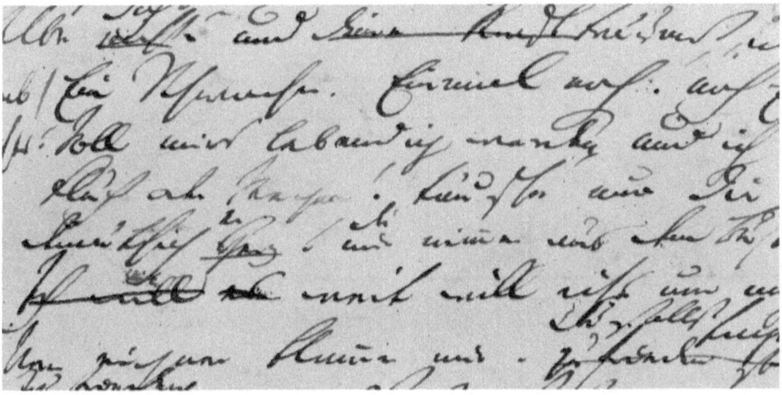

THREE

The Death of Empedocles

Second Version

IN THE SECOND VERSION of the mourning-play, which Dietrich Sattler dates between mid-April and mid-June 1799 (BA 7:90), Hölderlin tightens both the sequence of the dramatic incidents and the poetic line. The priest, Hermocrates, gains greater depth as a character, if only because of his enhanced psychological insight into the possible weakness—the Achilles heel, as it were—of Empedocles. The archon, now called Mecades, is for his part less seduced by the priest's machinations against Empedocles. The debate between Pausanias, Panthea, and Delia at the end is expanded and becomes increasingly tense. As Jochen Schmidt argues, Hölderlin clearly has sympathy for Delia's doubts about the legitimacy of the hero's suicide, even if Panthea ends this version by attributing a "supra-individual significance" to that death (DKV 2:1108). The problem of individual and collective destiny is developed more starkly here than in the first version. Can Empedocles' sacrifice truly alter the fate of his city? Can it mark a change of epoch for his people? Or is Hermocrates right in asserting that Empedocles has nourished himself on excessive light, that he has overstepped the line that limits mortal existence? Empedocles' self-accusations in this second version are accordingly more intense and less easy to dismiss. Hermocrates is not simply conniving when he claims that Empedocles "sees his fall advancing, seeks / To turn his back on his own life, a life that's lost / Its god, the god his careless mouth despatched" (ll. 216–18).

Yet Empedocles' flaw is not so much a matter of *nefas,* that is, of betraying the secrets of a mystery cult by uttering the "unspeakable." Rather, it becomes increasingly a question of the relation of humanity to nature as a whole. Hölderlin, in a letter to his brother Carl dated June 14, 1799, in which an important passage from one of Empedocles' soliloquies is copied out (ll. 395–428), associates the progress of culture with the feverish haste of mortals to better their situation in nature: "Even when they come into willful conflict with one another, it is because they are dissatisfied with their present, because they want things to be otherwise, and so they cast themselves sooner rather than later into nature's grave, speeding up the pace of the world" (CHV 2: 769; BA 7:86). Already one sees the central conflict of the third version taking shape here in the second, namely, the conflict between the destinies of an excessively intense individual and of the moribund collective, the city or nation in decline. Furthermore, Delia's lament near the end of this second version shifts the question away from culture in the direction of nature herself:

> Oh, why do you allow
> Your heroes all to die
> So readily, nature?
> All too gladly, Empedocles,
> Too happily you sacrifice yourself;
> While fate obliterates the weak, the others,
> The strong, feel it's all the same, to fall, to stand,
> And so they too grow feeble. (ll. 667–74)

When Panthea speaks of Empedocles' smilingly tossing his pearls back into the sea whence they came (ll. 727–28), one recalls that this was the deed of the haughty Egyptian queen Cleopatra, to whom the lyric poem "Empedocles" alludes. And well she might, adds the singer, but not the philosopher-physician who is close to nature, not Empedocles, and not the one for whom love forbids such emulation.

For the first 145 lines of this second version the translation follows the *Reinschrift,* that is, Hölderlin's copy in a neat hand designed for publisher and typesetter. After line 145 it reverts to his rough draft—hence the discrepancy in the numbering of the lines. Only the major emendations in the *Reinschrift* receive comment in the notes at the end of the book.

The Death of Empedocles
[Second Version]

A Mourning-Play
in
Five Acts

Persons in the Play:
Empedocles
Pausanias
Panthea
Delia
Hermocrates
Mecades
Agrigentians: Amphares, Demokles, Hylas

The setting for the play is partly in Agrigent, partly on Etna.

Act 1

Scene 1
Panthea, Delia

Scene 2
Chorus of Agrigentians in the distance,
Mecades, Hermocrates

MECADES
You hear the frenzied people?

HERMOCRATES
They seek him.

MECADES
The spirit of the man
Is powerful among them.

HERMOCRATES
I know; like parched grass
Humanity ignites.

MECADES
That one man moves the crowd this way seems
To me like Jove's lightning bolt when it afflicts
The forest trees, though still more terrifying.

HERMOCRATES
That's why we blindfold humankind,
That no one will be nourished
Too heartily on light.
Divinity dare not
Be made too present
To them, their hearts dare not
Encounter something vital.
Do you not know the ancient ones,
The ones they call the favorites of heaven?
They fed their hearts
On cosmic forces, and to these
Clairvoyant upward-gazing ones
Immortal things were near;

The proud ones therefore all
Refused to bow their heads
And nothing could withstand
Their virulence; whatever they
Confronted they transformed.

MECADES
And he?

HERMOCRATES
Precisely this made him
Too mighty; he grew too
Familiar with the gods.
Thus to the crowd his word resounds
As though from Mount Olympus;
They thank him
For having robbed the sky of
The flame of life,
Betraying it to mortals.

MECADES
They know nothing else than him, he
Should be their god,
Should be their king.
They say Apollo built
The city of the Trojans.
The people find it better yet when
A lofty mortal helps them get through life.
They say such senseless things
About him and they heed no law
Nor any need nor custom.
A wandering star our nation has
Become and I do fear
This is a sign of things
To come, things on which
His silent mind is brooding.

HERMOCRATES
Becalm yourself, Mecades!
He won't succeed.

MECADES
Are you then mightier?

HERMOCRATES
The one who understands them
Is stronger than the strong.
And this rare man I know full well.
Too fortunate he was while growing up;
And from the start his own
High sense of self indulged itself;
The slightest thing can set him off; he will
Regret his having loved the mortals overmuch.

MECADES
I too have sensed that not
Much time remains to him,
And yet it may be just enough;
He'll fall, but only once he's won.

HERMOCRATES
And yet already he has fallen.

MECADES
What are you saying?

HERMOCRATES
Do you not see? The poor
In spirit have distracted his own lofty spirit,
The blind have foiled their seducer.
He tossed his soul into the crowd, betrayed
The gods' own favors amiably to the vulgar,
And yet, by way of vengeance, empty echoes in
The lifeless hearts of fools were aping all he said.
He bore it for a time, he bit his tongue,
Was patient, did not know
What ailed him; meanwhile the crowd's
Inebriation waxed; they shuddered when
They saw how moved he was by
His own words; they said:
We never hear the gods speak so!
And names I will not name for you
These knaves bestowed on that proud mourner.
And in the end the man who thirsts imbibes the poison,
Poor creature; he cannot endure his thoughts when he's
Alone and yet can find none equal to himself;

He takes some consolation from the happenstance
That they adore him; blinded, he becomes like them,
The soulless superstitious ones;
His force abandons him,
He walks into the night and does not see how he
Can help himself, and that's when we help him.

MECADES
Are you sure about all this?

HERMOCRATES
I know him.

MECADES
An arrogant harangue of his occurs to me,
A speech he made quite recently down in
The marketplace. I know not what
The people had been telling him; I came
Just then and stood aside. You honor me,
He answered them, and you are right to do so;
For nature cannot say a word;
The sun and air and earth and all her children live
Like strangers to each other, as though
Alone and not belonging.
True, the ever forceful ones
Do wander in the spirit of the gods;
These free, immortal powers of the world
Surround the transitory lives
Of others; and yet
Like plants out in the wild
In untilled ground, in
The womb of gods is sown
The seed of mortals;
Its nourishment is meager; dead the soil
Would seem if that One were not found
To minister to it, awakening life,
And mine is the field. In me alone
The mortals and the gods are fused
In force and soul, becoming one.
More warmly the eternal powers embrace
The striving heart, more forceful flourish those
Who feel within themselves the spirit of the free,

And it awakens! For I
Befriend the strange, my word bestows
A name on what's unknown, and I
Receive the love of all who live as I
Go here and there; what one man lacks I
Dispense, taking from another; I
Unite and I ensoul, I transform and I
Rejuvenate the halting world,
And am like no one and like everyone.
Thus he spoke in arrogance.

HERMOCRATES
That is not much. Worse things slumber in him.
I know him, know them all, the all-too-fortunate
And coddled sons of heaven, those who
Feel nothing other than their own souls.
Yet once disruption touches them—
So easily the tender are destroyed—
Then nothing soothes them any longer, wildly
It burns, the laceration in them, beyond all healing
The heart ferments. So it is with him! as quiet as he seems,
There glow within his breast, ever since the wretched folk
Enflamed his lofty spirit, desires that tyrannize.
It's him or us! We do no harm when
We sacrifice the man. He must go down
In any case!

MECADES
Oh, don't rile him! Don't give it any room, let
It suffocate, the cloistered flame! Let him go!
Don't give him cause! and if for all his arrogance
He cannot find his way to deeds of insolence,
If he can sin in word alone,
He'll die a fool and will not damage us,
At least not much.
A forceful opposition makes him terrifying,
Can't you see, that's exactly when
He feels his power, that's exactly when

HERMOCRATES
You fear him; you fear everything, poor man!

MECADES
I'd only like to spare myself the rue,
Would gladly salvage all that can be saved.
The priest need not concern himself with that, he knows
It all, the saint who sanctifies whatever he may touch.

HERMOCRATES
You upstart! Know me well before you dare
Blaspheme me. The man must fall, I tell you, and
Believe me, were he salvageable I would save
Him sooner than you would. For he is closer
To me than you. Yet learn this: more
Corrosive than the sword and flame is
The spirit of man, so godlike, when it
Cannot keep still and thus preserve
Its secret unexposed. If it can keep its peace
And rest within its depths, if it can offer what
Is needed, it is beneficial; a holocaust
If it should break its bonds.
Away with him who bares his soul
And his soul's gods, him who recklessly
Would speak what never should be spoken, him
Who treats his gifts most hazardous
Like water to be spilled and wasted; that is worse
Than homicide, and you, you're speaking up for him?
It is his fate. He formed it for
Himself; thus he should live it, thus he
Should die it, in pain and madness snared
Like all who tell such godlike secrets,
Inverting all, delivering to human hands
Concealed and ruling principles!
Down with him!

MECADES
Yet must he pay so dearly who commended
His best gifts with all his soul to mortals?

HERMOCRATES
Perhaps he did, yet Nemesis will not default.
Perhaps he spoke with eloquence, perhaps
He also mocked the life that's chastely silent,
Extracting gold from depths of earth, exposing it

To light of day; perhaps he used things that
Cannot be granted for the use
Of mortals; on account of it he'll be
The first to perish—has it not
Already blurred his senses, has it not
Already ravaged his entire soul,
His tender soul, and in the presence of his people?
How is it that this self-empowering one
Emerged from one who would share all?
The generous man! how is he now transformed
Into the insolent man, the one who treats
Both gods and men with sleight of hand?

MECADES
Your speech is terrifying, priest, yet your
Dark words seem true to me. Let it be as you say!
You may engage me to the task. And yet I do not know
The way he might be seized. A man may have
Enormous stature, yet it won't be hard to censure him.
To be the equal of the overpowering one, who like
A sorcerer manipulates his people, this seems
To me another matter, Hermocrates.

HERMOCRATES
His magic's fragile, child, he's made it easier
For us to manage than he had to. For at
The fitting hour his melancholy altered;
His proud and quietly indignant sense
Became his own worst enemy; had he
The power, he would spurn it; he merely mourns,
However, sees his fall advancing, seeks
To turn his back on his own life, a life that lost
Its god, the god his careless mouth despatched.
Assemble all the people for me; I'll accuse him
Call down the curse upon him, say they should
Be terrified of their old demigod, should
Agree to ostracize him to the wilderness;
And there, returning never, he will grant
Me restitution, for he has told far more
Than is permitted to the mortals.

MECADES
What blame then will you heap upon him?

HERMOCRATES
The words you have recounted to me will
Suffice.

MECADES
With this pathetic accusation you
Would turn the people from his soul?

HERMOCRATES
The weakest accusation, if but the time be right,
Has force, and this one's not so slight.

MECADES
I fear that if before the crowd you should accuse
The man of murder, it would not change a thing.

HERMOCRATES
But that's the very point! a deed done openly
They would forgive, these superstitious ones;
Unseen malignancy's the thing for them
Uncanny it must be! a thorn thrust in
Their eye, that will move the louts.

MECADES
Their heart still clings to him, you won't constrain,
Won't steer them all that easily. They love him!

HERMOCRATES
They love him? yes, indeed! as long as he still blooms
And radiates
                    they feed on him
But what are they to do with him now he's in
Despair, in ruins? There's nothing in the man
That's now of use to them, nothing to abbreviate
Their stretch of time; the field's been harvested.
It lies abandoned; as they please, wild windstorm
And our own footpaths trample and traverse it.

MECADES
Well, go on, enrage him! enrage, and watch what happens!

HERMOCRATES
Precisely what I hope to do, Mecades! he is long-suffering.

MECADES
And so the patient one will win?

HERMOCRATES
Precisely so!

MECADES
I see that you have no respect; you'll devastate
Yourself and me and him and everything.

HERMOCRATES
The schemes and dreams
Of mortals truly I do not respect!
They want to be like gods, adore themselves
Like gods, and yet it only lasts a little while!
Are you afraid the suffering one, long-suffering one,
Will win them over?
He'll make the fools indignant towards him
His suffering they will acknowledge as the heavy price
He pays for his betrayal; no mercy will they show;
Why gratitude, when one they once adored
Turns out to be a weakling just like them?
He'll get his just deserts and why did
He ever mix in their affairs,

MECADES
I wish that I had nothing more to do with this, priest!

HERMOCRATES
Have faith and do not shy from what is necessary.

MECADES
Yet there he comes. Attempt it by yourself alone,
You errant spirit! You may lose everything.

HERMOCRATES
Let him be! away!

[SCENE THREE]

EMPEDOCLES
You came into my stillness softly wandering
You found me out within my darkling halls
You amiable one! you came as I had hoped
And from afar, transforming all above the earth
I sensed your imminent recurrence, lovely day
And my familiar friends, you energetic forces of
The heights—and you are close to me
Again, as once before you blessed ones
You never-erring trees within my grove!
You grew in sweet repose and daily drank
From heaven's source you humble ones
With light and sparks of life replete
The ether pollinating all your blossoms.—

O intimate nature! I have you now before
My eyes do you still know your friend
The one you deeply loved am I now lost to you?
The priest who brought you living song
Like sacrificial blood that's gladly shed?

O by the sacred founts,
Where waters from the earth's vast arteries
Are gathered, where those who thirst
On summer days rejuvenate! in me
In me, you founts of life, you once
Converged from all the world's depths;
The parched then came
To me—why now is all
In mourning? am I alone?
And is it night outside, the daylight notwithstanding?
An eye that saw more lofty things than mortal eye
Is now struck blind, I grope about me—
Where are you, O my gods?
Woe! and do you leave me like
A beggar now
And this breast
That loves you, is attuned to you,
Why do you now repel it?
Why bind in narrow shameful bonds

The one born free, the one who is his own
And no one else's? and now in this sad state
He's set adrift, your erstwhile darling,
Who often was so blessed among the living
Could feel their life, ah, in that holy lovely time
Could feel it like his own heart beating with the world
And all its royal godly forces.
Condemned in his own soul is he now
To wander ostracized? friendless he,
The friend of gods? grazing on
His nothing and his night forever
Accepting unacceptable conditions like
Those weaklings down in timid Tartarus
Fettered to their works and days. What has
Befallen me? for nothing? ha! One thing
Alone then you must grant me, me the fool!
You are the man you always were and yet you dream
You are a weakling. Once again! Once again I
Must feel alive, I will it! be it curse
Or blessing! do not surrender ever all the force
Humiliated one! that dwells within your breast!
I want some space about me; dawn shall rise
From my own flame! You should be
At peace, you wretched spirit,
You prisoner! should feel free and grand and rich
In your own world—and once again you
Are lonely, woe, and lonely once again?

Woe! lonely! lonely! lonely!
And never will I find
You, my gods,
And never more will I return
To your life, nature! I am
The one you banished!—woe! since I
Did not respect you, raised
Myself above you; did you not
Embrace me once with your warm plumage
You tender one! and rescue me from sleep?
Did you not lure compassionately, flatteringly to
Your nectar the fool who shied from nurture,
That he at length imbibed and burgeoned
And blossomed; soon grown mighty and inebriate

He spurned you to your face—O spirit,
Spirit that nourished me, raised me, you
Have drawn unto your master, ancient Saturn,
A new Jupiter, a novel yet
A weaker and more insolent one, for
His evil tongue can only mock you now.
Is there nowhere an avenger; must I alone
Pronounce contempt and curse upon my soul?
Am I to be alone in this as well?

[Scene 4]
Pausanias, Empedocles

Empedocles
I feel the waning of the day alone, my friend,
It's growing dark around me now and cold!
I'm heading back, dear friend! though not to rest,
As when the bird that's happy with its prey tucks
Its head in order to awaken fresh and satisfied
From slumber; with me it's otherwise!
Yet spare me your lament!

Pausanias
You've grown so strange to me, my
Empedocles! do you not know me? and do I
Know you no more, you splendid man?—
You've changed so much, you have
Become a riddle to me, noble countenance;
May grief thus bend to earth oppressively
The favorites of heaven? Are you not one
Of these? behold the gratitude of everyone;
So mighty in dispensing golden joy was
No other, none like you, to his people.

Empedocles
It's true they honor me? oh, tell them all
To let that go.—It ill suits me, such

A victor's wreath, and its green leaves
Will only wilt as soon as they
Are severed from the stem!

PAUSANIAS
And yet you are still standing, fresh waters still
Are purling all about your roots, and mildly waft
The breezes through your crown; not
By dint of transitory things does your
Heart flourish; over you rule more
Immortal forces.

EMPEDOCLES
You remind me of my youthful days, beloved!

PAUSANIAS
The middle stretch of life to me seems sweeter.

EMPEDOCLES
The eyes are pleased to see that when the sun
Goes into steep decline, quickly vanishing, all things
Return to vision; they wish it back, the eyes
Of one who's grateful. Oh, times past!
Delights of love, when this soul of mine
Was roused by gods; like Endymion of old
The slumbering child opened wide his eyes,
Received the living, ever-youthful
Grand tutelary spirits of life—
O beauteous sun! human beings did not
Instruct me, it was my holy heart compelled me
Immortally to love immortals, drove me
To you, to you, I could not find a thing
More godly, lambent light! and as you refuse
To hoard your life within the compass of the day
As selflessly you rid yourself of all
Your golden plenitude, thus I, belonging to
The best of souls, to you, was happy to bestow all
That I possessed on mortals; openly, not timidly
I gave my heart as you give yours to earnest earth,
The fateful one, ah! to her in youthful joy
To dedicate my life to her until the very end
I often pledged my troth to her in hours intimate

I bound myself to her in union unto death.
The breeze then freshened differently within the grove
The mountain springs were gurgling tenderly, all
Your joys, O earth! as true as she is true
And warm and fully ripening in labor and in love,
You gave all this to me; and often when
I sat and gazed astonished up on silent mountaintops
And mused on man's kaleidoscopic madness
Too deeply moved by all your transformations
And sensed the time of my demise approaching,
The ether breathed to me as it did to you
A salve upon my love-torn breast, and
Like smoke that curls upward from the flame
My cares dissolved in endless heights of blue.

PAUSANIAS
O son of heaven!

EMPEDOCLES
I was this! yes! and now I would recount it,
Wretch that I am! would recall them all
Again unto my soul, the accomplishments
Of your ingenious forces, all the splendid powers
Whose comrade I once was O nature
In order that my mute and mortified breast might
Resound with every one of your vibrations;
Am I still this? O life! once they rushed to me, all
Your melodies arriving on the wing; did I not hear
Your ancient consonance, grand nature?
Alas! I the lonely one, did I not live
In company with this our holy earth and with this light,
With you from whom the soul refuses to depart
O father ether and with all that lives
The friend of gods who dwell on the Olympus of
The present? I've been ejected, I
Am altogether lonely, and woe is now the boon
Companion of my days, the partner of my sleep!
Blessings are not with me, go!
Go! do not ask! you think I'm dreaming,
Well, look at me! and do not marvel,
Dear boy, that I have sunk into decline;
The sons of heaven, at the instant

They have grown too fortunate,
Are meted out a curse that's all their own.

PAUSANIAS
I cannot abide
Woe! such talk! you? I cannot abide it,
You should not make my soul and yours
So anxious. It seems to me an evil sign when
The spirit that was always radiant
Is swallowed up in mighty clouds.

EMPEDOCLES
You feel it, then? It means that soon he must
Descend to earth in cloudburst.

PAUSANIAS
Oh, let the melancholy go, dear friend!
Oh, what did this one, this pure one, do to you
You gods of death! that now his soul should be
So clouded over. And do the mortals then
Possess nothing of their own, nothing anywhere,
And does cold terror penetrate their very heart, does
Eternal destiny prevail even in the bosom of
The stronger ones? Restrain the gloom
And exercise your power; you are the one
Who's abler than the rest; oh, see in
The mirror of my love the one you are
And ponder who you are, and live!

EMPEDOCLES
You know not me and you and death and life.

PAUSANIAS
I know so little, true, of death, I have
Not thought about it much.

EMPEDOCLES
To be alone, to be
Without my gods, is death.

PAUSANIAS
Let death go, I know *you,* and by your deeds
I knew you then; in their vast potency

I felt your spirit and its world
When oftentimes a single word from you
Upon a holy moment granted me
So many years of life.
A new enduring stretch of time began from that
Point onward for the boy. As when tame deer
Can hear the far-off forest's sounds, so that they think
Of home, thus my heart would pound when you,
Familiar with the purer days of yore, invoked
The gladness of the ancient primal world; for you
All destiny lay open; did you not draw with
Unwavering gaze the vast contours of the future
And right before my eyes, the way an artist adds
The missing piece and makes the painting whole.
The forces of grand nature are within your ken,
You are familiar with them all as mortal never was,
You can, at will, steer them all in quiet mastery.

EMPEDOCLES
Correct! I know it all, can master all.
I recognize it as my handiwork, I know it through
And through; I steer it as I like, for I'm
A lord of spirits, I'm everything that is alive.
The world is mine, and as servants are
Subservient, so are all the forces now to me,

                    she's become my handmaid
This nature, she needs a lord. And if
She still has honor, then it derives from me.
For what would be the sky and sea
And isle and star, and everything that lies
Before the eyes of humankind, what would
It be, this mummery of thrumming strings, did I
Not give it sound and speech and soul? what are
The gods and what their spirit if I do not
Proclaim them? now! say, who am I?

PAUSANIAS
Oh, mock yourself in melancholy tones, mock all
That grants a human being splendor, mock
Their actions and their words, obliterate
The courage in my breast and terrify the child

In me. But speak it out! you hate yourself
And hate what loves you, hate what would approach you;
You would be someone other than the one you are,
Are restive with your honor; you sacrifice yourself
To alien things. You will not stay, you want
To perish. Alas! in your breast there is even less
Tranquillity than there is in mine.

EMPEDOCLES
You innocent one!

PAUSANIAS
Why prosecute yourself?
What is it then? no longer make your sufferings
A mystery to me! it tortures me!

EMPEDOCLES
A human being should act with calm;
We should reflect, we should unfold
Enhancing, cheering all that lives about us
                    for full of high significance
Magnificent nature, bearer of the silent force,
Surrounds the one who intimates
That he must shape a world
That he may call
Her spirit forth, this human being suffers
Care within his breast and hope;
An overwhelming yearning
Its roots deep within him strives upward;
For he can do much and lordly is
His word; the world is then transformed
And under his hands

[THE TWO FINAL SCENES PLANNED FOR THE SECOND VERSION]

[Panthea, Delia]

PANTHEA
Insanity of humankind! you
Have spoiled his heart for him

You utter insignificance! what did
You ever give him in your poverty?
And now that he is yearning for his gods
The fools are thunderstruck, as though they had
Created for the man his lofty soul. Not
In vain, O nature, did you bestow on him
All those gifts!
More transitory than the others are your favorites!
This I know full well!
They come, they grow to greatness, and no one
Knows how it happened; then they quickly vanish,
These fortunate ones! alas! but let them go!

DELIA
Yet is it not a lovely thing
To dwell with human beings; my heart
Knows nothing else, finds its repose
In this one thing; but mournfully obscure
Before my eyes looms the end
Of this incomprehensible man, and you
Encourage him to part, Panthea?

PANTHEA
I have to. Who will tie him down? who
Will tell him, You are mine;
The living one is all his own,
His spirit is his only law,
And should he seek to save the honor of
The mortals who have scorned him, should
He tarry, when
His father ether opens wide
His arms to him?

DELIA
Behold! how splendid and
Hospitable is our earth.

PANTHEA
Yes, splendid, and now more splendid still.
Not deprived of gifts should
A bold one take his leave of her.
He surely lingers still on one of

Your verdant heights, O earth
You changeable one!
And still he gazes down across the hills
Onto the open sea and takes
His final joy from this. We shall perhaps
Espy him nevermore. Good child!
Of course it hurts me too and gladly would
I have it otherwise yet I'm ashamed of this.
Let him do it! Is it not holy thus?

DELIA
Who is the young man
Coming down the mountain!

PANTHEA
Pausanias. Alas! Must we then meet
Again this way, you fatherless one!

Pausanias, Panthea, Delia

PAUSANIAS
Where is he? O Panthea!
You honor him, you too seek him,
Would see him one more time
The fearsome wanderer, the one alone
To whom it is allotted that he walk that path
With fame which is accursed for all others.

PANTHEA
Then is it pious in his case and grand
This greatest of all terrors?
Where is he?

PAUSANIAS
He bade me go and since that time
I've not seen him again. I called to him
In all the rocky clefts, but did not find him.
Surely he'll return. He promised as
A friend to me to stay into the night.
Oh, may he come! Faster than

An arrow on the wing our best beloved hour flies.
We shall be joyful then, shall be with him again
You will be, Panthea, and she,
The noble stranger who
Will see him only once, the splendid meteor.
Of his death, you weeping ones,
You have heard!
You mourners! Oh, see him
In his flourishing, the lofty man,
Learn whether what is mournful and
What mortals find so terrifying is not
Alleviated by an eye that's blessed.

DELIA
How is it that you love him, yet you begged
The earnest man in vain? Mightier than he is your
Request, dear boy! and it would have been
A lovely victory for you!

PAUSANIAS
How could I have won? He wounds
The soul in me when he
Replies, proclaims his will.
The failure of his plan alone would give
Me joy. That's it: the more the wondrous man
Insists on what's his own, the louder cries
My beating heart. It is
No vain persuasion, do believe me,
When he empowers
His own life.
For oft when he was silent
In his own world,
And proudly self-sufficient, I saw him in
A darkling intimation; my soul stirred
And brimmed, though I could feel not
A thing; it almost made me anxious,
The presence of the man no one could touch.
Yet once the word had leapt decisive from his lips
It was as though the sky resounded joyously in him
And me alike, and raising no objections
I was seized yet never felt more free.
Ah, even if he were to go astray, all the more intensely

Would I then recognize in him an inexhaustible truth
And should he die his genius will escape his ashes
More brilliant then than ever to my eyes.

DELIA
You ignite, magnificent soul, from the death of this
Magnificent man; yet the hearts
Of mortals also sun themselves and gladly so
Beneath a milder light; their eyes remain
Transfixed by what endures. Oh, tell me what
Remains of living and of lasting? Fate tears
The tranquil ones away, and if, intimating this,
Some would be daring, their friends
Will soon enough discourage them,
As young folk watch their hopes expire.
No living thing remains
In bloom—alas! observe the best as they
Step over to the side of the eradicating gods
Of death; these best depart with joy
And make us feel ashamed
To tarry here among the mortals!

PAUSANIAS
Do you condemn

DELIA
Oh, why do you allow
Your heroes all to die
So readily, nature?
All too gladly, Empedocles,
Too happily you sacrifice yourself;
While fate obliterates the weak, the others,
The strong, feel it's all the same, to fall, to stand,
And so they too grow feeble.
You splendid man! what you have suffered
No slave can undergo, and poorer still
Than other mendicants you
Have scoured the countryside,
Yes! it's doubtless true that those

You most repudiate are not
As wretched as the ones you love when
Humiliation touches them, you gods!
He took it well—

PANTHEA
Is it not so?
Why should he not?
For always and ever must
The overpowering
The genius survive—did you think
The scourge would slow him down? to one in pain
It speeds his flight, and like the driver of a chariot,
When on the course the chariot's wheels begin
To smoke, the man in danger hurtles all
The faster toward his victor's wreath!

DELIA
Are you then so full of joy, Panthea?

PANTHEA
Not only in the blossom, not only in the purple grape
Does holy force inhere; nourishment
Of life derives from sorrow too, my sister!
Life drinks the way my hero does,
Imbibing gladly from the cup of death!

DELIA
Woe! is that the way you would
Console yourself, dear child?

PANTHEA
Oh, no! my only joy would be,
If what we fear must come to pass, that it
Should happen in a holy, splendid way.
For have not myriad heroes,
Like him, gone to the gods?
In shock, and wailing loudly, came
The people from the mountain; I saw
Not one who would have wanted to blaspheme,
For unlike someone in despair
He did not flee in secret, they heard it all, and

The sorrow on their faces glistened in the light
Of words he spoke to them—

PAUSANIAS
Is that not the festive way that shooting stars
Go down, and, drunk with light,
The light of stars, the valleys glimmer?

PANTHEA
It's true that he goes down most festively—
The earnest one, your favorite, O nature!
Your faithful one, your sacrifice!
They love you not who tremble in the face of death,
Deceptive care has tied the blindfold tight
About their eyes; upon your heart
Their own heart beats no longer, they wilt
In separation from you—O holy universe!
The living! the intense! to you with thanks
That he might bear you witness, deathless one!
He smiles and tosses all his pearls into the sea
From which they came, this bold one.
That is how it had to happen.
Thus wills the spirit,
Time ripens and nears it,
For, if only once,
We blind ones required a miracle!

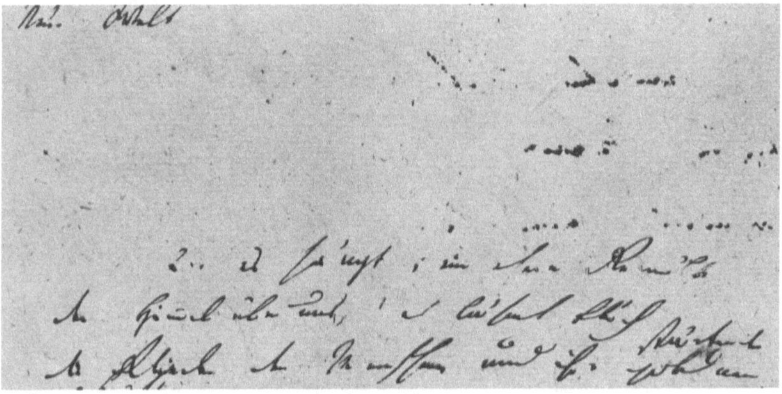

FOUR

Essays toward a Theory of the Tragic

The Tragic Ode
The General Basis [of Tragic Drama]
The Basis of Empedocles
The Fatherland in Decline

THE FOLLOWING FOUR ESSAYS toward a theory of the tragic relate directly to *The Death of Empedocles.* Three of the four Hölderlin wrote between the second and third versions of the play—clearly to develop his own thinking about the path the drama should take. The fourth essay, once given the title "Becoming in Passing Away," but now usually cited by its opening phrase, "The Fatherland in Decline," Hölderlin jotted into the notebook that contains the third version of the play and the "Sketch toward the Continuation of the Third Version."

The three essays composed between versions two and three of the play are contiguous. The first, which opens with the words "The tragic ode begins in supernal fire," describes the course of an ode from its initial enthusiasm, through a confrontation with obstacles to that mood, to a conclusion that rejoins the initial—now chastened and enlightened—enthusiasm. The second, which bears Hölderlin's own title *Allgemeiner Grund* ("The General Basis"), goes on to discuss the tragic *dramatic* poem, in which the obstacles confronted by the tragic hero are elaborated quite starkly in the central conflict of the drama. In "The General Basis" Hölderlin develops his notion that the dramatist must seek in some foreign world, that is, in dramatic material derived from some remote time and place, an experience analogous to his or her own. Finally, the third essay, called by Hölderlin *Grund zum Empedokles,* "The Basis of Empedocles," applies the general structures he has elaborated to the drama he is working on at the moment. Empedocles, born to be a singer or poet, is compelled by his times to become a sacrificial victim. Although the great Sicilian unites nature and art in his very person, he does so too intensely and too singularly; the problem of destiny, moreover, cannot be solved by a single individual, certainly not if the intensity of such exceptional individuals shows them to be far ahead of their time. Something is thus deceptive about the figure of Empedocles, as the character Manes, in the third version of the play, will attest. If the times are out of joint, the tragic hero or heroine cannot rejoin them—not in either sense—and certainly cannot salvage an entire epoch.

"The Fatherland in Decline" is an untitled sketch. (Dietrich Sattler, Michael Knaupp, and Jochen Schmidt derive the title from the essay's opening words; Friedrich Beissner, in StA, gives the essay the title *Das Werden im Vergehen* ["Becoming in Passing Away"], and it is often discussed as such in the older secondary literature.) The holograph of "The Fatherland in Decline" appears near the end of the *Stuttgarter Foliobuch,* immediately after the choral ode "New world," which concludes the third version of the play. It is jotted down as a narrow column on the right side of the final recto pages of that notebook, with the rest of the page left blank, presumably to leave room for a continuation of either the drama itself or the "Sketch toward the Continuation of the Third Version." Knaupp (CHV 3:396) believes that "The Fatherland in Decline" was written *after* the "Sketch," and Sattler (BA 8:119) at least suggests the same; by contrast, Schmidt (DKV 2:1198) argues that the essay must have been written *before* the "Sketch." All agree that it is closely associated with the word "Future" in that "Sketch," inasmuch as it concerns itself with a new world taking shape from the ashes of the old.

Such a consolation—the hopes for a new world—was not the result of an abstraction, nor did it come easily. When Hölderlin's friend Johann Gottfried Ebel, an enthusiastic Jacobin, returned utterly disillusioned from an extended stay in Paris, Hölderlin consoled him in a letter with the following words: "Every fermentation, every dissolution, necessarily has to lead to either annihilation or a new organization; but there is no annihilation; hence the youth of the world has to return again from our decomposition" (CHV 2:643). In the essay "The Fatherland in Decline," Hölderlin completes the itinerary of the foregoing essays: tragedy involves the conflict between an exceptionally talented hero or heroine and a world that ultimately cannot accept or even withstand his or her intensity. In this last essay—here removed from its strict chronology, which would place it at the end of the third version of the play—Hölderlin moves decisively in the direction of a philosophical-historical understanding of the tragic.

A word about the incomparable difficulty of all these essays: Dietrich Sattler, in a moment of uninhibited enthusiasm, says that they represent "the unconquered mountain peak of dialectical thinking, in contrast to Hegel's dialectic, which is but an awkward travesty of it" (BA 8:6). Students of Hegel will balk at such a claim, at least until they become more familiar with the work of Schelling and Hölderlin. At all events, one must concede the rebarbative difficulty of Hölderlin's essays. That difficulty can be explained away neither by the haste in which Hölderlin composed them nor by the interruptions to Hölderlin's work on them, which were many and varied (see BA 8:35–98; 119–25). Perhaps the present translation ought to have interrupted the page-long sentences and simplified the often nightmarish syntax. Yet an effort has been made here to preserve the velocity and momentum of the thinking, and these are inseparable from the style of the writing. The translation occupies a slope far below the peak, which it only dreams of scaling; it remains caught up in the respect and the reserve that Kant associates with the sublime. Of course, one must remember that Hölderlin himself regarded these essays as nothing more than efforts to clarify tragic drama as such and to shed light on the mystery of Empedocles' thinking and his deed.

The Tragic Ode

The tragic ode begins in supernal fire; pure spirit pure intensity has overstepped its boundaries, has failed to moderate sufficiently those alliances in life that necessarily and thus even without fire incline to contact, as it were, alliances that through their quite intense attunement tend to excess rather than moderation when it comes to consciousness, reflection, or physical sensuality; through excess of intensity, therefore, conflict has arisen, a conflict that the tragic ode conjures up at the very outset in order to depict what is pure. The ode then advances as by natural action from one extreme, that of differentiation, to the other, that of not differentiating at all with respect to what is pure, the supersensuous, which seems to acknowledge no sort of neediness; from there the ode falls into a pure sensuality and a more modest intensity, because the original more lofty more godlike bolder intensity appears to it to be extreme, and also because the ode can no longer merely fall into that degree of excessive intensity from which, in its initial tone, it took its point of departure; for the ode has experienced, as it were, the place to which that tone has been leading; it has to transcend the extremes of differentiation and nondifferentiation, advancing to that tranquil lucidity and sensibility in which it will assuredly come to appreciate the necessity of struggle, that is, struggle for a lucidity that itself requires a more enhanced striving; thus the ode will come to appreciate that its initial tone and its proper character are opposition, and it will recognize that it must pass over into its opposite if it is not to end tragically in this modest state; yet because the ode appreciates its opposite as such, the idea that unifies both opposites now emerges more purely, the primal tone is found once again, and with lucidity; thus from that point on the ode advances once again by means of a moderate and freer reflection or sensibility, more assured more liberated more thoroughgoing (which means having attained the basis of an experience of, and insight into, the heterogeneous), returning now to its initial tone.

The General Basis [of Tragic Drama]

What the tragic dramatic poem expresses is the most profound intensity. The tragic ode too presents intensity in its most positive distinctions, in actual opposites; however, these opposites are at hand merely in the form and unmediated language of sensibility. The tragic poem veils the intensity in the presentation to a greater extent, expressing it in distinctions that are more stark, inasmuch as it expresses a more profound intensity, a more infinite divinity. The sensibility no longer expresses itself immediately; it is no longer the poet and his or her own experience that comes to the fore, although every poem, including the tragic, must indeed have proceeded from poetic life and poetic actuality, that is, from the poet's own world and soul, because otherwise the proper truth everywhere goes missing; nothing at all can be understood and brought to life if we are unable to transpose our own inmost heart and our own experience to the foreign analogical material. Thus in the tragic dramatic poem too the divinity that poets sense and experience in their own world expresses itself; the tragic dramatic poem too is for the poets an image of the living, of that which is and always was present to them in their own life; yet this image of intensity everywhere denies its ultimate basis, and has to do so, to the degree that it everywhere approximates to the symbolic realm; the more infinite and ineffable the intensity is, that is, the closer such intensity comes to the *nefas*, and the more rigorously and more coldly the image has to distinguish among human beings and their felt element in order to arrest the sensibility within its boundaries, the less is the image capable of expressing that sensibility immediately; it has to deny sensibility in both its form and material; the material has to be a bolder more foreign likeness and exemplar of that sensibility, while the form has to withstand something more like a counterposing and separating. A different world, foreign surroundings and characters, are called for, and yet, as with every likeness of a bolder sort, all these things must be adapted to the underlying material all the more intensely; they are heterogeneous only in the extrinsic configuration, for if this intense affinity of the likeness to the material, that is, the characteristic intensity that lies at the basis of the image, were not visible, its displacement or foreign configuration could not itself be explained. The more alien these foreign forms are, the livelier they have to be; and the less the poem's visible material can be likened to the underlying material, that is, to the inmost heart and world of the poet, the less may the spirit, the divine, as the poets sensed them in their world, be denied in the artifice of the foreign material. Yet also in the case of this foreign, more artificial material, the intense, the divine, dare not and cannot express itself otherwise—as long as the sensibility that lies at its basis grows increasingly intense—than through a correspondingly greater degree of differentiation. Therefore (1) the mourning-play in both its material and form is dramatic, that is, (a) it contains a third element, namely, the different, more foreign material that the poets have chosen, material quite distinct from their inmost heart and their own world, because they found that foreign material to be sufficiently analogous for the investment of their total sensibility into it, thus preserving the poets' sensibility within it as in a vessel, indeed all the more assuredly as the analogous material becomes increasingly foreign; for the most intense sensibility is exposed to what is transitory to the degree that it has not denied truly temporal and sensuous relationships (and it is therefore a law in lyric poetry as well, even if the intensity in its case is in itself less profound and is thus easier to retain, that one must deny one's own physical and intellectual context). For that very reason the tragic poets renounce altogether their own person, their subjectivity, precisely because they express the most profound intensity; they also renounce the object that is present to them, conveying it to a foreign personality, a foreign objectivity (and even there where the underlying total sensibility exhibits itself most, in the leading personage, who sets the tone of the drama, and in the principal situation, where the drama's object, namely, destiny, expresses its mystery most tellingly, and there where it best takes on the figure of homogeneity with regard to its hero, precisely there where homogeneity grips the hero most strongly, even there

* * *

and the deleterious success achieved by false attempts at a manufactured pure intensity in the inmost heart are once again not treated in terms of the *autonomous activity* of the one who suffers; rather, they are treated by a new attempt, whether appropriate or inappropriate, performed by another, who conveniently comes forward and treads the selfsame path, occupying a niche that is but a single stage higher or lower; thus the inmost heart, beleaguered by these false attempts at improvement, is not merely disturbed in its own self-activity but is altered still more by the forestalling action of something alien and even false, and is therefore determined to undergo a more tumultuous reaction.

The Basis of Empedocles

When life is pure, nature and art oppose one another merely harmoniously. Art is the blossom, the perfection of nature; nature first becomes divine when it is allied with art, which differs from it in kind but is in harmony with it, first when each is everything it can be and when each allies itself with the other, supplying what the other lacks, and lacks necessarily if it is to be everything it can be as a particular; at that point perfection is achieved and the divine stands at the midpoint of the two. The more organizational, more artistic human being is nature's flowering; the more aorgic nature, when it is felt in its purity by human beings who are organized purely and educated purely in their mode of being, grants them their feeling of perfection. Yet such a life is at hand only in feeling, and is not a matter of cognition. If it is to be knowable it must depict itself by separating itself off from itself in the excess of intensity in which opposites mistake themselves for one another, such that the organizational, which surrendered itself too much to nature and thereby forgot its essence and its consciousness, passes over into the extremes of autonomous activity, art, and reflection; by contrast, nature, at least in the effects it exercises on the reflective human being, passes over into the extreme of the aorgic the inconceivable, the insensible, the unbounded, until both sides, advancing in their reciprocal yet opposite directions, unite with one another in a primordial way, as though encountering one another at the commencement, except that nature has become more organized through the shaping and cultivating human being, through the cultural drives and formative forces in general, whereas, by contrast, the human being has become more aorgic, more universal more infinite. This feeling belongs perhaps among the loftiest of things that can be felt, and it arises when the two opposites encounter one another, namely, the universalized spiritually vital artistically pure aorgic human being and the magnificent configuration of nature. The feeling pertains perhaps to the supreme level of human experience, because the harmony that human beings feel now reminds them of the earlier, reversed pure relation, and they feel themselves and nature in a twofold way, though now the alliance is more infinite.

At the midpoint lies the death of the individual, namely, the moment when the organizational dispenses with its ego, its particularized existence, which went to the extreme; the aorgic dispenses with its universality, not in ideal mixture, as it was at the commencement, but in its real supreme struggle; such dispensings occur when the particular, having gone to its extreme, increasingly universalizes itself and becomes active against the extreme of the aorgic; the particular has to tear itself away from its midpoint more and more, while the aorgic, acting against the extreme of the particular, has to concentrate itself more and more; it achieves for itself with ever greater success a midpoint, thus becoming something superlatively particular, *at which point the organizational that has become aorgic appears to find itself again and to revert to itself by fastening onto the individuality of the aorgic, and the object, the aorgic, appears to find itself when, at the very moment it takes on individuality, the organizational too finds itself at the uttermost extreme of the aorgic, so that in this moment, in this birth of supreme enmity, supreme reconciliation appears to be actual. Yet the individuality of this moment is but a product of supreme strife, and its universality is but a product of that supreme strife;* thus, as the reconciliation appears to advene, and as the organizational has its impact on this moment in a manner that is once again its own, and likewise the aorgic has its impact, the result is that the impressions made by the organizational, that is, by the individuality contained in this moment that originates aorgically, will once again become more aorgic, whereas the impressions made by the aorgic, that is, by the universality contained in this moment that originates organizationally, will once again become more particular; the outcome will be that the unifying moment, like a mirage, will dissolve more and more; because it reacts aorgically against the organizational, the moment distances itself increasingly from the organizational; yet precisely because of this, and because of the death of the moment, the warring extremes from which the moment came to be are more beautifully reconciled and united than they ever were in the life of the moment; this, because the unification is now not in an individual and therefore not excessively intense, since the divine no longer radiates sensuously, and since the felicitous fraud of unification ceases precisely to the degree to which it was too intense and singular; thus both extremes, of which the one, the organizational, is repelled by the transitory moment and is thereby elevated to a more pure universality, whereas the other, the aorgic, passes over to this moment, thus necessarily becoming for the organizational an object of tranquil observation, and the intensity of the past moment now comes to the fore with greater clarity, universality, steadfastness, and capacity for differentiation.

In this way, Empedocles is a son of his heavens and of his period, a son of his fatherland and of the massive oppositions of nature and art in which the world appeared to his eyes. A human being in whom those opposites are united *so* intensely that they become *one* in him, divesting themselves of their original distinguishing form and thus reversing themselves, so that whatever in his world passes for more subjective and is at hand more as particularity, that is, as distinguishing, thinking, comparing, shaping, organizing and being organized, is in *him* more objective, so that, in order to designate it in the strongest possible way, he is more capable of making distinctions and of thinking, comparing, shaping, organizing and being organized *when he is less at home in himself;* and *to the extent that he is less conscious of himself* the ineffable comes to speak in and for him, and for and in him the universal, the less conscious, attains the form of consciousness and particularity; by contrast, whatever for the others in his world passes for more objective and is at hand in a more universal form, that which tends not to make distinctions and is less likely to suffer distinctions, that which has less to do with thought, namely, the incomparable, that which is less susceptible of being shaped, the more disorganized and disorganizing in him and for him is more subjective, so that he suffers fewer distinctions and makes fewer distinctions, is less capable of thinking while working his effects; he is more incomparable and less susceptible of being shaped, more aorgic and more *dis*organizational when he is more at home in himself, whenever and to the extent that he is more conscious of the fact that in him and for him speaking attains the unspoken or the ineffable, that in him and for him the more particular and the more conscious aspects assume the form of the unconscious and universal, so that these two opposites become one in him, inasmuch as in him they reverse their distinguishing forms and, to the extent that in the original feeling they are quite distinct, thus also unite—

such a human being can have reached maturity only on the basis of the supreme opposition between nature and art, and as (ideally) the excess of intensity comes to the fore on the basis of intensity, so also does *this real excess of intensity* come to the fore on the basis of enmity and supreme conflict; in this conflict, the aorgic takes on the modest figure of the particular and thus appears to be reconciled with the hyperorganizational, with the organizational taking on the modest figure of the universal and thus appearing to be reconciled with the hyperaorgic and the hypervital, only because both sides interpenetrate most profoundly and touch one another in their uttermost extremes, compelled from hence in their outer form to take on the configuration the semblance of things opposed.

Thus Empedocles, as was said, is the result of his period; his character points back to the period that produced him. His destiny exhibits itself in him as in a momentary unification, one that has to dissolve in order to become something more.

According to everything we know about him, he appears to have been born to be a poet; he therefore appears in his subjective and more active nature already to have had that unusual tendency to universality which in other circumstances, or through insight and avoidance of conceding too strong an influence to this tendency, leads to that tranquil observation, that perfection and thoroughgoing determinacy of consciousness, by means of which the poet espies a *totality;* likewise a fortunate gift appears to lie in his objective nature, in his passivity, for even without diligent and well-instructed ordering and thinking and shaping he is inclined to order, thought, and form, to that malleability of the senses and of the inmost heart that is able to absorb all things easily and quickly in their totality and in a vital way, a quality that grants artistic activity more to say than to do. Yet this predisposition was bound not to remain in its appropriate sphere, bound not to work its effects within that sphere; it was bound not have an impact in its own way and according to its own measure, within its appropriate limits and in its purity, thus allowing its accord, through its own free expression, to become the more universal accord, the accord that would simultaneously be the determination of his nation; the destiny of his time, the massive extremes in which he matured, did not call for song, in which the pure can still be readily taken up in an ideational depiction that lies between the figures of destiny and primordiality, taken up quite readily, that is, if the times have not yet become too far removed from the pure; nor did the destiny of his times demand the authentic deed, which to be sure does have an immediate impact and which thus does lend a hand, but which is also one-sided, all the more so the less it *exposes* the whole human being; the times demanded a *sacrifice* in which the whole human being becomes actual and visible, a sacrifice in which the destiny of his times appears to dissolve and the extremes appear to unite actually and visibly in one, although precisely on that account they are united too intensely, and in which therefore the individual goes down in an idealized deed and has to do so, inasmuch as in him the sensuous unification shows itself to be the proleptic product of calamity and conflict; such a unification dissolved the problem of destiny, which, however, is a problem that can never be dissolved visibly and never by an individual, inasmuch as the universal would founder in the individual, and (which is worse than all the great movements of destiny, and which, when taken by itself, is quite impossible) the life of a world would be expunged in a singularity; whereas, by contrast, if this singularity, as a proleptic result of destiny, itself dissolves because it was too intense and actual and visible, the problem of destiny is dissolved in the same way *materialiter,* although *formaliter* otherwise, since precisely the excess of intensity, which was originally produced by good fortune, albeit only ideally and as an experiment, but which through supreme conflict has now become actual, to that extent and precisely for that reason actually cancels itself in all its levels forces and implements in which the original excess of intensity, the cause of all conflict, canceled itself; thus the force of the intense excess actually evanesces, and a more mature, true, and purely universal intensity remains.

Thus Empedocles was to become a sacrifice of his time, *the problems of destiny in which he grew up were to be apparently solved, and this solution was to show itself to be an apparent solution a temporary solution, as is the case more or less with all tragic personages,* all of which, in their characters and in their utterances, are more or less attempts to solve the problems of destiny; they all cancel themselves to the extent and to the degree that they are not universally valid, if it is also the case that their role their character and their asseverations of themselves represent something transitory and momentary, so that the ones who apparently dissolve destiny most completely exhibit themselves most conspicuously in their transitoriness and in the implacable progress of their efforts to be a sacrificial victim.

In what way, now, is this the case with Empedocles?

The mightier the destiny constituted by the opposites of art and nature, the greater the tendency in them to individualize themselves more and more, to gain a firm point, a foothold; such a time seizes upon all individuals and demands that they persist in trying to find a solution for as long as it takes, until they find someone in whom destiny's unknown requirement and covert tendency exhibit themselves visibly and as already attained; on the basis of that particular one alone, the dissolution that has been found will have to pass over into the universal.

Thus in Empedocles his time individualizes itself; the more it does so, and the more scintillating and actual and visible the riddle that appears to be dissolved in him grows, all the more necessary does his downgoing become.

1. The very spirit of art in his people, a spirit that was generally quite vital and vigorous in its attempts, had to repeat itself in him more aorgically more boldly with fewer limitations more inventively; on the other hand, the glowing stretch of sky and the luxuriant Sicilian landscape had to exhibit

themselves for him and in him more tellingly and in a way that was more powerfully felt; as soon as he was seized by both sides, the one side, the more active force of his essential self, had to enhance the other as its countereffect, so that the spirit of art was nurtured by the sensitive parts of his inmost heart and was thus compelled to advance ever farther.—

2. Among his fellow Agrigentians, who were hyperpolitical, extremely litigious, and always calculating, under the social forms of their innovative, ambitious city, a spirit such as his, which always strove to invent something complete and whole, was compelled quite strongly to become a spirit of reform; yet also the anarchical self-reliance in which each citizen pursued a cause unique to him, without bothering himself about the particular problems of the others—these things had to affect him more than anyone else, given his multifaceted, self-sufficient nature and his extraordinary vitality, making him less convivial and more solitary, prouder and more his own person; and these two sides of his character also must have reciprocally enhanced and magnified one another.

3. The boldness of a free spirit sets itself in ever-waxing opposition to the unknown, to that which lies beyond the ken of human consciousness and action, all the more so if the original, intense feeling of the people was that they were united with the unknown, that is, if they found themselves driven by a natural instinct to defend themselves against the too powerful, too profoundly approachable influence of the element, to preserve themselves from oblivion of self and from total alienation; such free-spirited boldness, with its negative ratiocination concerning the unknown, or its ignoring it altogether, which is so natural in a haughty people, had to go a step farther when it came to Empedocles, who was by no means made for negation; rather, he had to try to master the unknown, had to seek self-assurance; his spirit had to struggle against sheer serviceability, so much so that he was forced to try to comprehend the nature that overwhelms us, to understand it through and through, becoming conscious of it in the way he was able to be conscious of himself, certain of himself; he felt compelled to struggle toward a sense of identity with nature, and so his spirit had to assume an aorgic configuration in the highest sense of the word; he had to tear himself away from himself and from his point of equilibrium, always penetrating his object so excessively that he lost himself in it as in an abyss, while, viewed from the opposite side, the entire life of the object had to seize his abandoned inmost heart, which had only become more and more infinitely receptive because of the boundless activity of his spirit; with him the object had to become individuality, had to grant him his particularity, and this particularity had to enter thoroughly into accord with itself precisely to the degree that he had surrendered himself in his spiritual activity aimed toward the object; and so, in him, the object appeared in a subjective configuration, just as he had taken on the

objective configuration of the object. He was the universal, the unknown, the object the particular. And thus the contest between art, thought, and the human character's compulsion to order, on the one hand, and the less conscious nature on the other, appeared to have been settled, seemed to have been united in one in their uttermost extremes, to the point where these extremes exchanged the very form that distinguished the one from the other. This was the magic with which Empedocles entered on the stage of his world. The nature that dominated his free-spirited contemporaries, nature in all its might and with all its delights, dominated them all the more violently to the extent that they abstracted themselves from her to the point of nonrecognition; that very nature, with all her melodies, came to appear in the spirit and in the mouth of this man, and so intensely and ardently and personally, as though his heart were her own, and as though the spirit of the element dwelled among mortals in human guise. This is what lent him his special grace, his grandeur, his divinity; every heart that was moved by the storm of destiny and every specter that was flitting here and there, restless and without guidance in the enigmatic night of those times, flew to him; and the more humanely he associated with them, growing closer to their own essence, with that extraordinary soul of his making their concerns his own, and after that soul had appeared to them as divinely configured but then returned to them in a form that was more their own, even and precisely then they worshiped him. This fundamental tone of his character showed itself in all his relations. They all took on that tone. Thus he lived in supreme independence, in that relation which prescribed for him his own path, without the more objective, more historical indicators, so that the external circumstances that conducted him along that selfsame path, as essential and as indispensable as they were in bringing him to the forefront and causing him to act in ways that otherwise would have remained mere thoughts in him, nevertheless, and in spite of all the conflict that the sequence of his involvements with them seemed to entail, it all resulted in an encounter with his own freest determination and his very own soul; and no wonder, since precisely this determination is also the most intrinsic spirit of the circumstances, inasmuch as all the extremes in these circumstances took their departure from that spirit and reverted to it once again. The destiny of his time, in its initial and ultimate problem, is dissolved in his utterly independent relation to it. To be sure, from that point onward this apparent solution begins in its turn to cancel itself and thereby comes to an end.

In this independent relation, and in that supreme intensity which constitutes the fundamental tone of his character, he lives with the elements, whereas the world around him lives in supreme opposition to them; his contemporaries live in that free-spirited refusal to think about or to acknowledge in any way that which lives; that is one side of the matter, while the other side is that their approach to the encroachments of nature remains under the supreme dominion of sheer serviceability. In this independent relation he lives (1) as a human being possessed of a refined sensibility in general, (2) as a philosopher and a poet, and (3) as a solitary who cultivates his gardens. Yet in this he would not yet be a personage designed for a drama; he would have to confront destiny not merely in universal relations but also by means of his independent character; he would have to resolve destiny in his particular relations and in his most particular occasions and tasks. But just as he stands in intense relation with the living character of the elements, so also does he stand in intense relation with his people. He was not capable of their negative, violent spirit of renovation, which can only oppose and strive against implacable, anarchic life, which for its part is impatient with every attempt to influence or cultivate it; he had to go a step farther, and in an effort to bring the living under some kind of order, he had to strive to grasp it in its inmost core with his own essence; with his own spirit he had to try to become equal to the human element, with all its inclinations and drives, to grow equal to its soul, to all that is ungraspable and unconscious and involuntary in it; precisely in that way his will his consciousness, his spirit, which transcended the usual human boundaries of knowledge and action, had to lose themselves and become objective, and whatever he wanted to give he first had to find, since, viewed from the other side, the objective reverberated in him all the more purely and profoundly the more open his inmost heart remained, open by virtue of the fact that this intellectually active man had surrendered himself to the particulars as well as to the universal.

Thus he played the role of a religious reformer and a man politically engaged; in all the activities he devoted to those areas he displayed his typical proud and enthusiastic commitment; to all appearances, expressed already in his exchanging the positions of object and subject, he solved for himself all that is destined. Yet in what can this expression consist? What is it precisely in such a relation which satisfies that portion of the population that at the outset is merely incredulous? And everything depends on this expression. For on account of it that which unites must go down, precisely because it comes on the scene too visibly and too sensuously, and can do so only by expressing itself in some quite particular point and in some specific given case. They have to see the single unifying factor between themselves and this man. How can they do so? Is it that he heeds them to the uttermost point? But in what respect? In that respect which concerns the unification of the extremes in which they are living and which plague them with doubts. However, if these extremes arise in the conflict between art and nature, then before their very eyes he must reconcile nature with art precisely in that respect which is most out of reach for art.—The fable takes this as its point of departure. He does it with love, and against his own will;* he passes the test; now they believe that all is accomplished. This is how he comes to realize what they are. The deception in which he lived, as though he were at one with them, now comes to an end. He pulls back, and they grow cold toward him. His opponent uses this, brings about his banishment. His opponent, great in his natural disposition, as is Empedocles, tries to solve the problems of his time in a different, more negative way. Born to be a hero, he is inclined not to unite the extremes but rather to rein them in and tie their reciprocal relation to something enduring and firm, something in the midpoint between them, holding each extreme within its limits by letting each one act on its own. His virtue is the intellect, his goddess, Necessity. He is destiny itself, with the difference that in him the contending forces are firmly tied to a consciousness, to a clear divide, which counterposes those forces in a lucid and secure manner, solidifying them in a (negative) ideality and granting them one sole direction. In Empedocles, art and nature unite in extreme antagonism, the active in excess becomes objective, and the subjectivity that has been lost is replaced by the profound encroachment of the object; by contrast, art and nature unite in his opponent through an excess of objectivity, of being-outside-itself, and of reality (in such a climate, in such an uproar of passions and transformations of the original situation, in such a dominant fear in the face of the unknown), in a courageous, open heart, which has to stand in for the active and formative force, since the subjective here attains the more passive form of patience, endurance, steadfastness, security; and if the extremes, either by their skill in holding out or in some extrinsic way, assume the figure of tranquillity and of the organizational, then the subjectively active must now become the organizing factor, must become the element; thus here too the subjective and objective have to exchange their configurations and become united in one.

* because the fear of becoming positive had to be quite naturally his greatest fear, arising from the feeling that the more he himself actually expressed intensity the more he would surely go down.

The Fatherland in Decline

The fatherland in decline, nature and humanity insofar as they stand in a specific reciprocal relation, one that constitutes a *particular* world that has become the ideal and the very nexus of things; to that extent it is dissolving, so that from it and from the generation that remains, along with the remaining forces of nature—nature being that which constitutes the other principle, the real—a new world may take shape; it will be a novel yet still reciprocal relation, precisely in the way that the decline itself came to pass on the basis of a pure yet particular world. For the world of all worlds, which forever *is* all in all, *depicts itself* only in the fullness of time—or in downgoing or in the moment, or, considered more genetically, in the coming-to-be of the moment and the commencement of time and world; and such downgoing and commencement is something like the language expression sign depiction of a living yet particular whole, which works its effects precisely with a view to the whole, as in the case of language, where very little or nothing of what subsists may be vital when viewed from one side, whereas, viewed from the other side, everything appears to depend on it. A mode of relating and a *type of material* predominate in what subsists vitally; however, inasmuch as all other relations can be intimated in what subsists, the possibility of all relations prevails in the transitional period; yet the particular mode of relating is to be taken or drawn from the transitional period, so that by means of the particular set of possible relations, taken as infinity, the finite effect comes to the fore.

This downgoing or transition of the fatherland (in the sense intended here) is felt down to the very extremities of the subsisting world, so that at the precise moment and to the precise degree that the subsisting world dissolves, the incipient, youthful, possible world can also be felt. For how could the dissolution be apprehended without unification? If the subsistent world is to be apprehended as it is in fact apprehended, in its dissolution, then *the unexhausted* and *inexhaustible* in its *relations* and *forces* must be felt at the same time all the more strongly; and it must be a matter of the dissolution of the *relations* being felt through the *forces,* rather than the other way around; for nothing comes from nothing; and this, taken straightforwardly, means that whatever passes into negation, to the extent that it passes out of actuality and is not yet something possible, can work no effects.

But *the possible,* which enters into *actuality,* and does so precisely as *the actuality is dissolving,* does have an impact; it effects both the apprehension of the dissolution and the remembrance of what has dissolved.

From this arises the thoroughgoing originality of every genuinely tragic language, its enduring creativity . . . the emergence of the individual from the infinite, and the emergence of the finitely infinite, that is, of the individual eternal, from both; this is what grasps and animates not what has become incomprehensible and wretched but the incomprehensibility and the wretchedness of dissolution as such, the death struggle itself, which is grasped and animated by means of the harmonious, the comprehensible the living. In this the individual eternal expresses, not the initial raw pain of dissolution, which is felt in its depths by sufferer and spectator alike, felt as *still too* unfamiliar; in this initial pain the newly emergent, the ideal, is indeterminate, more an object of trepidation than anything else, since in contrast to it the dissolution in itself subsists, *radiates* as the real nothing and as the dissolving that has been caught in a state between being and nonbeing, that is, caught in the turning of necessity.

The new life, which was to dissolve and did in fact dissolve, is now actually the ideally *old,* the dissolution of which was necessary, exhibiting its peculiar character between being and nonbeing. In the state between being and nonbeing, however, the possible is everywhere real and the actual ideal, and in free artistic imitation this is a frightful yet divine dream. Thus dissolution, as necessary, when seen from the point of view of ideal remembrance becomes as such the ideational object of the life that has recently unfolded; it is a glance cast back along the path that had to be traversed from the outset of the dissolution up to the point from which, on the basis of nascent life, a remembrance of what has dissolved can follow, and from that, as an explanation and as a unification of the gaps and the contrasts that occur between the new and the bygone, a remembrance of dissolution itself can succeed. Such ideational dissolution is not met with trepidation; its points of commencement and end are already fixed, located, secured; for that reason such dissolution is also more secure, more inexorable, bolder; it depicts itself thereby as what it properly is, namely, a reproductive act by means of which life traverses all its points; in order to attain the entire sum of those points it does not tarry on any one point but dissolves its attachment to each in order to reproduce itself in the next—it is only that the dissolution becomes increasingly ideal as it removes itself from its point of commencement, or, by contrast, increasingly real as the production advances, until in the end, out of the sum of these sensations of passing away and originating, run through infinitely in a single moment, a feeling of life as a whole comes to the fore; out of this feeling, the sole excluded item, which at the outset was dissolved in remembrance (because of memory's need for an object in the most accomplished state) now also comes to the fore; and after this remembrance of what has dissolved, of the individual, unites with the infinite feeling of life by means of the remembrance of dissolution itself, and after the gaps between them have been filled in, there should emerge from such unification and comparison of the particulars of the past and the infinite that is now presenting itself the new state proper the next step that is to follow upon what is bygone.

Thus in the remembrance of dissolution the dissolution itself, because its two ends are steadfast, becomes the secure, inexorable bold act that it properly is.

Yet this ideational dissolution can be distinguished from the real dissolution also by the fact that it passes from the infinitely present to the finite past, so that in the following three points everything is more infinitely interlaced: (1) within each point of the same dissolution and production; (2) between one point in its dissolution and production and every other point; (3) between each point in its dissolution and production and the total feeling of dissolution and production; more infinitely interlaced, that is, in such a way that everything is more infinitely permeated touched implicated in pain and in joy, in strife and at peace, in motion and at rest, in configuration and disfiguration, so that celestial fire rather than an earthly blaze is at work.

Finally, yet again, because the ideational dissolution goes also in the direction that is the reverse of that from the infinitely present to the finite past, it differentiates itself from the real in that it can be more thoroughly determined; it does not proceed in anxious disquiet, hurriedly jumbling together into one a number of essential points of dissolution and production, nor does it wander timorously among inessential matters that can only hinder not only the feared dissolution but also the production, since hindrance here is properly fatal; nor does it restrict itself diffidently one-sidedly obstinately to a single point of the dissolution and production, once again embracing the cause of something that is genuinely defunct; rather, it treads its precise, straight, and open path, traversing in a thorough way each point of the dissolution and production with a view to what can be contained in it and in it alone, that is, with a view to what is truly individual about it; naturally, it does not force matters, does not foist onto any given point matters that do not belong there and that can only distract us, matters that are both meaningless to the point in question and insignificant in themselves; rather, it passes through the single point freely and completely in all its relations with the other points of the dissolution and production; it passes through everything that lies between the first two points that are *capable of* dissolution and production, namely, between the opposed infinitely new and the finite old, between the totality of the real and the ideal particular.

Finally, the ideational dissolution differentiates itself from the so-called actual (because the ideational passes in the reverse direction, from the infinite to the finite, *after it has gone from the finite to the infinite*) in that the actual dissolution, by dint of the ignorance concerning its points of termination and commencement, has to appear quite simply as the real nothing, so that everything subsistent, every particular, appears as the be-all-and-end-all; it thus comes to the fore as a sensuous idealism or Epicureanism, as Horace tellingly depicts it, although deploying this point of view merely for dramatic purposes, in his phrase *Prudens futuri temporis exitum* p.p.—thus the ideational dissolution finally differentiates itself from the so-called actual dissolution in that the latter appears to be a real nothing, the former, because it is a coming-to-be of the ideal individual in the direction of the infinitely real, and of the infinitely real in the direction of the individual ideal, attaining an ever greater import and harmony to the degree that it is thought of as a transition from one subsistent state to another; the subsistent also attains augmented spirit precisely to the degree that it is thought of as having originated from that transition, or as originating in the direction of that transition, so that the dissolution of the ideal individual comes to appear not as debility and demise but as burgeoning as growth; the dissolution of the infinitely new comes to appear not as an annihilating violence but as love; both together come to appear as a (transcendental) creative act; the essence of that act is to unite the ideal individual with the real infinite; thus the product of the act is the real infinite unified with the ideal individual, whereby the infinitely real assumes the configuration of the individual ideal, with the individual ideal taking on the life of the infinitely real, and with both of them uniting in a mythic state in which the transition, along with the opposition of the infinitely real and the finite ideal, comes to an end; this cessation occurs to the extent that the infinitely real attains enhanced life as the finite ideal gains in tranquillity; this state is not to be confused with the infinitely real that is lyrical; just as little is this state, which originates during the period of transition, to be confused with the individual ideal as depicted in epic; for in these two cases the state in question unites the spirit of the one with the sensuous concreteness of the other. The mythic state is in both cases tragic; that is, in both cases it unites the infinitely real with the finite ideal, and the two cases differ merely by degree; for, even during the period of transition, spirit and sign—in other words, the material of the transition together with the infinitely real, and the infinitely real together with the finite ideal (the transcendental together with the isolated)—are like ensouled organs with an organized soul, that is, they are a one in harmonious opposition with itself.

From this tragic unification of the infinitely new and the finite old there then develops a new individual, such that the infinitely new, by means of its having taken on the configuration of the finite old, individualizes itself now in its proper configuration.

The new individual strives now to isolate itself and to wrestle free from infinity precisely to the same degree that, from a second point of view, the isolated, old individual strives to universalize itself and to dissolve itself in the infinite feeling of life. *The moment in which the period of the new individual ends is there where the infinitely new* comports itself toward the old individual *as the dissolving yet unknown* power, just as in the earlier period the new, which is a still unknown power, comports itself toward the finite old; these two periods confront one another, the first as the dominion of the individual over the infinite, the unique over the whole, the second as the dominion of the infinite over the individual the whole over the unique. The end of this second period and the commencement of the third occur in the moment at which the infinitely new comports itself as the feeling of life (as I) toward the individual as object (as not-I),

---

After these oppositions, tragic unification of the characters, after the opposition of characters has tended toward reciprocity and reversal. After that, the tragic unification of both.

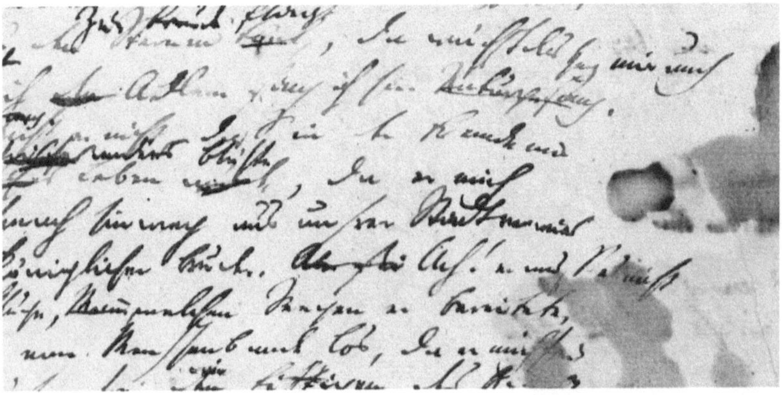

FIVE

Plan of the Third Version of *The Death of Empedocles*

IN HÖLDERLIN'S MANUSCRIPT (which is not yet the *Stuttgarter Foliobuch,* in which the third version itself appears), the plan of the third version follows immediately after the essay "The Basis of Empedocles." Hölderlin kept to the plan for the first three scenes of the third version of the play, but then departed from it altogether. We notice first that Mount Etna is now to be the locale for the entire play: Agrigent is left far behind, and everything that occurred there in the first two versions will in the third merely be reported. According to the plan, the play is to open with a scene in which Empedocles is alone—a soliloquy is obviously called for here. In the second scene, Pausanias is to join him; at the culmination of that scene they are to part. The third scene calls for the arrival of "the old man," *der Greis.* The name Manes does not appear in the plan, but this is the old man (perhaps identical to "the wise man" of the plan) that Hölderlin has in mind.

The most important innovation in the plan of the third version is that Empedocles now must confront an "opponent," *den Gegner.* This is the opponent of which "The Basis of Empedocles" had spoken. Clearly, Empedocles' opponent is to be a more worthy partner in the dramatic conflict than either Critias/Mecades or Hermocrates could be. True, the opponent is "inferior" to Empedocles, and initially he succumbs to his desire to banish the superior man; as the plan has it, however, he soon regrets his action and is quick to follow the crowd in seeking Empedocles' return. The opponent, as in the earlier versions, is the archon-king of Agrigent; he is now to be "heroically reflective," his intellect devoted to practical action and the "clear divide." Whatever his limitations, he does have an influence on Empedocles, who toward the end of the plan is described as "heroic, ideational," that is, as combining the best epic and meditative or reflective qualities.

Tellingly, the opponent is now said to be the *brother* of Empedocles. Brotherhood is their "secret bond" and "unique situation." The family quarrel that Hölderlin early on had envisaged for the play is now to be a dispute between brothers. (One thinks of brothers in the Greek tragic houses of Argos and Thebes, of Thyestes and Atreus, and of Eteocles and Polyneices.) Furthermore, Panthea is now said to be Empedocles' and the opponent's *sister.* Their closeness is also indicated by the fact that both Panthea and Empedocles are described as "naive, ideational," meaning that they are closer to the worlds of philosophy and poetry than politics. (Rhea/Delia, meanwhile, has disappeared—unless one may say that she has been absorbed into the Tiresias-like character of the old wise man in version three.) The later scenes of the play—scenes never written—are to center on a quarrel among the three siblings, principally a quarrel between Panthea and the king-archon that now begins to involve Empedocles. The final lines of the plan reintroduce Empedocles' proximity to and distance from "the people," who in the end can only reinforce his desire to end his life in the crater. The relation of the Agrigentian crowd to the decisive intrafamilial quarrel remains unclear.

Note that whereas the plan has "the old man" disappearing from the play, so that the two brothers and their sister may confront one another directly, without a "mediator," the third version of the play itself will present him—the old man, the wise man—as something more than a sibling, indeed, something closer to a second self or alter ego for Empedocles. Or perhaps a much older, indeed ancient, brother.

The various editions reproduce the plan of the third version of *The Death of Empedocles* with many differences, most of them having to do with the precise form of the text on the page; the translator has integrated the sundry versions here, silently, into a compromise form. An effort has been made, however, to allow the many gaps in the plan to stand. No doubt Hölderlin intended to return to the plan in order to flesh out various scenes.

Plan of the Third Version of *The Death of Empedocles*

Etna
1.
Empedocles

2.
Empedocles, Pausanias

The parting

3.
Empedocles, the Old Man
Telling his story.

The Wise Man. I fear the man who, to the gods

Why rage against the time that gave me birth,
Against the element that raised me
Oh, learn to understand the path I tread,
Empedocles leaves.

Pausanias, the Opponent. The latter, preeminently in order that his own ambitions may find their beginning, and because of the undecided character of the situation after the people's falling-out with Empedocles, but also of course because of his hatred of Empedocles' superiority, is induced to take the exaggerated step of convincing the people to banish Empedocles; now that the people appear to miss Empedocles, and now that the opponent too misses his grandest object, the one that he, as an inferior, would like to have at his side; now also because of the secret bond that unites him and Empedocles, the feeling of their original and unique situation, and the feeling of a tragic determination that is shared by both of them—all this causes him actually to rue the banishment; thus when the people utter the very first word of their dissatisfaction over Empedocles' banishment, he himself proposes that they invite him to return again. Nothing that happens should last forever, he says, a day does not endure without an end, nor a night; after the proud man has tried to accept the lot of mortals, he may now be permitted to live once again. Pausanias

The Old Man, the King

The Old Man.
reflective, ideational.

King heroically reflective.

Messenger.

The Old Man.
The king pleads with his brother p. p.

The king, overwhelmed, affirms it.
Yet he also no longer wishes to be advised, wants to have no mediator between his brother and himself, and so he tells the old man to go away.
Go now, I need no mediator.
Whereupon the old man actually does leave.
The king's monologue. Enthusiasm of the son of destiny.
Empedocles and the King

Empedocles
mine is this region p. p.

King
let the raving man be. p. p.

Empedocles
Yet, clever man, one mother suckled us.

King
How long has it been?

Empedocles

Who can count the years—but

Transition

from the subjective to the objective.

When the king wants to leave, a messenger comes to meet him, announcing that the people are approaching. In his agitation he intones the felicitous song of blessing but then passes over into indignation; he commands the armed soldiers to conceal themselves so that at the very first sign he gives them p. p. at the end, the arrival of his sister and Pausanias is announced.

The Sister, Pausanias

Sister naive, ideational.

She is looking for Empedocles.

Pausanias

Empedocles

naive, ideational

The sister inquires of the king.
wants to reconcile the two
speaks of the people.
begs Empedocles to turn back.

Wounds Oblivion

Empedocles

heroic, ideational

To forgive is everything.

Pausanias sees the people's representatives approaching. The sister fears the outcome—the ambivalent crowd, Empedocles' quarrel with them, and her other brother's quarrel with her, the quarrel between the two brothers that only now appears to be beginning.

Empedocles

remains calm, consoles her. this evening, he says, should be peaceful, cool breezes blow, the messengers of love, and amiably the youthful sun has descended from the heights of heaven to sing its vespers there, and its lyre is full of golden tones!

Representatives of the People

They encounter him in their truest form, just as he himself saw them, as they mirrored themselves in him; they crowd him close, the man whose death is his love, his intimacy, in order to chain him to themselves as firmly as he once was chained; but the closer they come to him with their spirit, and the more he sees himself in them, the more is he strengthened in that direction of his mind which by now has come to rule in him.

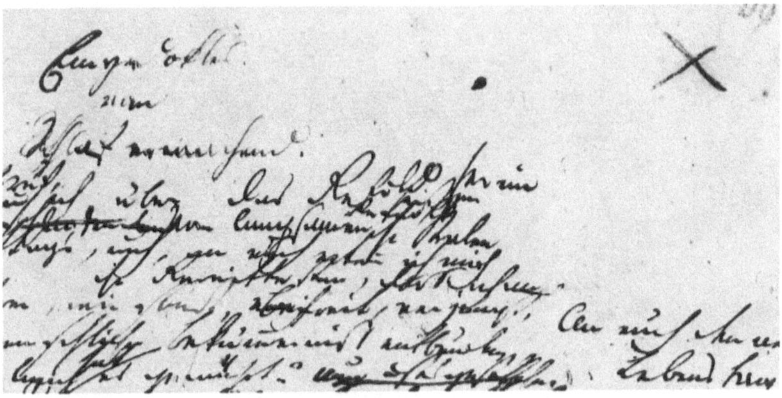

SIX

The Death of Empedocles

Third Version

According to Michael Knaupp (CHV 3:136), Hölderlin probably made his first entry into the so-called *Stuttgarter Foliobuch* in December 1799. That first entry, regardless of the dating, was the third version of *The Death of Empedocles.* Hölderlin began not on the first page of the notebook but well into it: the third version begins on the fifty-ninth verso page and ends on the seventy-fourth. Immediately following it are the "Sketch toward the Continuation of the Third Version" and the essay "The Fatherland in Decline," with which the notebook ends. In the first 118 pages of the *Stuttgarter Foliobuch* appear some of Hölderlin's most important poetological essays, composed after "The Fatherland in Decline," among them the particularly important essay "Once the Poet Has Become Equal to the Spirit" (also known as "The Poetic Spirit's Manner of Proceeding"), "The Lyric Poem as a Semblance of the Poem of Ideas" (also known as "Distinguishing the Poetic Genres"), and the so-called "Alternation of Tones." Also contained in these first 118 pages are second drafts of some Hölderlin's most important poems from the years 1798 to 1799, among them, "Diotima," "The People's Voice," and "To the Germans," along with the first versions of "Rousseau" and "The Poet's Calling." Knaupp observes that Hölderlin continued to work in this notebook through the winter of 1803–1804, up to the *Nocturnes* (*Nachtgesänge*). Hölderlin's practice was to write in his notebooks not only from front to back but also from back to front, and to insert work wherever a page was blank—he was often out of money *and* paper, Dietrich Sattler notes wryly (BA 8:5). Indeed, to get a full idea of the complexity of Hölderlin's creative life—in which practical concerns, professional plans, initial drafts of poems, and analyses of Greek meters interrupt and interpenetrate one another, one should examine the *chronological* presentation of the theoretical essays and third version of *Empedocles* in Sattler's Bremer edition (BA 8:35–127).

The theoretical speculations contained in "The Tragic Ode," "The General Basis," and "The Basis of Empedocles" surely leave their mark on the third version of the play. It begins with a monologue by Empedocles, who is already on Etna, far removed from Agrigent, and ends with the unresolved conflict between the Sicilian magus and his Egyptian doppelgänger, Manes. Jochen Schmidt notes that whereas the first two versions of the play exhibit Empedocles' "inner development," moving from a largely negative motivation for his "ideal deed," namely, his guilt, frustration, and rage, to a free and affirmative heroic will that can bless the world and the earth, the third version is devoted to a challenging of Empedocles' self-proclaimed affirmative resolve. If the *second* version shows a development in the character Hermocrates, who is no longer the contemptible, conniving priest but a far more serious opponent, the *third* version completes that development: Manes is "an interior voice of Empedocles himself, testing him, demanding an accounting" (DKV 2:1096). Schmidt confirms the reading of Max Kommerell, who emphasizes that in the third version the very notions of Empedocles' guilt and penitential death vanish; these notions are replaced by the idea of what one might call "the ferment of time," *die Gärung der Zeit* (MK 324, 327; cf. Manes in l. 364: *Es gärt um ihn die Welt,* "The world around him bubbles in ferment."). The "accounting," in other words, does not have to do with the *nefas* of Empedocles, but with a far greater issue—that of the destinies of nations as well as of exceptional individuals in historical time. One has the sense that no matter how much Manes and Empedocles are opposed, Manes's words can quite readily be integrated into the speeches of Empedocles himself. True, Manes is called both an "opponent" and an "evil spirit," yet the "Sketch toward the Continuation" envisages the Egyptian priest affirming and celebrating Empedocles after his leap into Etna. Perhaps it is the proximity of Manes and Empedocles that Jochen Schmidt means to indicate when he writes, "At its very kernel, the tragedy is monological" (DKV 2:1108). Perhaps because of this same proximity Philippe Lacoue-Labarthe says that *The Death of Empedocles* is ultimately less a piece for the theater than "an exercise in eloquence," "an oratorio without music" (quoted at TA 277). Be that as it may, with the long soliloquies of both Manes and Empedocles at the end of the third version, *The Death of Empedocles* becomes a meditation on the rise and fall of civilizations and historical epochs within "the ferment of time," not a depiction of the life and death of individuals. While a poet is chosen to sing the swan song of the dying age, a threnody devoted to "the fatherland in decline," that individual is also a sacrificial victim—something very much resembling a scapegoat. A scapegoat, perhaps, who sings the goat song of tragedy. Whether there can be "a unique one" who conjoins nature and art in such a song, one who reconciles sky and earth by way of love, bridging the gap between his or her passing world and the still inchoate world to come, and achieving this precisely in one full deed, one ideal and deadly deed at and as the end—the play leaves us with such questions carefully posed and rigorously unanswered.

The Death of Empedocles
Third Version

[Persons in the Play]

Empedocles
Pausanias, *his friend*
Manes, *an Egyptian*
Strato [formerly Critias, Mecades], *ruler of Agrigent, brother of Empedocles*
Panthea, *sister of Empedocles*
Followers [of Strato]
Chorus of Agrigentians

[ACT 1, SCENE 1]

EMPEDOCLES
(emerging from sleep)
To you I call across the fields that you
May come eluding sluggish clouds, you hot rays
Of midday, you ripest rays, that I may know
Through you this new day of my life.
For things are different than before! gone, gone are
My trials with human beings! as though
I'd grown strong pinions, with me all is well and airy
Up here above it all, and rich enough and glad enough
And splendidly I dwell here near the fiery chalice,
Filled with spirit to the brim and wreathed
With flowers he himself has cultivated
My father Etna offers me his hospitality.
And as the subterranean storm celebrates
By reaching to the cloudy precincts of
The blood-related Thunderer, flying heavenward
With joy my heart too flourishes;
With eagles here I sing the canticle of nature.
He did not think that here in unfamiliar country
Another life would bloom in me
When shamefully he drove me from our city
My royal brother. Ah! he did not know,
The clever fellow, the blessings he bestowed
On me when from the bonds of humankind he
Declared me free, as free as soaring wings of heaven.
And that was only right! that's why it was fulfilled!
With scorn and curse the nation girded up its loins,
The nation that was mine, and turned against my soul
And ostracized me; not without effect I still can hear
The clamor of a hundred voices in my ear,
The chilling laughter, when the dreamer,
The jester, went weeping on his way.
O judges of the dead! I well deserved it!
And it was salutary; poison heals the sick
And one sin punishes the others.
For much from my youth onward have I sinned
I never loved humanity in fitting human ways,
I served as fire and water blindly serve;
In turn my fellows never met me as a human being

Till finally they dared humiliate me to
My face; they seized me, as you did once
Long-suffering nature! you too possess me,
You have me; between the two of us
The old love kindles once again
You call, you draw me close and closer to yourself.
Oblivion—oh, like a happy sailing ship
I've left the lee shore,

And when the wave would whelm me, then
My mother's arm embraces me; oh what have I
To fear, is there anything to fear. Others may
Be terrified of this. For it is the death of them.
O you! well known to me, you thaumaturgic
Frightful flame! how noiselessly you dwell,
Here and there you flit, shying from yourself,
You flee yourself, you soul of all that lives!
From me you'll hide, O fettered spirit, no more,
I'll see you clearly in the light, for I am not afraid.
And, yes, I want to die. This is my right.
Ha! Youth! like daybreak all around me now
And down below the rage that roared storms by!
Down, down with you, you thoughts of accusation!
O care-filled heart! I need you now no more.
Up here there's no more pondering. It calls,
The god calls—

(he then becomes aware of Pausanias)

and this all-too-faithful one I
Must also liberate; my path is not his.

[Scene 2]

Pausanias, Empedocles

Pausanias

By now and not in vain, dear friend, I
Have scouted all about our new homeland.
The wilderness is sacred to me,

you too are pleased by this brave fortress, our Etna.
They've banished us, humiliated you,
You good man! and you must believe

For some time now they could not suffer you, and in
The midst of their own rubble you shone too intensely
In their dark night a light too bright for desperadoes.
Now they want to end it all left undisturbed
A storm offshore has caught them unprepared
Their polar star's obscured, their ship sails in circles.

I knew it well, divine man, from you all arrows are
Deflected, while other men are struck and thrown.
And harmlessly, as on the caduceus serpents coil at play
The fickle crowd you helped to educate
Has always played about you, the crowd
You held within your heart, you loving man!
Now! let them go! may they falter as they shy
Away from light, stumbling on the ground
That bears them, and craving all, fearing all
Run themselves ragged; let the brushfire burn
Till it goes out—we'll dwell here tranquilly.
Yes! tranquilly we'll dwell; they open mightily
Before us here, the holy elements, bestir
Themselves without exertion, always in
The same inspiring measure, here about us.

EMPEDOCLES

You holy elements!
On firm shores surging then reposing
The ancient sea, and mountains all ascending
To heed the roaring of their streams; winds respire
And rush within the wood from vale to vale below.
While here above, the lingering light, as ether stills
The spirit and the more mysterious yearnings that
Lie deeper in the breast, yes, son! up here
We'll dwell most tranquilly!

PAUSANIAS

You'll stay
Upon these heights, you'll live in your own world;
I'll serve you well and see to all our needs.

EMPEDOCLES

My needs are very few, and I myself
From this point on would rather see to them.

PAUSANIAS
But friend! already I've assembled
Some of what you'll need at least at first.

EMPEDOCLES
Do you know what I need?

PAUSANIAS
As though I did
Not know what satisfies a man so easily pleased.
A life that's come to need its intimacy
With nature, a life familiar with her, will find
The smallest things are most significant.
Yet as you slept on bare earth here
Beneath the scorching sun I had to think
A softer bed at cool of night and
Security of walls would be far better.
Then too, we objects of suspicion here
Are almost too near the others' dwellings.
I did not want to leave your side for long
And so I hurriedly ascended; luckily I found
As though designed for you and me a quiet house
Concealed within a gorge and shaded by thick oaks.
There among the shadows of the mountains near
A bubbling spring, and verdant all around,
A cornucopia of herbs, and for your bed
Dry leaves and grass in rich excess. There none
Can harm you; it's steep and still, the very place
For your reflections; and when you sleep
The grotto for the two of us will be a sacred precinct.
Come, see for yourself, and don't say I'm no use to you
In times to come; to whom else could I be of use?

EMPEDOCLES
You're too useful.

PAUSANIAS
How could I be?

EMPEDOCLES
You too
Are far too faithful; you're a foolish child.

PAUSANIAS
You can say so if you like; I know nothing wiser than
Belonging to the one for whom I saw the light of day.

EMPEDOCLES
How can you be so sure?

PAUSANIAS
How not be sure?
What reason did you have back then when I
Was like an orphan on a shore that bred no heroes;
I sought a patron god, was wandering wretchedly;
What reason to extend to me your hands, good man?
For what good reason with your power, tranquil light,
And with an eye unerring did you rise
Before me, banishing my sad twilight?
Since then I've been another, I've been yours,
And closer to you, more solitary with you;
Near you my soul can wax felicitous and free.

EMPEDOCLES
No more of that!

PAUSANIAS
Why? what is it? how can
A friendly word abash you, my dear friend?

EMPEDOCLES
Go! obey me, be silent now and spare me
Don't you too stir up my heart.—
Have not you all transformed my memory into
A dagger? and now they marvel still, they speak up
And confront me with their questions.
No! you are guiltless—my son! it's only that
I cannot bear what crowds me close.
Tell yourself whatever story pleases you,
For me the past has passed, it is no more.

PAUSANIAS
I know full well what's passed for you,
Yet you and I remain to one another.

EMPEDOCLES
But speak to me of other things, my son!

PAUSANIAS
What else do I possess?

EMPEDOCLES
And do you understand me?
Away! I've told you this before and tell you now
Again, it is not good of you to thrust
Yourself so uninvited on my soul,
You're clinging to my side as though you knew
Of nothing else in your anxiety.
You have to know I don't belong to you, nor you
To me; the paths that you will tread
Are not mine; it flowers for me elsewhere.
And what I am intending now is not a matter of today,
For at my birth, already then, it was concluded.
Look up now and be brave! what is merely one
Will shatter; love dies not at budding time,
And everywhere in open joy life's
Great tree shares its luxuriance.
No bond that's sealed in time remains as is,
We have to part, my child! do not
Delay my destiny, do not procrastinate.

Behold! the image of ecstatic earth,
Divinity itself, is present in you, boy,
It rushes raging, sweeps through every land,
Transforms itself in youthful, lithe, and pious
Earnest forms, the energetic circle dance in which
The mortals celebrate the spirit of their ancient father.
Then go and wander without tumult as befits
A human being, and think on me at eventide alone.
What suits me is the silent hall, mine is
The spacious chamber looming high above,
For I need rest, too sluggish now
To entertain the quick-change play of mortals are
These limbs of mine; if once upon a time
My youthful jubilation sang its festive song
The thrum of fragile strings has now succumbed.
O melodies above me! it was all in jest!
And childishly I dared to imitate your song,
A distant anesthetic echo it resounded in me
Incomprehensibly—
Now, godly voices, I hear you all more earnestly.

PAUSANIAS
I do not know you anymore, can only mourn,
And everything you say is like a riddle to me.
What have I done, what have I done to you
That you should treat me as you please
And that your heart should take some nameless joy
In driving off its sole and final friend.
Rejection never was the plan when we, despised,
Together, banished to the wilderness of night,
Slipped past the houses of mankind
And friend! was I not there when
The tears of heaven's rain assailed
Your face and did I not observe you
When you smiled and dried your rags
At midday underneath the scorching sun
On shadeless sands where you left traces
Hour after hour like a wounded deer
Inscribing them with blood that dripped
From naked soles upon your stony path
Alas! it was not for this I left my home and drew
Upon me curses from my father and my nation,
That you, arriving here to dwell and rest
Toss me aside as though I were an empty vessel.
And would you travel farther on? where to? where to?
I'll wander with you, though unlike you I do not stand
In steadfast league with all the forces of beloved nature
To me, unlike you, the future is not open
Yet soaring joyful out into the night divine
The pinions of my mind will flex and
Will not fail before the gazes of the mighty.
Yes! for even if I were a weakling I would be
As strong as you, if only for the love of you.
Divine Heracles! even if you plummeted
To seek below the violent ones, to
Conciliate defeated Titans, plunging down
From that peak there into the groundless gorge,
And if you dared to penetrate abyssal precincts
Where patiently before the day begins the heart
Of earth conceals itself, where all her pains she tells,
Our darkling mother, tells you, nocturnal one,
The son of ether! I'd follow you below.

EMPEDOCLES
So stay!

PAUSANIAS
What do you mean?

EMPEDOCLES
You gave yourself to me;
You're mine; and so you must not question!

PAUSANIAS
So be it.

EMPEDOCLES
And tell me once again my son will you give your
Life's blood to me, your blood and soul forever?

PAUSANIAS
As though I had been speaking drowsily
Resisting sleep the moment when I promised you
Precisely that? Incredulous! I say it and repeat it,
This too, this too is not a matter of today,
When I was born it was concluded.

EMPEDOCLES
I am not who I am, Pausanias,
My stay will not be counted off in years,
A shimmer only, quickly passing, a fading note
Within the symphony of strings—

PAUSANIAS
That's how
They always sound, vanishing together into thin air!
And their reverberations echo in a friendly way.
Do not beguile me any longer! let that go,
Bestow on me the honor that is mine!
Have I not borne enough deep pain inside,
How can you think of further hurt!

EMPEDOCLES
O all-sacrificing heart! and this one
For my sake flings away his golden youth!

And I! O earth and sky! behold! still
Still you are near, although the hour flies,
And still you bloom, you, my eyes' rejoicing.
Things still are as once they were, I hold you in
My arms as though you're mine, indeed, my prey,
And once again the lovely dream befuddles me.
Yes! it would be splendid if into the pyre's flames
Thus arm in arm instead of one left all alone
A festive pair at end of day went off companionably
And gladly I would take the one that here I loved,
The way a noble stream sweeps all its tributaries
Into the depths below, libations to the holy night.
Yet better it would be if each of us pursued
His own path, as divinity has meted out,
Less guilt there is in this, no damage done.
And meet it is and just that everywhere
A human being's mind stands on its own.
Then too—more lightly and securely does
A man endure his burden when alone.
The forest oaks grow old this way; no one of them,
However great its age, can know the others.

PAUSANIAS
As you will! I shall not strive against you.
You speak to me and what you say is true and loving
This final word from you is suitable to me.
And so I go! your tranquillity I'll not
Disturb in times to come; you are right
To say my mind is not designed for silence.

EMPEDOCLES
But now, my friend, you are not angry?

PAUSANIAS
With you? With you?

EMPEDOCLES
What is it then? ah, yes! Do you know where to go?

PAUSANIAS
Command me.

EMPEDOCLES
It will have been my last command,
Pausanias! my lordship now is at an end.

PAUSANIAS
My father! counsel me!

EMPEDOCLES
So many things I should
Relate, and yet I keep them from you. It seems
My tongue well-nigh refuses mortal talk,
Rejects all words that speak in vain.
Behold! my best beloved, it is otherwise with me
And soon I'll breathe more easily, and as the snow
On Etna's peak, exposed there to the sunlight,
Grows warm and glistens, starts to melt,
Then plunges till the rainbow, goddess Iris, blooms
And spans her cheerful bridge across the waterfall, thus
The thaw and plunging of the waters from my heart, thus
The tumbling echoes here of all that time heaped up in me
And all that's heavy falls, and falls, and brightly flowers
Ethereal life above me.
Now walk with courage, son, for I bestow
With kisses promises upon your brow,
The dim horizon there reveals the hills of Italy,
The Roman lands, so rich in deeds,
You'll flourish there where men exhilarate
The moment when they meet upon the racing course,
A heroes' city there! and you, Tarentum! your
Fraternal halls, where often I was drunk
With light while wandering with my Plato
And to us youths the years seemed ever new
And every day commencement in our sacred school.
So visit him, my son, and greet him there for me
His friend of old down at his homeland's stream
The flowering Ilissus, where he dwells.
And if the soul in you refuses rest, then go
Inquire of my brothers far away in Egypt.
You'll hear the earnest thrum of strings
Urania plays and all their shifting tones.
So many things await you that are luminous

And grand; you'll learn that mortals standing
Face to face are but images and signs
Yet this will not disturb you, my dear friend!
They'll open for you there the book of destiny.
Go! fear nothing! everything recurs. And what
Is yet to happen already is accomplished.

[Scene 3]

Manes, Empedocles

Manes
Now! do not delay! don't ponder any longer
But pass away! yes, pass! that we may have some quiet
And a brighter day, mirage!

Empedocles
What? whence?
Who are you, man?

Manes
A mortal just like you.
I'm sent at the propitious time to you who think yourself
The darling of the sky, to indicate the heavens' wrath,
The wrath of god, the god who won't be named in vain.

Empedocles
Ha! you know him?

Manes
I told you many things upon
The banks of the far Nile.

Empedocles
And you? you here?
No miracle in that. Ever since I died to all the living
The dead rise up to greet me.

Manes
The dead do not reply to questions that you put to them.
And yet if you should need a word, pay heed.

EMPEDOCLES
I heed the voice that's long been calling me.

MANES
So *that's* the way it speaks to you?

EMPEDOCLES
Why this talk, stranger!

MANES
Yes! a stranger here, and in the midst of children.
For that's what all you Greeks are. I've often said so
In earlier times. But don't you want to tell me
How you fared with your own people?

EMPEDOCLES
Oh, why remind me? Why dredge it up again? Things went
Precisely as they should have.

MANES
I knew that in
Advance, and long ago I prophesied it to you.

EMPEDOCLES
Well, then! why do you delay it? why threaten me
With all the flames of god, the god I know,
The god I serve, if only as a plaything, and you
Blind man! presume to judge my holy right.

MANES
What you go to encounter I'll not alter.

EMPEDOCLES
And so you came to sate your curiosity?

MANES
Speak not in jest, and honor this your festival,
Enwreathe your head and decorate
The sacrificial beast that does not fall in vain.
For death, the sudden steep, is there from the beginning,
As you know well; and to the baffled ones, to those

Who are your kin, it has long since been allotted.
Your will declares it! let it be! Yet you should not
Abandon me and go down thoughtlessly, not as you are;
I have a word that you must ponder, my besotted friend!
For one alone in our time is it fitting; one being
Alone ennobles your black sin.
That one is greater than I am! for as the vine
Bears witness to the earth and sky when, saturated by
The lofty sun it rises from dark soil, thus
This being grows, a child of light and night.
The world around him bubbles in ferment, and all
Disruption and corruption in the mortal breast
Is agitated, and from top to bottom; whereupon
The lord of time, grown apprehensive of his rule,
Looms with glowering gaze above the consternation.
His day extinguished, lightning bolts still flash, yet
What flames on high is inflammation, nothing more;
What strives from down below is savage discord.
The one, however, the newborn savior, grasps
The rays of heaven tranquilly, and lovingly
He takes mortality unto his bosom, and
The world's strife grows mild in him.
The human being and the gods he reconciles;
Again they live in close proximity, as in former times.
No sooner has the son appeared, that he may not
Surpass his parentage, and that the holy spirit
Of life may not remain in shameful fetters
On his account, forgotten up above, the unique one
Now turns aside, although he is the idol of his times,
Destroys himself, so that a pure hand executes
Whatever of necessity befalls the pure one;
He shatters his own fortune, now too fortunate for him,
Restores whatever he possessed unto the element
That glorified him, gives it back now wholly cleansed.
Are you that man? the very one? are you this?

EMPEDOCLES
I know you by your gloomy words, and you
Who are all-knowing recognize me too.

MANES
Oh, tell us who you are! and who am I?

EMPEDOCLES

Can it be so, that still, still you tempt me, coming as
My evil spirit, descending on me here at such an hour?
Why not let me go in hushed tranquillity, man?
You challenge me, you irritate, that I
Might walk my holy path enraged?
A boy I was back then, my eyes did not know what
Mysterious things were under way from day to day,
Surrounding and bedazzling me, the great
Configurations of this world, the joyous ones that stirred
The inexperienced and slumbering heart within my breast.
Astonished oftentimes I heard the waters' flow and saw
The sun burst into bloom; I saw our silent earth
At youthful day catch fire from that sun.
A hymn was in me, splendidly it soared,
My twilit heart I poetized in prayers
When I gave names to all these strangers
The present ones, the gods of nature; to me
The spirit showed itself in words and images
Felicitous, to solve the mysteries of life.
The years passed uneventfully; I grew, while other things
Prepared themselves for me. For far more violent
Than inundating waters, savage waves of humankind
Came crashing down against my breast; in all that din
I came to hear the voice of my poor people.
And while I paced in silence in my halls
At midnight rose in tumult their lament
They stormed across the fields, and weary unto death
With frenzied hands they tore down their own homes,
They razed their desecrated and abandoned temples;
When brother fled from brother, when lovers passed
Each other by in ignorance, when fathers failed
To recognize their sons, when human words no more
Were understood, nor human laws, that was when
The meaning of it all assailed me and I trembled:
It was my nation's parting god!
I heard him, and upward to unspeaking stars
I gazed, the place from which he had descended.
And then I went to placate him. For us there still
Were many radiant days. It still seemed at the very end
We might invigorate ourselves; and thus consoled
By memories of the Golden Age, that all-confident

And brilliant morning full of force, the frightful melancholy
Was lifted from me and from my people also;
We sealed with one another free and firm bonds,
Appealing to the living gods in supplication.
Yet often when I donned the crown of all the people's thanks,
And when the nation's soul approached me ever closer,
Crowding me alone, again the melancholy stole upon me.
For when a country is about to die, its spirit at the end
Selects but one among the many, one alone through whom
Its swan song, the final breaths of life, will sound.
I had an intimation, yet served the spirit willingly.
And now it has transpired. To mortals I belong
No more. Oh, the termination of my time!
O spirit! you who raised us, you who secretly
Prevail beneath the sun as well as in the clouds,
And you, O light! and you, our mother earth!
Here I am, tranquil, for I await that which
Prepared itself so long ago, my new hour.
No longer now in images, not as before among
The mortals steeped in sometime happiness,
In death I'll find the living one; today
Will be the day I meet him, for on this day
The lord of time inaugurates a festival and sends
A sign for me and for himself, a cloudburst.
Do you feel the calm about us now? do you sense
The silence of the sleepless god? await him here!
At stroke of twelve he will accomplish it for us.
For if as you have said you are the Thunderer's
Familiar, and if your spirit's of a single mind with his,
And if you know the path and wish to walk it,
Then come with me and banish dire loneliness;
The heart of earth lamenting to itself, remembering
Their ancient unity, the darksome mother reaching out
Her arms of fire, stretching toward the ether;
And if the ruler comes in his bright ray
We'll follow him, to signify that we are blood
Related, going down in holy flames together.
If you yourself would rather tarry at a safe remove,
However, why not grant me what is mine?
If this is not allotted to you as your own, why
Deprive me of it, why disrupt! My gratitude
To you, you tutelary spirits, who when I began
Were close to me, you far-projecting ones! You I thank

For granting me release; the long count of my sufferings
Here ends; emancipated from all other obligations,
I go to meet my free death, obey divine law!
For you it is forbidden fruit! so leave me and depart,
And if you cannot follow me, at least you shall not judge!

MANES
The pain inflames your spirit, you poor man.

EMPEDOCLES
Well then, feckless friend, why not heal it?

MANES
How is it with us? are you quite sure of what you see?

EMPEDOCLES
You tell me, you who see all things!

MANES
Let us remain at peace, my son! and let us always learn.

EMPEDOCLES
You taught me once; now learn from me today.

MANES
Have you not told me everything?

EMPEDOCLES
Oh, no!

MANES
And now you'll go?

EMPEDOCLES
I'll not go yet, old man!
From this green earth and her beneficence
My eye should not depart deprived of joy.
And even now I'll think on times gone by,
On friends of early days, those dear friends
Now far away in Hellas' happy cities,
And on my brother too, who cursed me, it
Was bound to happen; leave me now; over there
When daylight's down, you'll see me once again.

[CHORUS]

New world

and it looms, a brazen vault
the sky above us, curse lames
the limbs of humankind, and the nourishing, gladdening
gifts of earth are like chaff, she
mocks us with her presents, our mother
and all is semblance—

Oh, when, when will it open up
the flood across the barren plain.

But where is he?

That he conjure the living spirit

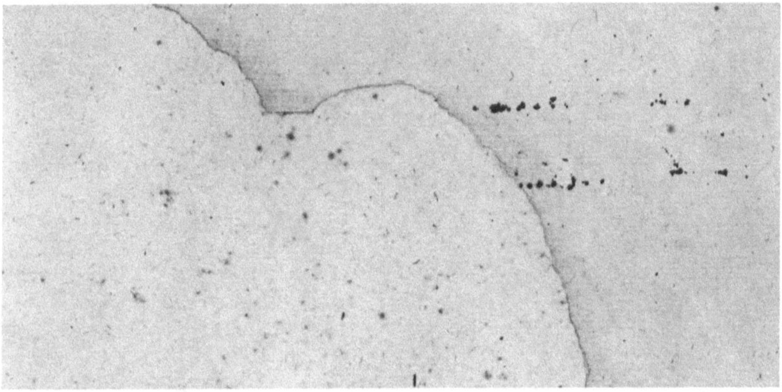

SEVEN

Sketch toward the Continuation of the Third Version

THE SKETCH TOWARD THE continuation of the third version of *The Death of Empedocles* appears in the *Stuttgarter Foliobuch* immediately after the choral ode, "New world," which concludes version three of the play as we have it. The sketch does not refer to the three scenes of act 1 that were already composed, but tries to move ahead with the concept of the play. New to the sketch are the names Strato, the king-archon of Agrigent and the brother of Empedocles, and Manes, the "old man" of version three. On the page prior to that on which the sketch begins, Hölderlin notes the following cast of characters:

Empedocles
Pausanias, his friend
Manes, an Egyptian
Strato, lord of Agrigent, brother of Empedocles
Panthea, his sister
Followers . . .
Chorus of Agrigentians

Strato is clearly meant to be that "opponent" of which "The Basis of Empedocles" speaks. Recall the augmented role that the "king" was to play, according to the plan for the third version. Yet there is some evidence in the following sketch—which is the very last document surrounding the intended mourning-play that we possess—that Manes, the Egyptian priest, is to play an even more significant role in the tragedy. We have seen how in the third version the "old man" challenges Empedocles' very identity; here, in act 4, scene 3 of the sketch, that same old man, Manes, and not Strato, is "astounded by Empedocles' speeches" and confirms Empedocles' vocation. In the final scene, it is again Manes who proclaims Empedocles' ultimate will. No doubt, then, Hölderlin intended to have Empedocles respond to Manes's challenges to his identity, and this reply was to have convinced Manes and everyone else. Max Kommerell comments, "The invention of Manes, as one who is the equal of Empedocles in his opposition to him, one whose words concerning Empedocles in the final phase of the play are entirely valid, makes the essence and the death of Empedocles a pure necessity. Manes knows Empedocles unconditionally on the basis of infinite being; he derives the sense of Empedocles from the collective course of time" (MK 338).

Finally, we note in the sketch Hölderlin's intention to add more choral odes to acts 2 and 3 of the play. It is as though he is increasingly taking classical Athenian tragedy as his model. Sophocles had always been of supreme importance to him, and in a few years he would be devoting his final creative energies to translations of Pindar's Odes and Sophocles' *Oedipus the Tyrant* and *Antigone.* Those translations, along with the extraordinary "Notes" that accompany the Sophoclean tragedies, are the works toward which *The Death of Empedocles* is heading. Students of Hölderlin's efforts to create a mourning-play for modernity—and for postmodernity—will want to follow him there.

Sketch toward the Continuation of the Third Version

Chorus Future.

Act 2
Scene 1
Pausanias, Panthea

Scene 2
Strato His Followers

Scene 3
Strato alone

Chorus ?

Act 3
Empedocles, Pausanias, Panthea, Strato, Manes
Strato's Followers, Agrigentians
Chorus ?

Act 4
Scene 1
Empedocles, Pausanias, Panthea

lyric or epic?

Scene 2
Empedocles

heroic elegiac

Scene 3
Manes, Empedocles

lyrical heroic

Manes, who has experienced all, the seer, astounded by Empedocles' speeches and by his spirit, says that Empedocles is the one who has been called, the one who kills and who gives life, the one in and through whom a world dissolves and in the same instant renews itself.

The human being who felt his country's downgoing so mortally was also able thus to sense its new life.

Scene 4
Empedocles

heroic lyrical

Act 5

Manes, Pausanias, Panthea, Strato, Agrigentians, Strato's Followers

On the following day, at the festival of Saturn, Manes wants to proclaim to all of them the ultimate will of Empedocles.

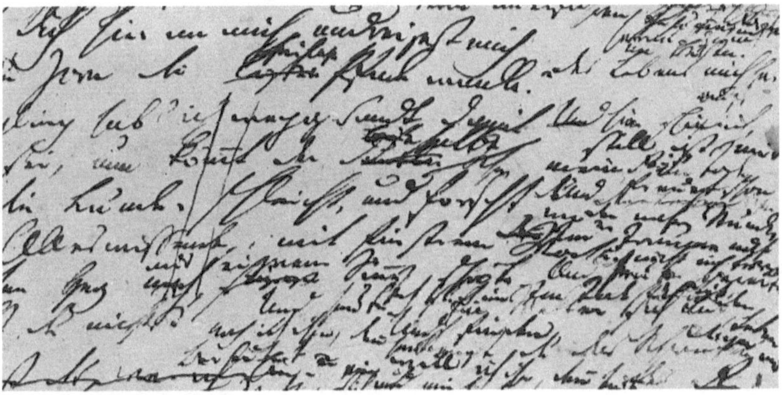

Facsimile Pages from
Der Tod des Empedokles

THE FOLLOWING PORTFOLIO presents twelve pages from Hölderlin's manuscripts of the three versions of *The Death of Empedocles.* A brief description of the contents of each page is provided. The portfolio offers readers a glimpse of the manuscripts—in all their complexity—and provides a sense of the poet's manner of composition and emendation. The debt we owe to the patient and skilled editors who over the years have pored over these pages is great indeed. One may justly single out Dietrich Sattler, whose Frankfurter Hölderlin-Ausgabe (FHA) offers a variorum edition of the holograph, yet each editor—from Christoph Theodor Schwab and Gustav Schwab, Wilhelm Böhm, and Norbert von Hellingrath, among others in the nineteenth and early twentieth centuries, down to Beissner, Knaupp, Sattler, and Schmidt in our own time—has made worthy contributions.

In the captions to the facsimile pages, English words appearing in brackets ([ ])are those that precede the direct quotation; German and English words in braces ({ })are words that Hölderlin crossed through, usually replacing them with the word or phrase that follows.

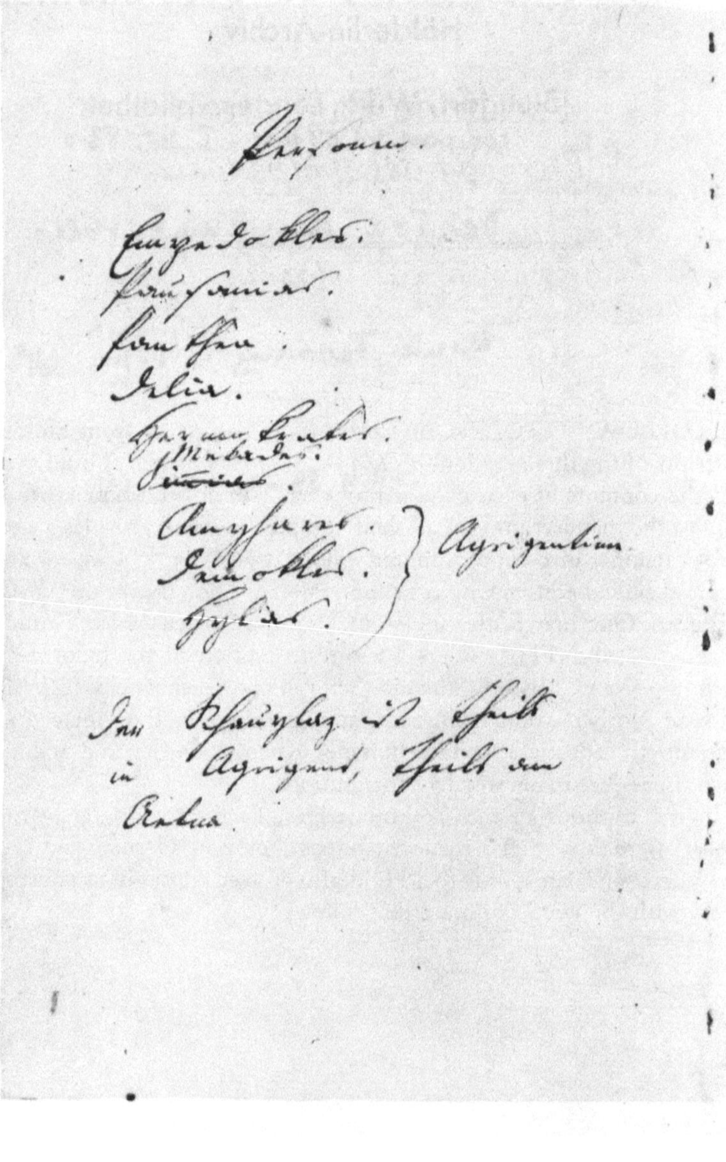
Personen.
Empedokles.
Pausanias.
Panthea.
Delia.
Hermokrates.
Mekades.
Amphares.
Demokles.
Hylas.
Agrigentiner
Der Schauplaz ist theils in Agrigent, theils am Aetna.

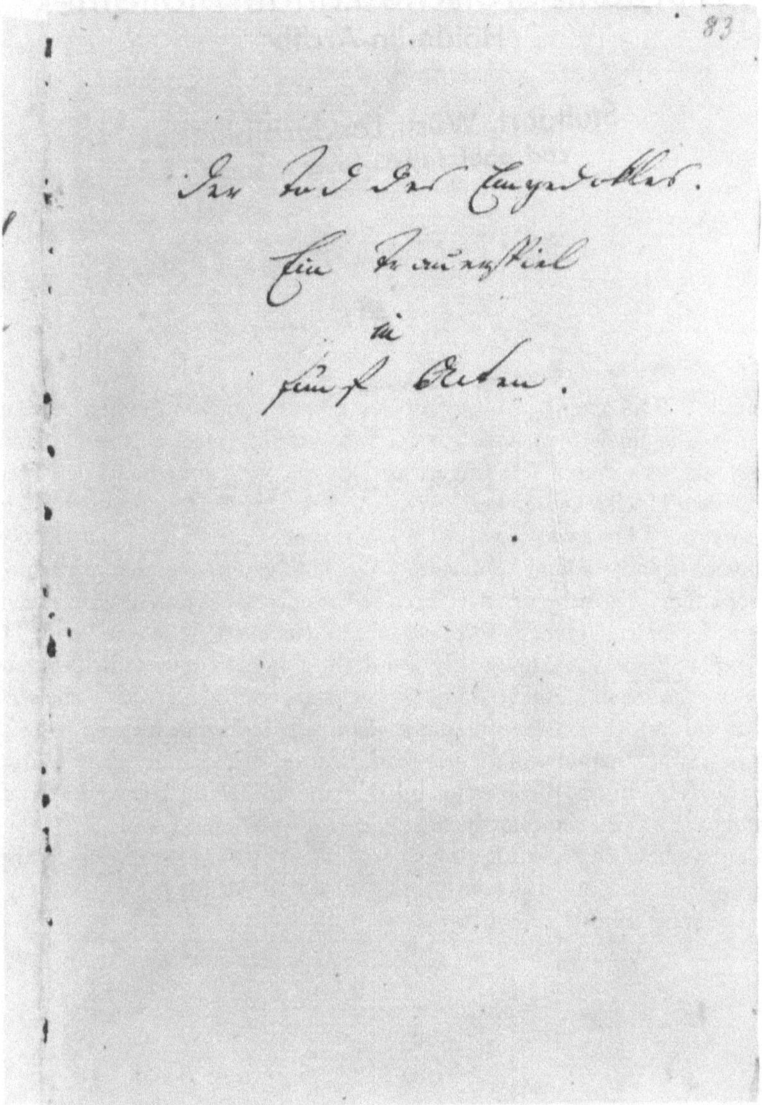

Facsimiles 1–2. The title page (recto) and list of persons in the play (the opposite verso) for version two, taken from the *Reinschrift* or neat copy designed for the printer. *Der Tod des Empedokles: Ein Trauerspiel in fünf Acten.* Note the name of the archon in version one, *Kritias,* crossed through and replaced by *Mekades.* Below the list of characters, the scenes are described: "Der Schauplaz ist theils in Agrigent, theils am Aetna," "The scene is partly in Agrigent, partly on Etna."

Facsimile 3. The opening of Empedocles' first soliloquy in the first version, ll. 279–94. The final three lines are the most readily recognizable: "O innige Natur! ich habe dich / Vor Augen {und du} kennest du {mich} den Freund noch / Den Hochgeliebten kennest du mich nimmer?" In translation: "O intimate nature! I have you now before / My eyes {and you}, do you still know {me} your friend, the one / You deeply loved, do you know me now no more?" The opening lines, however, have been reworked several times, so that the first line of the finalized text, "In {die} meine Stille kamst du leise wandelnd," "Into {the} my stillness you came softly wandering," is extremely difficult to make out: note the second, indented line on the page, continued then in the second half of the third line. After the name "Empedokles" what we read instead is: "Du riefst mich herauf—in meiner Ruhe drunten / Zu meiner Ruhe kamst du leise wandelnd hinab," "You called me to come up—in my repose down below / To my repose you came softly wandering down below." These are, of course, first attempts at the opening line. Incredible as it may sound, the following pages of the soliloquy are even more difficult to decipher, filled as they are with the most minute emendations.

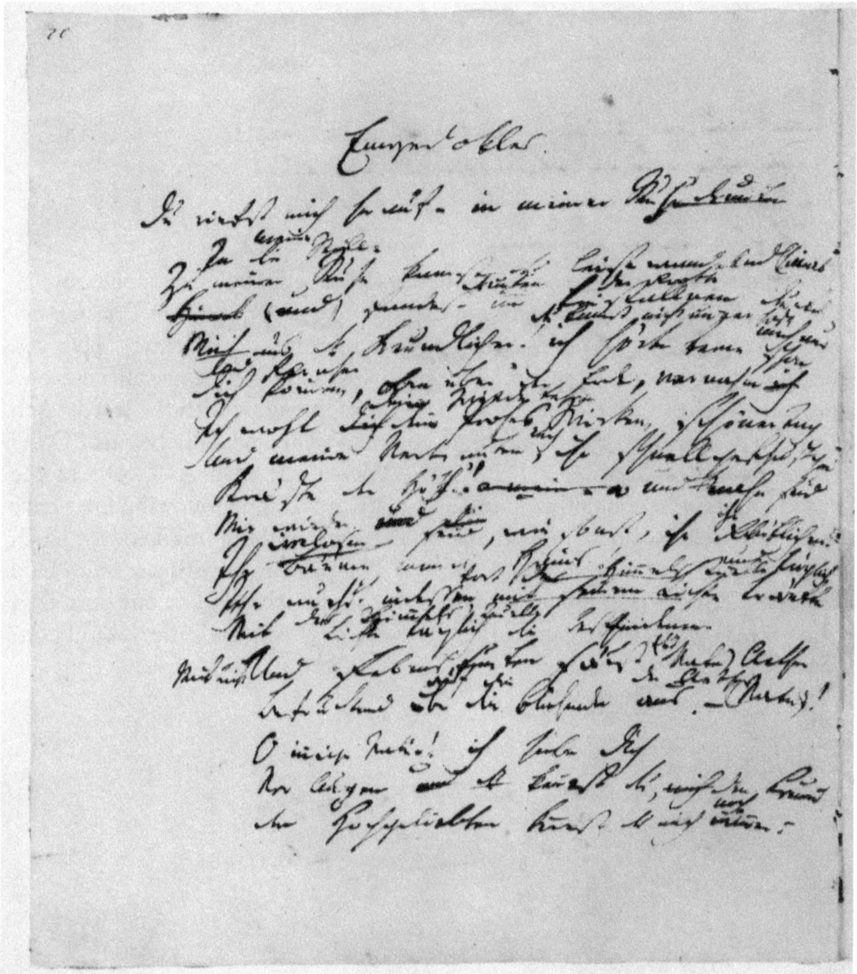
Empedokles.

Facsimile 4. This is the continuation of Empedocles' first soliloquy, ll. 295–313. The first two lines are not difficult to make out: "Den Priester, der lebendigen Gesang, / Wie frohvergossnes Opferblut, dir brachte?" "[Do you not know] The priest who brought you living song / Like sacrificial blood that's gladly shed?" The next line of the holograph begins with the words "Ach sonst!" but these are crossed through, so that the line actually begins, "O bei den heiligen Brunnen, wo sich still / Die Wasser sammeln . . . ," "Oh, by the sacred founts, where quietly / The waters gather. . . ." The following lines have been intensely reworked—perhaps they were initially marked for such reworking by the curlicue line to the left? The page ends with the line, "Und keines andern ist? {Ich dulde es nicht} dulden sollt' ichs," "[The one born free, who on his own is / His own] and no one else's? {I will not suffer} Am I condemned / To suffer this. . . ."

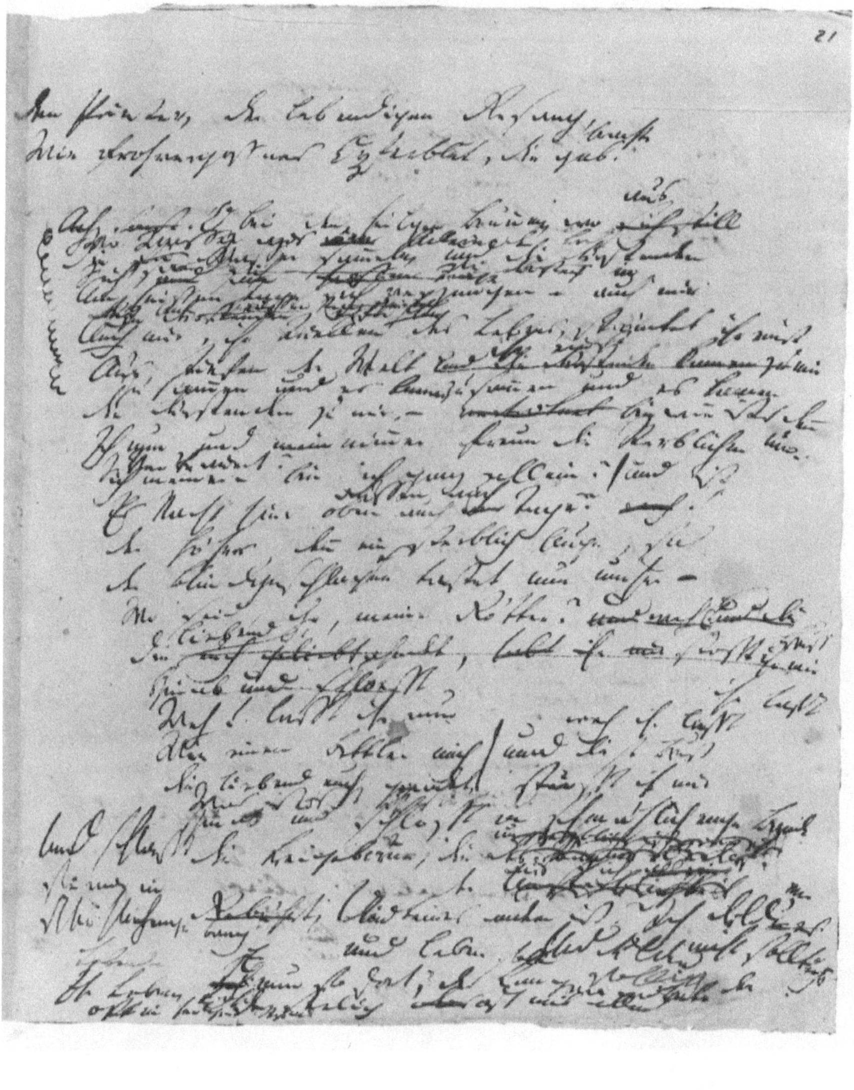

Facsimile 5. Empedocles' final soliloquy in version one begins "Ha! Jupiter Befreier!" "Ha! Jupiter Emancipator." Lines 1880–1902 appear on this page. The last two words are "Schauderndes Verlangen," "Shuddering exaction." The second word has been crossed out for reasons of meter; it reappears on the following page of the manuscript. The final nine lines of the page, beginning with "O darum," are relatively clear, and they are presented here so that readers may try to follow them: "O darum ward {ein wirksam Leben dir} das Leben dir so leicht. / {Versagt} Daß du {in Einer heilgen That} / Des Überwinders Freuden all{e} {fändest?} / In Einer vollen That am Ende fändest? / Ich komme. Sterben? nur {ein Schritt} ins Dunkel ists, / Ein Schritt, und sehen möchtst du doch, {getreues} mein Auge! / Du hast mir ausgedient, dienstfertiges! / Es muß die Nacht itzt eine Weile mir / Das Haupt umschatten. Aber freudig quillt / Aus muthger Brust die Flamme. Schauderndes / {Verlangen!}" "Is that why {an efficacious life was denied you} life was so carefree for you, so / That you {would find in one holy deed} would find the joys of overcoming all / In one full deed and at the end? / I'm coming. Dying? it's only {one step} into darkness, / One step; and still you'd love to see, O {faithful} eye of mine! / You've served your time with me, most serviceable eye! / And now must night awhile surround / My head in shadow. Yet joyous leap / The flames from an intrepid breast. Shuddering / {Exaction}!" The words that jut into the left margin four lines from the bottom are, "Ein Schritt," "One step," which the poet is moving to the next line for reasons of meter, or perhaps emphasis.

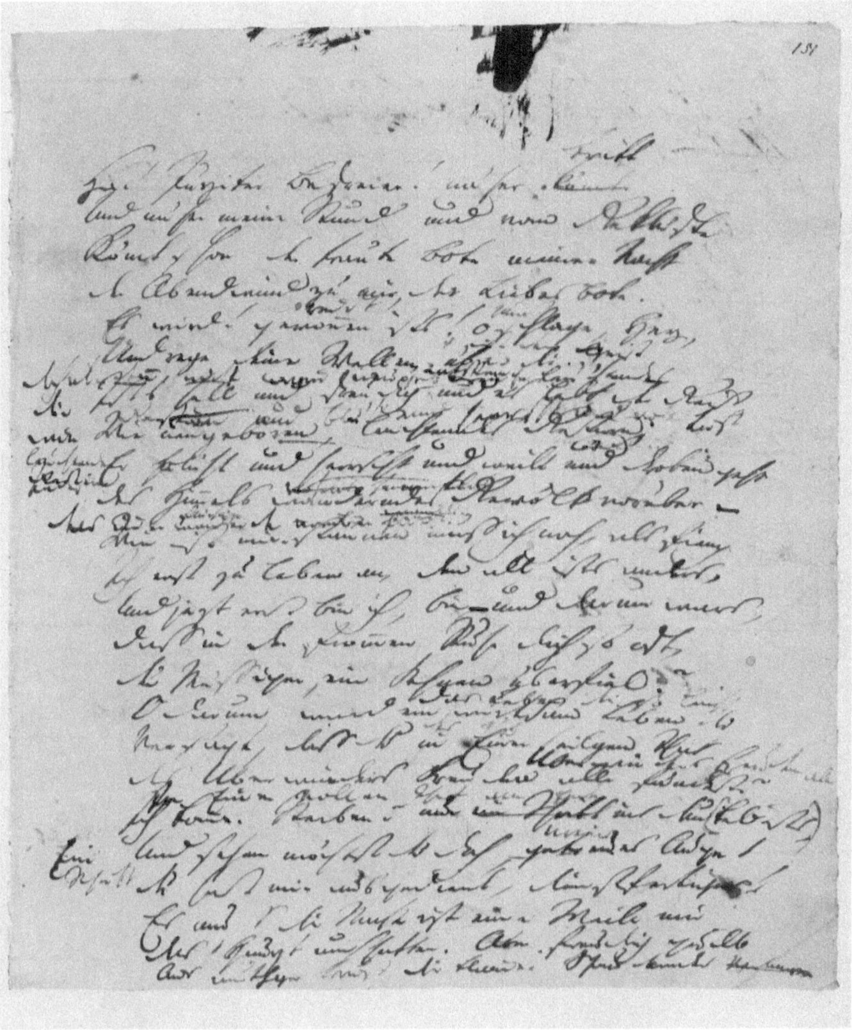

Facsimile 6. In the second version of the play, Empedocles' first soliloquy is much the same as in the first version, at least until the antistrophe begins. This facsimile shows lines 314–39. At midpage are seven lines that jut into the left margin. They emend the lines that follow the phrase, "Unduldbares duldend gleich den Schwächlichen, die," and they read, "Ans Tagewerk im scheuen Tartarus / Geschmiedet sind. Was daherab / Gekommen? um nichts?" In English, the preliminary phrase, "Accepting unacceptable conditions like / Those weaklings," continues in the margin, ". . . down in timid Tartarus / Fettered to their works and days. What has / Befallen me? for nothing?" The final two lines, separated by an empty line, are the final line of the penultimate strophe and the first line of the final one, "Und wieder einsam, weh! und wieder einsam? // Weh! einsam! einsam! einsam!" "[And once again you] / Are lonely, woe, and lonely once again? // Woe! lonely! lonely! lonely!"

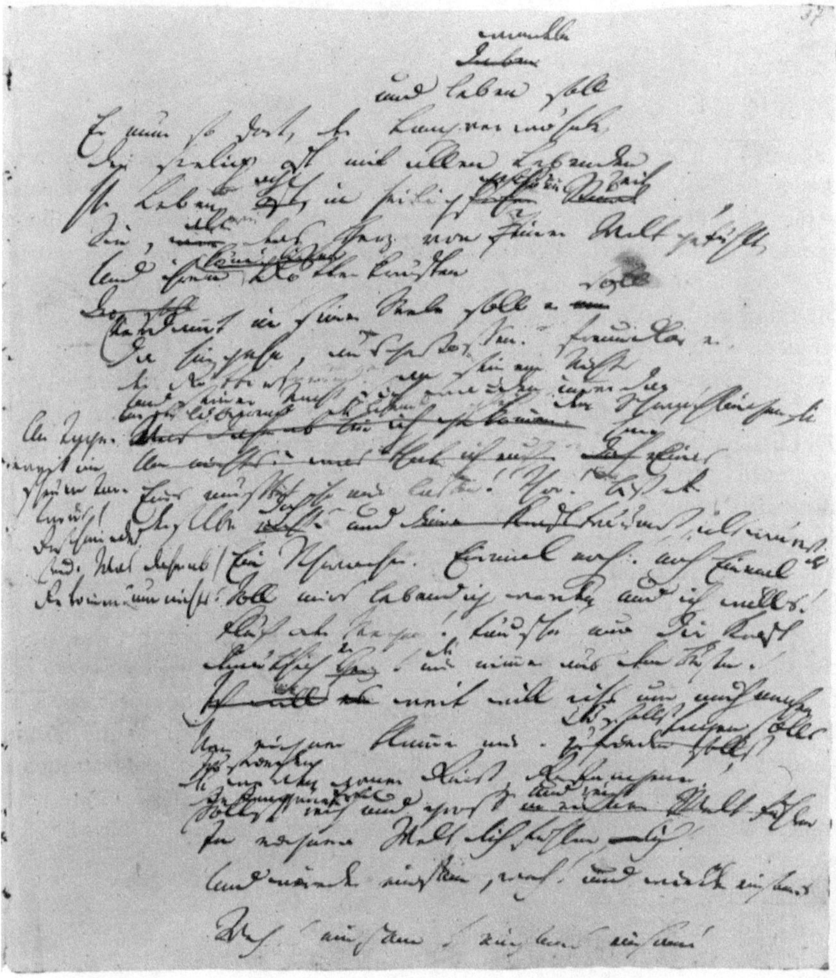

Facsimile 7. This facsimile shows the continuation and conclusion of Empedocles' first soliloquy in version two, lines 340–61. This relatively clear page begins, "Und nimmer find ich / Euch meine Götter." (Yes, what looks like a capital R in the final word of the second line is a capital G!) The text continues, "Und nimmer kehr ich / Zu deinem Leben, Natur! / Dein Geächteter!" Superimposed above the line is the word "weh!" The line continues: ". . . hab ich doch auch / Dein nicht geachtet, dein / Mich überhoben." From this point on, the crossed out words and the emendations proliferate. The English, so far, "And never will I find / You, my gods, / And never more will I return / To your life, nature! I am / The one you banished!—woe! since I / Did not respect you, raised / Myself above you. . . ." The first words to be crossed out are "der Bote dich," whereupon two words are left standing, "hast du," with the final crossed out words "nicht mich." The next line begins with "Umfangend, wie mit warmen Fittigen." In English, ". . . {your messenger above you} did you {not me} not / Embrace me once with your warm plumage."

The bulk of Hölderlin's holograph has to be deciphered this way, laboriously, phrase by phrase, in an effort to see where the excised passages are clearly replaced by other material, so that the sense of the lines is clear. The final three lines of Empedocles' soliloquy are relatively easy to glean: "Ist nirgend ein Rächer, und muß ich denn allein / Den Hohn und Fluch in meine Seele sagen? / Muß einsam seyn {?} auch so?" "Is there nowhere an avenger; must I alone / Pronounce contempt and curse upon my soul? / Am I to be alone {?} in this as well?"

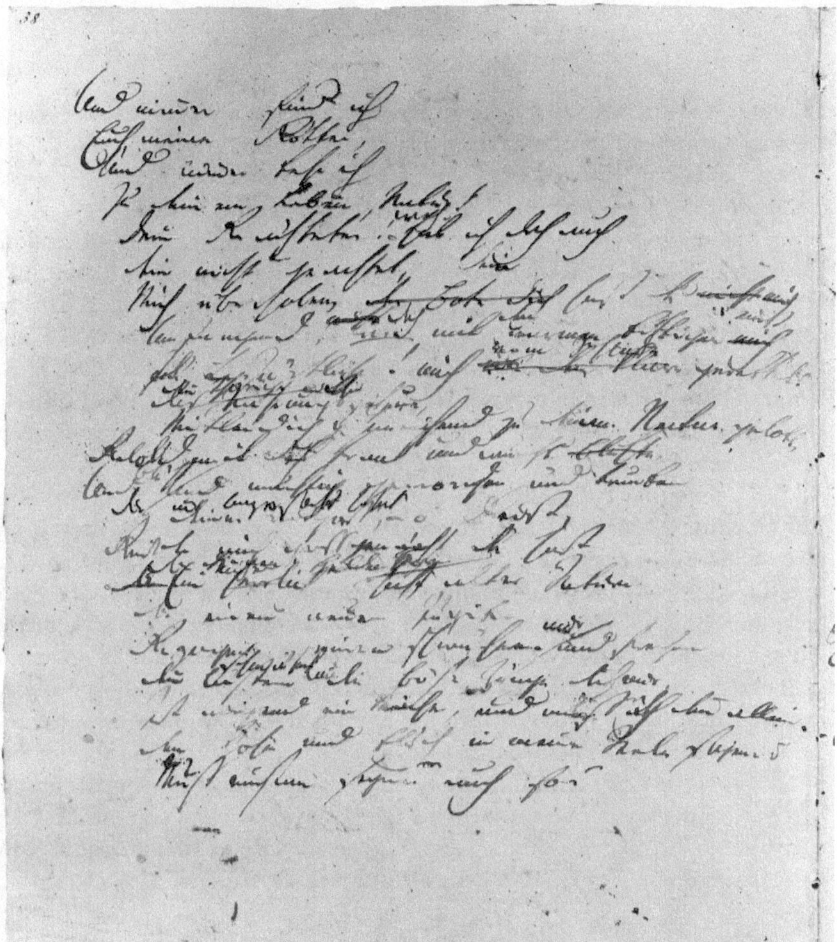

Facsimile 8. Here is the first soliloquy of Empedocles in version three—where the soliloquy opens the play as such. The first words, centered on the page, are a stage direction: "Empedokles / vom / Schlaf erwachend," literally, "Empedocles / from / sleep emerging." Note that the text of the *Stuttgarter Foliobuch,* which Hölderlin is using for the first time when composing his third version, although beginning well into the notebook, is far more cramped than it is in the other manuscripts. The handwriting is reduced in size by half. This of course makes deciphering the lines even more difficult than in the case of the first two versions. The soliloquy begins: "Euch {kenn'} ruf ich über das Gefild herein / {Aus schlafendem} Vom langsamen Gewölk{,} ihr heißen Stralen / Des Mittags. . . ." "{You I know} To you I call across the fields that you / May come {from slumbering} eluding sluggish clouds, you hot rays / Of midday. . . ." Note that Hölderlin does not find the next phrase of this third line, "ihr Gereiftesten, daß ich" "you ripest rays, that I," until he has written some seven additional lines of text. The darker ink shows that he has gone back to line three, only at that point finding "you ripest rays." In other words, these early lines of what may be called Hölderlin's "sovereign" style, the style of the late hymns, no matter how much the end-product seems to flow, do not come easily to the poet. The phrase "ihr Gereiftesten, daß ich" is finally completed by those first words scribbled into the right margin: "An euch den neuen / Lebenstag erkenne." The opening four lines now read, in translation, "To you I call across the fields that you / May come eluding sluggish clouds, you hot rays / Of midday, you ripest rays, that I may know / Through you this new day of my life." The final line on the page (l. 32) reads, "Beim Todtenrichter! wohl hab ichs verdient!" "O judges of the dead! I well deserved it!"

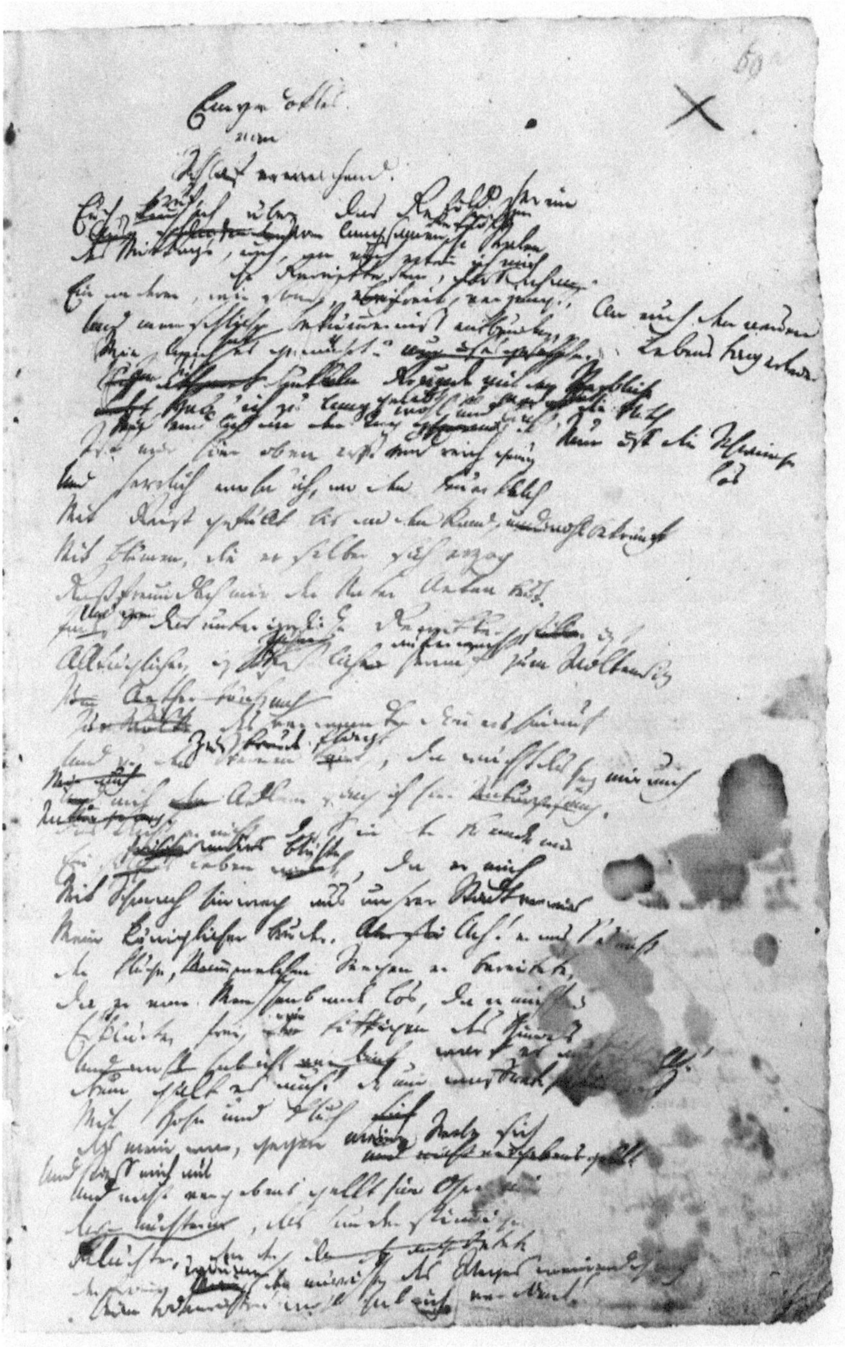

Facsimile 9. This facsimile presents some dialogue between Empedocles and Manes (in the holograph called simply *Greis,* "old man") and the beginning of Manes's long speech. Entire pages of preliminary efforts to compose the scene between "the old man" and Empedocles are not shown here, so that the "cleanliness" of this page is deceptive. The page opens with Empedocles' words, "Was mahnst du mich? Was rufst du mir noch einmal? / Mir gieng es wie es soll." "Oh, why remind me? Why dredge it up again? Things went / Precisely as they should have." Manes's long speech begins below midpage: "O scherze nicht! und ehre doch dein Fest, / Umkränze dir dein Haupt und schmük es aus, / Das Opferthier, das nicht vergebens fällt." "Speak not in jest, and honor this your festival, / Enwreathe your head and decorate / The sacrificial beast that does not fall in vain." At this point the crossed out words and emendations begin. "{Der Tod is jedem Unverständigen / Von Anbeginn ist ja der jähe, /} Der Tod, der jähe, ist ja von Anbeginn, / Das weist du wohl, den Unverständigen / Die deinesgleichen sind, zuvor{gesetzt}beschieden." "{Death is for everyone who does not understand / From the beginning, yes, is sudden, is there at the beginning.} For death, the sudden steep, looms from the beginning, / As you know well; and to the baffled ones, to those / Who are your kin, it has long since been {placed before them} allotted." The final three lines on the page read, "Ich hab ein Wort, und diß bedenke, Trunkner! / Nur Einem ist es Recht, in dieser Zeit{.} / Nur Einer adelt {sie, die} deine schwarze Sünde." "I have a word that you must ponder, my besotted friend! / For one alone in our time is it fitting{.}; one being / Alone ennobles {it, the} your black sin."

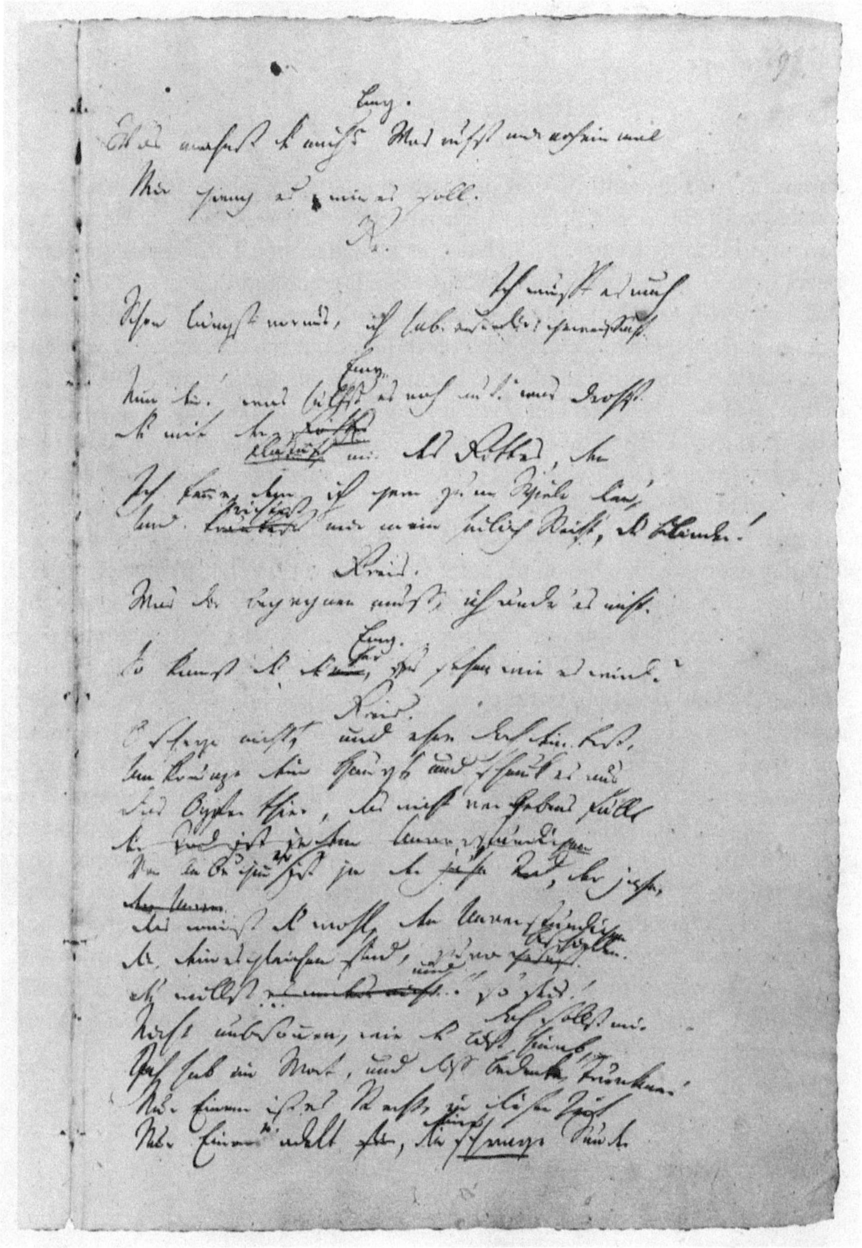

Facsimile 10. The continuation of Manes's long speech appears on this page, starting with the words, "Ein größrer ists, denn ich! denn wie die Rebe / Von Erd' und Himmel zeugt. . . ." "That one is greater than I am! for as the vine / Bears witness to the earth and sky. . . ." The large margin on the left suggests that Hölderlin was expecting to make many changes to the old man's speech. Yet the page is relatively clean. The tenth line from the top, repeating the first four words of line nine, marks the beginning of the most remarkable passage of the speech: "Der Herr der Zeit, um seine Herrschaft bang, / {Der Geist} Thront finster blikend über der Empörung. / Sein Tag erlischt, und seine Blize leuchten, / Doch was von oben flammt, entzündet nur / Und was von unten strebt, die wilde Zwietracht." "The lord of time, grown apprehensive of his rule, / {The spirit} Looms with glowering gaze above the consternation. / His day extinguished, lightning bolts still flash, yet / What flames on high is inflammation, nothing more; / What strives from down below is savage discord." The final two lines on the page, which carry over onto the next page (see facsimile 11), are, "Und nahe [added: wieder] leben, sie, wie vormals {wieder}. / Und daß {er}, wenn er erschienen ist, der Sohn. . . ." "And [added: again] they live in close proximity, as in former times {again.} / No sooner has {he} the son appeared. . . ." Note in the bottom margin some added lines. These are not from Manes's speech, but from Empedocles' response to it on the next page: Hölderlin ran out of room on that recto page and so completed the line in the margin of this, the previous verso page. Empedocles says: ". . . kennst du das Schweigen / Des Himmels, des schlummerlosen Gotts? erwart. . . ." Here the page is exhausted, and the line is concluded on the present facsimile page: ". . . ihn hier. Um Mitternacht wird ers vollenden." In English, "[Await] him here. At stroke of twelve he will accomplish it for us." (See FHA, *Supplement II: Stuttgarter Foliobuch*, 170–72. (My thanks to Marianne Schütz of the Hölderlin-Archiv for solving this puzzle.)

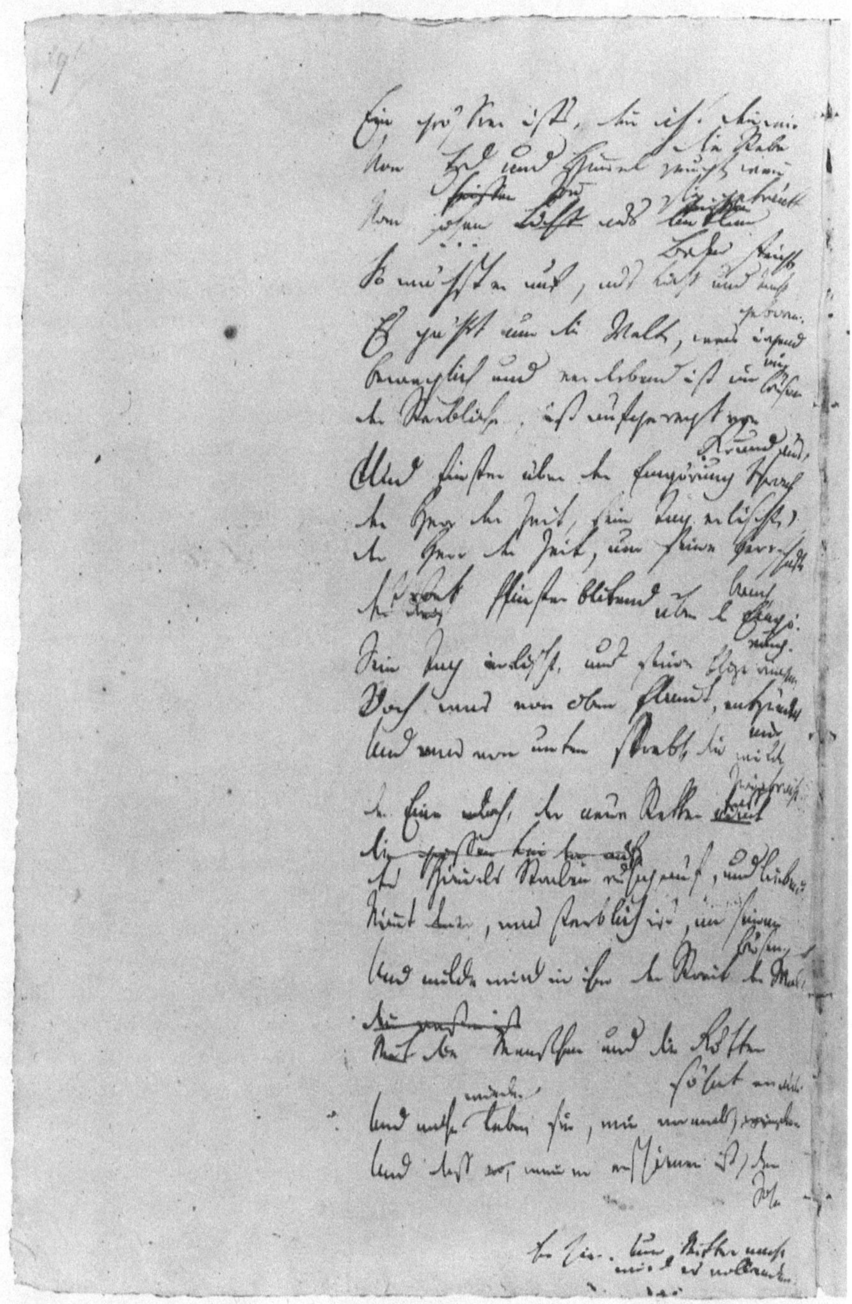

Facsimile 11. The final lines of Manes's speech appear here, along with some dialogue and the beginning of Empedocles' long reply to the "old man." (Note that here, on the lower half of the page, the margin has been richly used.) Manes continues, "Nicht größer, denn die Eltern sei, und nicht / Der heilge Lebensgeist gefesselt bleibe / Vergessen über ihn, dem Einzigen, / So lenkt er aus, der Abgott seiner Zeit, / Zerbricht, er selbst, damit durch reine Hand / dem Reinen das Nothwendige geschehe. . . ." ". . . that he may not / Surpass his parentage, and that the holy spirit / Of life may not remain in shameful fetters / On his account, forgotten up above, the unique one / Now turns aside, although he is the idol of his times, / Destroys himself, so that a pure hand executes / Whatever of necessity befalls the pure one. . . ." The final line of Manes's speech—almost a taunt—appears ten lines down the page: "Bist du der Mann? derselbe? bist du {der} diß?" "Are you that man? the very one? are you {he} this?" Immediately before Empedocles' long reply to Manes, we see a repetition of the taunt, with which the "old man" closes: "O sage, wer du bist! und wer bin ich?" "Oh, tell us who you are! and who am I?" Empedocles' final soliloquy begins: "Versuchst du noch immer mich und {lässest,} kömst, / Mein böser Geist, zu mir in {dieser} solcher Stunde{,}?" "Can it be so, that still, still you tempt me, {letting} coming as / My evil spirit, descending on me here at {this late} such an hour?" The final line on this page, stricken from the speech, is, "Eins will ich auch dir rathen, alter Mann!" "One thing too I'll counsel you, old man." In the right column appears what still today seems a sudden alteration in the tone and content of the speech: "Ein Jüngling war ich . . . ," "A boy I was back then. . . ." See ll. 397ff. These lines sketched into the right margin continue at the very bottom of the page: ". . . kennst du das Schweigen / Des Himmels, Des schlummerlosen Gotts? erwart. . . ." As noted above, this line is completed in the bottom margin of the *previous* page.

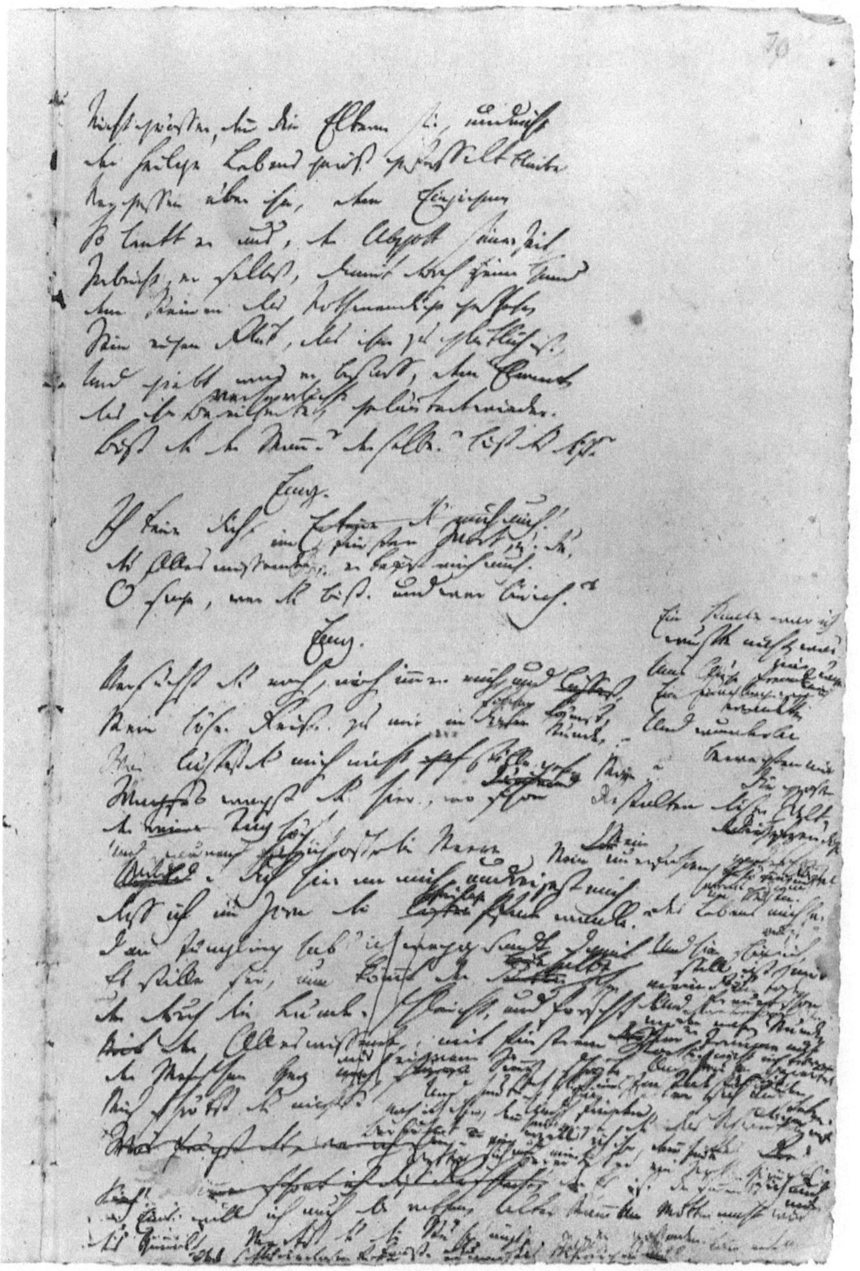

Facsimile 12. This sketch of the choral ode, "New world," not yet in metered verse, is fairly easy to decipher, in spite of the minuscule hand. The deleted words (in braces) may be translated as "golden," "fruits," "as," "with," and "But." The tear at the bottom left may have occurred during Hölderlin's lifetime, although this is uncertain. The page reads:

Neue Welt

u[nd] es hängt, ein ehern Gewölbe
der Himmel über uns, es lähmt Fluch
die Glieder den Menschen, und ihre {goldnen} stärkenden, die erfreuenden
Gaaben {Früchte} der Erde sind, wie Spreu, {als} es
spottet{e mit} unser, mit ihren Geschenken die Mutter.
u[nd] alles ist Schein—

{Ab} O wann, wann öffnet sie sich
die Fluth über die Dürre.

Aber wo ist er?

Daß er beschwöre den lebendigen Geist

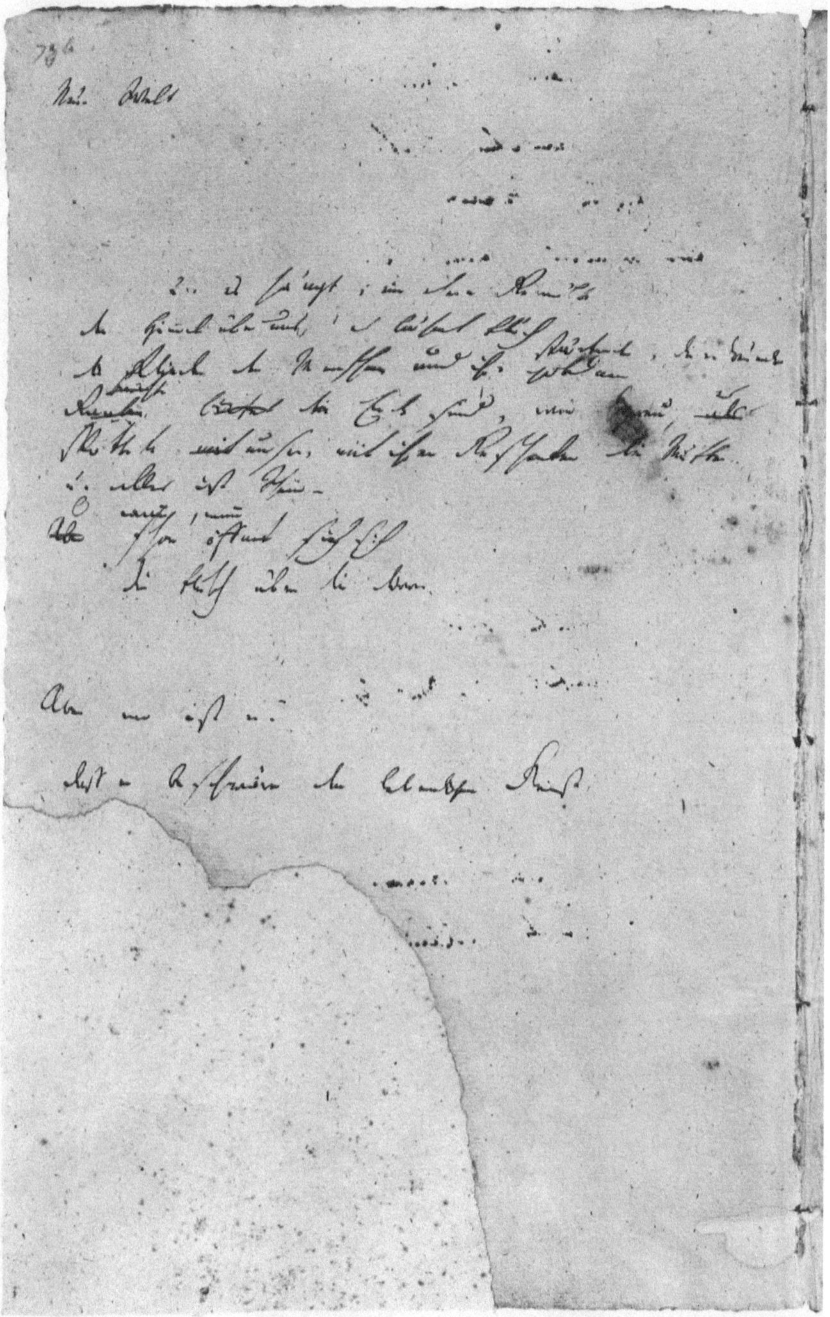

Notes

THE FOLLOWING NOTES on the three versions of the play, along with the plans, sketches, and essays surrounding them, are designated on the left side of the page by the number of the line of poetry or prose to which they refer. Many of the notes to the versions of the drama have to do with variants of the text as presented in the four principal German editions; only major discrepancies in the German text have been noted here, namely, those that alter the meaning in a significant way. I have also entered notes to identify various names, figures, and themes in Hölderlin's text that may be obscure to contemporary readers. For the key to works cited, see the Preface.

Notes to *The Death of Empedocles,* First Version

lines 1–73 Hölderlin begins to write this first version in prose form, only gradually finding his way to the iambic pentameter that will then dominate in it.

lines 4/5 Both Jochen Schmidt (DKV 2:279) and Michael Knaupp (CHV 1:769, 3:331) follow Friedrich Beissner by changing *Rhea* to *Delia* throughout act 1; I have followed Dietrich Sattler here (FHA 12:30, 179), altering the name *Rhea* only when Hölderlin himself does, namely, in the final (the ninth) scene of act 1. (Hölderlin's initial designation of Panthea and Rhea at the outset of the first version as "two priestesses of the Vesta" seems to have become almost immediately superfluous.) Schmidt's speculation that Hölderlin replaces the Titaness Rhea with a figure of Apollonian restraint—*Delia* being derived from the isle of Delos, the birthplace of Apollo—while at first convincing, becomes increasingly problematic as we hear and take to heart Rhea's (or Delia's) objections to Panthea and Pausanias. Rhea represents that fidelity to the earth and to the maternal side of Empedocles' inheritance that only a Titaness could embody. If *Delia* does refer to Apollonian restraint, perhaps it does so as a suspicion concerning Empedocles' eagerness to abandon the earth for the sky.

8–10 Diogenes Laertius notes that Empedocles' grandfather—of the same name—won the horse race competition at the Olympic games in 496 B.C.E. Hölderlin's conflation of the generations—as of horse and chariot racing—is the first of a series of deliberate anachronisms that characterize all three versions of the play.

16 FHA (though not CHV) inserts *drängten* before *strebten herauf,* "thrust[,] strove upward," breaking the line after *herauf.*

50–57 Diogenes Laertius, in his *Lives and Opinions of Eminent Philosophers* (DL 8:69), tells the story of Empedocles' having healed an Agrigentian woman named Pantheia, whom the doctors had given up for lost. Having identified a source of warmth in her belly, the physician preserved her life, even though she had been without pulse or breath for days. This account was also important for Friedrich Nietzsche's early attempts to compose a drama on Empedocles' life: see D. F. Krell, *Postponements,* 111 n. 11.

55 FHA and CHV cut the phrase "and scarcely did I need to draw a breath." See FHA 12:30 and CHV 1:770.

104 The name *Pausanias* is mentioned in Diogenes Laertius (DL 8:60ff.) and is the addressee of Empedocles' fragments "On Nature" (DK B1).

115 After the exclamation "Sophocles!" FHA and CHV cut to l. 119. See FHA 12:36 and CHV 1:772. Here as elsewhere I am sympathetic to Schmidt's and Beissner's reluctance to excise entire lines, even when Hölderlin appears to offer replacement material.

169 FHA 12:39 notes that Hölderlin is now searching for a trisyllabic name to replace *Rhea,* but again insists that the name *Delia* does not appear until scene 9 of act 1, at ll. 944–45.

172–73 FHA assigns the dialogue of Critias throughout scene 2 to the "Archon." This is significant because not only the name but also the characterization of the archon—Critias, Mecades, Strato—is in flux from each version of the play to the next. By the time we arrive at version three, the king-archon will be held to be a worthy opponent of Empedocles—indeed, his brother.

174 See the earlier note on Delia at l. 169.

189–90 DK B112, recorded by Diogenes Laertius (DL 8:62), contains the remarkable proclamation by Empedocles, "As for me, I walk among you as immortal god, no longer a mortal," ἐγὼ δ' ὑμῖν θεὸς ἄμβροτος, οὐκέτι θνητός πωλεῦμαι. This hubris is the subject of Hölderlin's marginal note. Schmidt (DKV 1:1143–44) observes that the modern concept of the "genius" in, for example, Kant and Goethe reawakens for modernity the Athenians' discomfiture in the face of every exceptionally gifted person—every Alcibiades, to cite but one name. Empedocles is doubtless such a man for the Agrigentians. The question of hubris—that is, of Empedocles' having uttered what is unspeakable, literally the *ne-fas,* the "Do not speak"—is one of the decisive questions raised by the mourning-play. As Panthea has already pointed out, however, what may be hubris for some is but a lovers' quarrel for others.

196 FHA and CHV excise this line.

212–15 "Yet he is not the first. . . ." The allusion is to Tantalus—and perhaps to every tragic hero and heroine thereafter, for example, those of the houses of Atreus and Labdacus, from Agamemnon, Orestes, and Electra to Laius, Oedipus, and Antigone. Tantalus, a wealthy Lydian king, the son of Zeus (and a Titaness) and the father of Pelops and Niobe, is one of Hölderlin's favorite mythic characters. A darling of the gods, invited to share their table and their secrets, Tantalus betrays the gods and suffers the consequences. He insults his father Zeus either by stealing ambrosia and nectar in order to share them with mortals—this account in Pindar (First Olympian Ode, 54ff.) makes Tantalus an avatar of Prometheus, the benefactor of humankind—or by betraying the secrets of the gods to mortals (once again a Promethean account, this one in Ovid's *Metamorphoses* 6:13 and in Seneca's *Thyestes,* l. 90), or finally by serving up to the gods a stew containing his own son Pelops. (Interestingly, this most horrific account of Tantalus's crime appears also in the First Olympic Ode of Pindar, indeed, immediately after a passage on Charis [see the note on ll. 1066–67, below] that Hölderlin copied into his manuscript of the first version of *The Death of Empedocles,* as though that passage were to serve as a motto for the work as a whole; Pindar's extended account of Tantalus's crime, in ll. 35–111, thus assumes even greater importance for Hölderlin's mourning-play than has been supposed.—But to return now to the myth.) Zeus kills his son Tantalus and condemns him to the underworld, where he is tormented (or "tantalized") by food and drink that are perpetually out of his reach. Hölderlin was long fascinated by this figure, who begins as a scion of the gods but then offends them and winds up being punished severely. As an erstwhile favorite of the gods, Tantalus seems indeed to tantalize them: for what otherwise have the gods to do with mortals? Why should the gods share their table, their table talk, and their secrets with this exceptional man—except because he is in fact a demigod? If Tantalus soon enough incurs their wrath, it is difficult to know whether the cards have been stacked against him from the outset. Plato mentions

Tantalus often in the dialogues as a fateful character, one whose reversal from wealth to squalor is reflected, as Socrates says in *Cratylus* (395d-e), "quite correctly and quite naturally" in his very name: in the underworld, Tantalus hangs suspended, ταλαντεία, from a fruit tree, and a gigantic stone is suspended over his head; he is of all mortals "the most wretched," ταλάντατος. When in chapter 110 of *Moby-Dick*, "Queequeg in His Coffin," Melville has Captain Ahab cry, "O devilish tantalization of the gods!" the reader is unsure about the little word *of.* Who is tantalizing whom? All the reader knows is that it is time to worry about Queequeg. Hölderlin mentions Tantalus several times: in *Hyperion* (I, 2, Letter 26, Hyperion to Bellarmin, CHV 1:667), he writes that "it is not easier to be the friend of a demigod than it is to sit like Tantalus at the table of the gods"; Empedocles himself, in the first version of Hölderlin's mourning-play, cries, ". . . you have / Yourself to blame, you wretched Tantalus / The sacred precincts you've besmirched, / With haughty pride revoked the covenant, / Pernicious one!" (DKV 2:291, ll. 329ff.); Sophocles' *Antigone,* at l. 854 of Hölderlin's 1803–04 translation, cites Tantalus as Niobe's father—Niobe herself being one of Antigone's most significant self-projections; finally, in the famous letter to Casimir Ulrich Böhlendorff of December 4, 1801, in which Hölderlin discusses the relation of native gifts to foreign inspiration, a relation that is central to his theory of tragedy, he writes, "Oh, friend! the world lies more brightly before me than it used to, and more earnestly. . . . Now I fear whether in the end things will go with me as they did with Tantalus of old, who became more of gods than he could digest" (CHV 2:914). Volumes could be written about the strange verb *ward* here, "became," where we expect the verb "ate," even though in the end it was the grieving Demeter who ate what Tantalus served up to the gods. Perhaps the most tantalizing aspect of the myth of Tantalus, however, is the fact that early on he tantalized the gods to the point where they invited him—the child of Zeus—to *become* one of them. Arguably, the theme of tantalization has to do with Hölderlin's own self-identification as a singer of divine songs and with his own doubts that he may be a "false priest"; see, for example, *Wie wenn am Feiertage,* "As on a Holiday," ll. 69–73: "I grew near, to gaze on the celestial ones; / They themselves cast me down among the living / The false priest, into the darkness, that I / Might sing a warning song to those who can learn." In every poet who wants to be Empedocles hover the shadows of both a Tantalus and a Hermocrates.

221 After *sorg' ich,* "I fear," FHA (although not CHV) inserts the line: *Noch Einmal geht empört er tödlicher hervor,* "Outraged once again, it [that is, the insult] will come to the fore, deadlier than ever." Hölderlin first writes *tödtend,* then *tödlicher.* Much later, in the "Notes" to his translations of Sophocles, Hölderlin will distinguish between *tödlichfaktisch* and *tödtendfaktisch.* In Greek tragedy the spoken word can be

"factically deadly," as when Oedipus insults Jocasta and she flees to their chamber and hangs herself. By contrast, in later ages the word wounds and festers over time, or *mortifies,* working as a slow poison, "factically deadening." Although anachronistic, or as a gift of sheer retrospection, it may be interesting to contemplate Empedocles' chagrin as somewhere between antiquity and modernity, precisely as Matthew Arnold and others have claimed: perhaps the problem of Empedocles is the "translation" of mortification back to a more deadly factical word—the word that would effect his "ideal deed and at the end," his suicide.

225–27 Precisely who those "enthusiasts" of old are who "wandered throughout Asia bearing reeds for staffs" is not easy to say. Jochen Schmidt cites Diogenes Laertius, who in the introduction to his *Lives and Opinions* (DL 1:7–9) writes of the ancient magi—more ancient than the Egyptians—who taught that even the gods themselves were creatures of becoming rather than of being. See DKV 1:1144. Michael Knaupp (CHV 3:345) is reluctant to identify these magi with the Bacchants of Dionysos, yet perhaps he is too cautious. Nietzsche will have good reason to identify Dionysos as the god of becoming rather than of being, the god of tragedy par excellence. Hölderlin's Hermocrates is here in his own cynical way digging at the roots of the mystery cults. Readers should refer to Hölderlin's hymns *Der Weingott* and to the two versions of *Brot und Wein,* from the years 1800 to 1802. When in the seventh stanza of "The Wine God" and "Bread and Wine" (first version) the lines appear, "But they are, you say, like the wine god's holy priests, / Who roved from country to country in holy night," not thinking back to the "enthusiasts" of Hermocrates' speech is difficult. At all events, the contrast between the ancient enthusiasts of becoming and the Agrigentian priest is stark. Max Kommerell (MK 333) writes that Hermocrates is "the enemy of becoming, which he condemns to paralysis." Kommerell continues, "He terrifies all the courage that wishes to submit all that subsists to becoming once again, terrifies it back into the bondage that the priest forces onto all human beings in the face of the gods. For him, religion is anxiety, not a voluntary relation; he murderously uproots all the new beginnings that would have received Empedocles' blessing" (ibid.). Finally, in the most general terms, "A priest is one who establishes the boundaries between god and humanity as absolute, transposing all human feelings into fear, imprisoning human intimacy with the gods in scriptures that are set in stone; instead of genuine *mythos,* which is itself mobile and which moves community life to the point of profound agitation, the priest chooses the false security of sacerdotal regimentation" (MK 344).

236 After the phrase *den Lebenden,* "the things that live," FHA and CHV insert three lines:

Wie alles sich verlor so nimmt
Er Alles wieder, und den Wilden hält
Kein Sterblicher in seinem Toben auf.

When all is lost he takes
It all back again, and this wild man
No mortal can restrain in his wild ravings.

StA inserts these lines after l. 237, at the end of Hermocrates' speech. See Schmidt's commentary at DKV 2:1119.

279–325 When Hölderlin's Empedocles invokes nature he refers to the four elements—earth, air, fire (or ether), and water—that are attributed to the teachings of Empedocles of Acragas. See Aristotle, *Met.* A 3, 984a; see also DK B6, B21, and B38 on the four "roots." When Hölderlin's Empedocles speaks of the alternating *love* and *enmity* of the gods toward him, he seems to be alluding to the forces of love and strife, φιλία καὶ νεῖκος, within the sphere. See DK B17, B26, and B35. Very similar fragments were known to Hölderlin through Stephanus (see 21).

292 "O intimate nature!" The word *innig* is most often translated here as "intense," yet it also carries the meaning of intimacy. The word has often been translated, especially in the philosophical literature, as "interior," in the sense of the interior life of subjectivity. This is in my view quite misleading. Rather, *Innigkeit* suggests the intensity of ecstasy, of standing outside oneself. The confusion may arise from the association of *Innigkeit* with intellectual intuition. Here Max Kommerell's analysis is helpful:

> Tragedy in Hölderlin's sense is the genre that uncovers [*die enthüllende Gattung*]. For according to its very definition it contains an intellectual intuition, i.e., something that cannot be achieved by a concept, something that within poetic forms pertains to the mythic state of life—namely, the perception of the individual within the whole, as of the whole in the individual. Here we also have Hölderlin's concept of *Innigkeit,* which means an amicable dwelling-with-one-another of opposites. (MK 331)

Amicable and intimate, yes—but also intense to the point of ecstasy.

307 "Now struck blind." Compare Hölderlin's ode from 1800, *Der blinde Sänger,* "The Blind Singer," which begins:

Where are you, you aspect of my youth, which always
    Woke me at the morning hour, where are you, light?
        My heart is roused, yet spellbound I am still held
            In the holy magic of night.

The ode ends with the following paradox:

> Oh, take from me, so that I may bear it,
> The life, divinity, from my heart."

The blind singer is of course Homer, who depicts the gods and heroes of a nation and an entire age. Yet he is also Tiresias, the "balding seer," who sees the future only after he is blinded by a goddess—and why? for having been forgetful of the difference, one might say.

313–15 "Am I condemned / To suffer this; is my anemic soul in timid Tartarus / In thrall to ancient works and ancient days?" Tartarus, like Orkus, is a designation of the underworld. The reference to works and days reminds us of Hesiod's great poem; the bloodless souls remind us of Odysseus's famous descent into the world of the shades in Book XI of *The Odyssey*, or Aeneas's descent into "darkest Dis" in Book VI of *The Aeneid.* Hölderlin is doubtless transposing the bloodless, bootless hovering of shades in the underworld into a figure for the hustle and bustle of modernity. Toward the end "The Archipelago" of 1800–1801 (ll. 241–46), he writes of our race, tribe, or generation (*unser Geschlecht*):

> But woe! wandering in the night, as though dwelling in Orkus,
> Our tribe is without divinity. Each is fettered to his own
> Devices all alone, and in the clamor of the shop
> Each hears his own toiling away; like wild men,
> Arms raised in violence, ever hectic, yet forever
> Bootless, like Furies, remain the labors of the wretched.

316–17 FHA and CHV excise these two lines.

322–25 FHA, CHV, and StA cut these four lines.

326 Sattler's reconstructed text, followed also by CHV, eliminates the spaces before and after the phrase *O Schattenbild!* and proceeds immediately to the words *verbirg dirs nicht,* "conceal it not!" Schmidt also deviates significantly from Beissner's StA text here. The implication is that Hölderlin's holograph is particularly difficult to decipher at this juncture. Sattler's variorum text confirms this: see FHA 12:49–51, along with Schmidt's commentary at DKV 2:1119.

329 "You wretched Tantalus." See the previous commentary on ll. 212–15.

336 "That these celestial ones would serve you slavishly!" Hölderlin expresses his opposition to manipulative, calculative religiosity in many places. Jochen Schmidt cites "As on a Holiday" and the following lines from *Dichterberuf,* "The Poet's Calling":

For too long a time everything divine is serviceable
And all the powers of heaven are squandered, used up
The beneficent ones are at our pleasure, and we, thankless,
A sly race that thinks it knows what it is doing when
It is the sublime ones that cultivate the field, bestow
The daylight and the thunderer. . . .

Hölderlin's sense of *proper* religiosity derives from his "more intense study of the Greeks" (CHV 2:850–51). Greek poetry, he says, is not about entertainment but is devoted to "a sacred skill," *eine heilige Schicklichkeit*. Whether the Greeks are caught up in "enthusiasm" or are subdued by "sobriety," Greek poetry—and especially tragic dramatic poetry—produces "a jubilant liturgy [*ein heiterer Gottesdienst*]" (ibid.).

389 FHA and CHV excise this line.

393 FHA and CHV read:

Und feurigmild im Blumenothem weckte
Der stille Geist der Göttlichen mir zu.

And in flowers with their fiery mild waftings
The silent spirit of divinities awoke in me.

DKV also departs from StA in its reading of this line.

401 FHA and CHV delete this line.

406 FHA and CHV cut the phrase "I was!"

408 "Your splendid tutelary forces." *Geniuskräfte* are powers of genius, but it is the genius of nature to which Hölderlin here is referring. "Genius" throughout the play indicates the daimonic forces of nature; because the δαίμων is a tutelary spirit, I have translated *Genius* most often as "tutelary." In the essays composed between versions two and three, Hölderlin will call these *Geniuskräfte* or daimonic energies the *more aorgic* forces of nature.

418 "O father ether!" The fiery light of the brilliant sky, αἴθηρ, is for almost all the early Greek thinkers—Empedocles among them—an exceptional element, sometimes identified with the sun itself. Later in antiquity, Lucretius invokes "the ethereal sun" (*On the Nature of Things*, 5:281, *aetherius sol* [cf. 5:458–59, *aether / ignifer*]). Empedocles' fragment B38 refers to "the Titan Ether" who embraces in his grasp earth, sea, air, and everything else, περὶ κύκλον ἅπαντα. Certainly by the

time of the Stoics the ether is held to have a close relation to the rarefied breath-soul, πνεῦμα, and is thus taken to be the exceptional micro-macrocosmic element. Even in antiquity ether was addressed as father, *pater aether.* Line 65 of "Bread and Wine" repeats the apostrophe "O father ether!" as does a poem that is contemporaneous with *The Death of Empedocles,* "To the Ether."

420 FHA strikes this bracketed line. StA and CHV retain it—and without brackets. Whether or not Hölderlin marked it for excision is therefore uncertain.

445–48 FHA (although not CHV) excises the extended metaphor of the "caged deer," cutting the line after the phrase "for the boy," moving directly to the words "Did you not limn the lines, etc."

466 This is the line to which Beissner (see Reclam, 174) appends the marginal note on "original sin." Sattler and Knaupp attach that note to Empedocles' entire response to Pausanias. See FHA 12:60, 192, and CHV 1:783. Schmidt's DKV reproduces the note only in the commentary (DKV 1:1147), arguing that it pertains to lines that Hölderlin had himself marked for excision, namely:

> Ich sollt es nicht aussprechen, heilge Natur!
> Die du den Reinen gegenwärtig bist,
> Und unbekannt den Übermütigen.
>
> I should not utter it aloud, holy nature!
> You who are present to the pure,
> And unknown to the arrogant.

Hölderlin is struggling to portray Empedocles' crime, or *nefas,* throughout this first version of the play in a "genetically vital" way. The first words of the excised lines, however, were originally *Ich kann nicht,* "I cannot"; Hölderlin then changed them to *Ich sollt nicht,* "I should not." Empedocles thus shifts from the theme of his current incommunicable suffering to the past event of his unspeakable crime, his "original sin." Yet precisely as Empedocles cannot express his pain to Pausanias, a pain that derives from his unspeakable sin, so Hölderlin cannot formulate the crime, cannot *write* it out, cannot *stage* it, as it were.

467–70 FHA and CHV strike these four lines.

473–77 FHA and CHV excise these five lines.

523–25 FHA and CHV cut these three lines.

530–31 These two lines, along with the blank space between ll. 529–30, are excised by FHA. See FHA 12:64–65, 195. CHV deletes l. 529 but retains ll. 530–31.

570–71 Compare the renderings in FHA 12:196, ll. 539–41, and CHV 1:787, ll. 540–41.

615–16 FHA and CHV excise these two lines.

625–50 As Jochen Schmidt indicates, Hermocrates' banishment of Empedocles (which begins at l. 592) appeals to certain classic formulae: to banish is equivalent to *aqua et igni interdicere alicui,* "to forbid someone water and fire." Hölderlin expands the formula to include the elements of earth and air as well. It is therefore as though Hermocrates' curse turns Empedocles' conception of the four elements or "roots" against the philosopher in a cruelly ironic way.

659–60 FHA (although not CHV) reads:

> Im Griechenlande drüben, an den Ufern
> Italias, da grünen Hügel auch, etc.
>
> In Greece, across the sea, on the shores of
> Italia, hills grow green, etc.

710 One of the rare typographical errors in DKV: read *mit dir,* "with you."

746–57 FHA and CHV cut all but the final three words of these twelve lines. DKV itself brackets some of them, indicating that at some point Hölderlin intended to drop them. The marginal note "No curse!" testifies to his dissatisfaction with the lines. The problem of Empedocles' negativity and the task of an affirmative, ideal deed, even if that deed should be suicide, lie at the very heart of the drama. See Schmidt's commentary at DKV 2:1120.

763–64 "On the path / To Syracuse." Mount Etna lies some eighty kilometers northeast of Agrigent (as the crow flies), and Syracuse some ninety kilometers to the southeast. Empedocles' route to the volcano—in Hölderlin's surmise—is therefore quite indirect, first to the eastern coast of Sicily, then north, through Catania, to Etna—some 140 kilometers.

803 "This tender earnest daughter of the gods," *Die zärtlichernste Göttertochter.* Compare l. 24, above, in which the words *zärtlichernste Heroide,* spoken by Rhea (Delia), refer to Sophocles' Antigone. Panthea and Antigone alike are characterized by this strange and beautiful neologism—the elision of seriousness and tenderness.

808 Delos is the birthplace of Apollo, famous, like Olympia, for its Panhellenic games; this Cycladic island is, one may say, up to the present day still sacred to Apollo. Elis is that part of the Peloponnesus where Olympia is located—famous for its temples of Zeus and Hera, as well as for its games. For Hölderlin such games and the concurrent festivals were the very essence of religiosity and the foundation of sociopolitical harmony. In his *Gesang des Deutschen* he laments, "Where is your Delos, where your Olympia, / That we all might find ourselves gathered at the supreme festival?" In "The Wine God," as in "Bread and Wine," he expands his lament to include the ancient theaters and temples: "Delphi sleeps and where is there a sound of great destiny?" "Why do they too keep silent, the ancient holy theaters?" And, finally, bringing the lament home, the desperate cry, ". . . and what are poets for in destitute times"?

818 FHA and CHV cut this line.

854–55 All other editions delete these two lines.

859–67 FHA and CHV cut these nine lines, moving down to the phrase *selbst / Die Hütte, die mich hegte,* "not even my fair cottage."

873–74 FHA (although not CHV) deletes the words *es ist / Dein letzter Dienst!* ". . . for this will be / Your final act of servitude."

888–89 FHA (although not CHV) cuts this dialogue of the second slave.

919 Prior to this line, FHA and CHV expand the stage direction with these words: . . . *und gehet zögernd auf und nieder,* ". . . and pacing back and forth in hesitation."

940–44 FHA and CHV delete these five lines.

948a-b All other editions add these two lines:

> Nur bleibe still indessen—kann ich wohl
> Hinein?

See Schmidt's comments at DKV 2:1121–22.

955–57 FHA and CHV end l. 955 with the phrase *ich fass es nicht,* "I cannot grasp it," and cut ll. 956–57.

985–87 Panthea's speech here is obviously difficult to reconstruct: the editions vary here widely. StA has:

. . . An ihm sich auf. Ich lebte gern mit ihm
In meinem Sinn, und wusste seine Stunden.
Vertraulicher gesellte da zu ihm
Sich mein Gedank, und teilte mit dem Lieben
Das kindliche Geschäft—ach! grausam haben sie's
Zerschlagen, auf die Strasse mirs geworfen
Mein Heldenbild, ich hätte es nie gedacht.
Ach! hundertjährigen Frühling wünscht ich oft
Ich Törige für ihn und seine Gärten.

With thoughts of him. I lived so happily with him
Within my mind, and I knew all his hours.
For ever more familiarly did my thoughts
Flock to him, and lovingly we shared
Our childlike games—alas! how cruelly they've
Destroyed it, tossed it in the street, the icon of
My hero; I never would have thought it possible.
Alas! a century of springtime I often wished,
I was so foolish! for him and for his gardens!

After the phrase "I never would have thought it possible," FHA and CHV insert these lines:

So schmählich! o verblühet nur ihr Blumen
Des Himmels schöne Sterne, denn freudig glänzt'
Auch er—es muss hinab, was sterblich ist.

So shameful! oh, wither away now all you flowers
You shining stars of heaven, for he too once
Was glistening—all that's mortal must go down.

Finally, all other editions have these two lines as Delia's reply to Panthea:

O konntet ihr die zarte Freude nicht
Ihr lassen, gute Götter!

Oh, could you not allow her then to keep
This tender joy, you good gods?

For all this, see FHA 12:98–100, where the complexity of Hölderlin's emendations becomes clear.

1000–1 All other editions read: *Das Gift im Busen, das sie mitgegeben? / Das habt ihr ihm getan! o lasst mich nicht, etc.* I have altered the text of DKV to read accordingly; yet see Schmidt's objections at DKV 2:1124.

1024 "The shade that is my brother." In the *third* version of the play, Hölderlin will redefine the relationships between Empedocles, Panthea, and the archon: Empedocles will be called the brother of both; Panthea will no longer be the daughter who struggles against her father, but a sister who tries to reconcile her two brothers.

1066/1067 Into the interstices between acts one and two Hölderlin copied verses 31–34 of Pindar's First Olympian Ode, leaving it untranslated. The context of Pindar's lines is this: the singer has admitted that when human language glitters like water or gold, that is, when it reflects the light of the sun most dazzlingly, it can lead mortals astray. Deception lies not only in darkness but also in excessive light. Yet, having warned us of this, the poet now enters a demur ("But") and adduces a word in favor of Charis—dazzling beauty, radiance, grace, charm, and whatever else incites love:

Χάρις, ἅπερ ἅπαντα τεύ-
Χει τὰ μειλίχα θνατοῖς,
'Επιφέροισα τιμὰν,
Καὶ ἄπιστο ἐμήσατο πιστὸν
"Εμμεναι τὸ πολλάκις.
'Αμέραι δ' ἐπίλοιποι
Μάρτυρες σοφώτατοι.

Charis, who brings all
That's mild to mortals,
Also brings honor,
And makes us believe the unbelievable,
Which often does come to the fore.
Yet the days that are still to come
Are wisest witnesses.

1072–76 FHA (although not CHV) excises these five lines.

1080–81 FHA (although not CHV) drops these two lines after the phrase *In dieser Hütte,* "This cottage."

1082 FHA (although not CHV) deletes the phrase *Versuch es nur!* "Do try!"

1134 FHA (although not CHV) replaces the name Empedocles with *o Vater! Vater!*

1144–59 These lines are very important for the play, as Hölderlin's marginal note soon tells us. Here Empedocles is to be transfigured into a wholly affirmative character; all bitterness, all rancor, will now be overcome. The symbols of the stream's water and, a few lines later, the bunch of grapes, are significant. When Empedocles raises the gourd in praise of his gods, he is celebrating his departure from the world of artifice and his reunification with the gods of nature. Max Kommerell writes:

> It is a celebration of parting: once again the fruits of the meadow and the juice of the grape are tasted—Christ-like, albeit in thankfulness to the earth. What the earth *is* reveals itself here: ancient by destiny, mother of the gods and the theater for their games, but also a compassionate friend of the human soul. The earth means that the human being is the suffering of a god and that infinite being itself traces its orbit through the souls of humans, that the earth is the green hills of youth and the chasm of Etna, which receives all and is the goal of jubilant return. The stars and the ether are not on their own; they are the playmates of earth. (MK 343)

1167a-e All other editions continue without interruption:

> Und musstest du bis hier mich hergeleiten
> Dass unsrer Feierstunden keine sich,
> Auch diese nicht, uns ungeteilt verlöre,
> Wohl kauftest du um schwere Mühe sie,
> Doch geben mirs auch nicht umsonst die Götter.

See, however, Schmidt's commentary at DKV 2:1125–26, which attaches the marginal note *(weitere Ausführung der Freude, die ihm sein unglücklicher Entschluss gibt)* to a portion of Empedocles' speech that Schmidt regards as having been superseded. I have appended this note to the end of Empedocles' speech. Here once again the central conflict of the mourning-play is adumbrated: Empedocles must find joy in his "unhappy resolve."

1197–1201 FHA and CHV delete these five lines.

1231 FHA and CHV strike the words *und seine Götter*, "all our spirits' gods."

1252–63 FHA and CHV excise these dozen lines.

1270a All other editions begin with this line: *Ihr Unverschämten! anders wisst ihr nicht?* Yet Schmidt (see DKV 2:1226–27) may well be right to excise this line, which he says belongs to an earlier sketch of Empedocles' speech, in which the hero gives free rein to his anger and contumely. By contrast, the emendation that Schmidt accepts as replacing the earlier sketch is controlled and even aloof in tone. Here is the earlier, angrier text, following l. 1276:

O thut die Augen auf, und seht, wie klein
Ihr seid, dass euch das Weh die närrische
Verruchte Zunge lähme; könnt ihr nicht
Erröthen? o ihr Armen! schaamlos lässt
Den schlechten Mann mitleidig die Natur,
Dass ihn der Grössre nicht zu Tode schröke.
Wie könnt er sonst vor Grösserem bestehn?

Oh, open wide your eyes and see how small
You are, so that the pain may cripple
Your foolish, wicked tongues; are you unable
To blush? oh, you wretched ones! nature
Takes pity on the villain, letting him be shameless,
So that what's greater does not frighten him to death.
How else could he withstand the greater man?

1281–89 FHA and CHV strike these nine lines.

1298 All other editions delete this line, eliding ll. 1297 and 1299. Here I follow DKV.

1314 FHA and CHV relocate this line, placing it after l. 1318.

1345–52 "When a nation is to die / The Furies send one man alone who through / Deception lures the vital human beings to / Commit the evil deed he has devised, etc." These lines of Pausanias's are remarkable, inasmuch as they foreshadow the words of Manes in version three of the play. For Manes will assert that Empedocles himself is an imposter and deceiver—a mirage—insofar as he claims to be that "one man alone" who is called. See l. 323 of version three, along with the note on it. See also the use of the word *mirage* in the essay, "The Basis of Empedocles," and the note on that word.

1355 FHA and CHV strike this line and the final word of the preceding line, *sengt,* "scorches."

1358–60 FHA and CHV structure these three lines differently, condensing them to two.

1373 "Saturn's age." Cronos, the Roman Saturn, is associated with the Golden Age, a time when human needs were met by the great Titan and when human society was marked by peace and plenitude. Hölderlin's friend Schelling wrote about this period both early and late in his career, especially in his never published *Ages of the World* (1811–1815). Hölderlin felt himself drawn to the myth of the Golden Age throughout his work, especially in his novel *Hyperion* (for example, in the seventh letter of I, 1; CHV 1:633), but also in the poem "Nature and Art, or Saturn and Jupiter," where Saturn is particularly identified with nature, life, and time. One of the most important sources for both Schelling and Hölderlin was Plato's remarkable adaptation of the myth of the Golden Age in *Statesman*, 268c-274e. See also the note to ll. 1602–3, below.

1375–78 FHA and CHV delete these four lines, yet they are significant because of the confusion of curses here. Whereas earlier Hermocrates cursed and banished Empedocles, here the third citizen is accusing Hermocrates of having brought down Empedocles' curse on them all: "Why did you call upon our heads his / Inexorable curse, the curse he's laid on us, / Alas! he had to do it." FHA and CHV are here perhaps trying to remain true to Hölderlin's marginal note, "No curse!" Yet it seems best to retain the ambiguity and ambivalence of (Hölderlin's) Empedocles' relation to his fellow Agrigentians and to his own resolve.

1413, 1415 "Numa." Legend has it that Numa Pompilius was the second king of ancient Rome, ca. 715–672 B.C.E. According to ancient sources such as Livy and Plutarch, Numa ruled justly and wisely over the Romans, overcoming civil strife—precisely what the citizens of Agrigent are begging Empedocles to do.

1418 "The time of kings has passed forever." Empedocles' reply testifies to Hölderlin's firm republicanism. Max Kommerell (MK 345) notes the impression that this statement made on the young Nietzsche, who read Hölderlin's play while still in secondary school: in *Thus Spoke Zarathustra* ("On Old and New Tablets," no. 21), Nietzsche has Zarathustra speak these exact words.

1443 The citizens promise Empedocles "statues," and indeed the Frankfurt Plan speaks of a statue of Empedocles that is erected by the Agrigentians but then toppled when he falls out of favor. See also the allusion to statues in l. 1528, below.

1486–1587 This long speech by Empedocles, fragmentary in its second half (after Pausanias's exclamation, "O father!") but continuous during its first half, is essentially about rejuvenation, *Verjüngung*, or palingenesis. Several fragments of the ancient Empedocles speak to it: DK B125 says what we will hear Manes say in the plan to version three of the play, namely, that Empedocles "exchanges the figures," making the living die and the dead live; DK B126 refers to a female daimon (presumably Persephone, but perhaps Moira, or perhaps Aphrodite herself) who "cloaks" the souls of the dead in "unaccustomed flesh." Michael Knaupp and Jochen Schmidt devote long commentaries to the notion of palingenesis (CHV 3:86, DKV 2:1152–56), which we may summarize here. As with so many essential ideas of the Romantics, Johann Gottfried Herder is the principal source. A passage from Herder's treatise *Tithon und Aurora,* familiar to Hölderlin at least since the summer of 1794, reads: "The dotard in us is to die in order that a new youthfulness may sprout. 'But how is that to happen? Can a human being return to its mother's womb and be born again?' To this doubt expressed by old Nicodemus no other answer is possible than 'palingenesis!' Not revolution but a fortunate *evolution of the forces that are slumbering in us, the forces that rejuvenate us.*" (Herder, *Werke,* ed. Suphan, 16:122.) Such rejuvenation applies to both individuals and institutions. Further, in 1796 Herder had published in Schiller's journal *Horen* an essay with the title "Iduna, or the Apple of Rejuvenation"; *Iduna* was to have been the title of the journal Hölderlin was planning to edit during the time when both the second volume of *Hyperion* and *The Death of Empedocles* were being composed. (*Verjüngung,* rejuvenation, is also an important motif in *Hyperion.*) Palingenesis, literally, "becoming again," is a Stoic thought related to the notion of ἐκπύρωσις, the consumption of the old world order by fire. Out of the ashes of the old order, phoenixlike, emerges the new. (This idea dominates Hölderlin's essay "The Fatherland in Decline.") A delicate question from antiquity through modernity is whether the "new" is in any significant sense different from what has been, or whether periodicity and recurrence of the same characterize rebirth. All three drafts of Hölderlin's mourning-play touch on this delicate question. In Hölderlin's sketch "Palingenesis," written perhaps late in 1796, the idea of rejuvenation moves in two directions at once: forward with the advancing sun toward the accomplishment of the day, but also, altering the metaphor, tracing the stream back to its source in the distant ranges of the past (CHV 1:166–67). In sociopolitical terms, the French Revolution is of course the promise of rejuvenation through the elimination of the *ancien régime.* As in the case of the Revolution, however, *nature* plays a vital role in the desired rejuvenation of institutions. Indeed, the Revolution legitimates itself in a cult of *reason,* but a reason that is itself rejuvenated by *nature.* Liberty, equality, and fraternity are experienced in the harmony *of* and *with* a nature that has itself been emancipated. The Jacobins do not hesitate to support the construction of a *temple de la terre.* (Schmidt cites a work of art history by Hans-Christian and Elke Harten, the title and subtitle of which tell the story—*Reconciliation with Nature: Gardens, Liberty Trees, Republican Forests, Holy Mountains, and Virtue Parks in the French Revolution,* Rowohlt Verlag, 1989.) For Hölderlin, and for Hölderlin's Empedocles, the key word for nature, however, is "life," *das Leben.* And the key hope for life? Rejuvenation.

1489–90 FHA and CHV excise these two lines.

1501 "Achilles from the Styx." Achilles' mother Thetis dipped her son into the deadly Styx—holding him by his heel—to harden him against vulnerability and mortality.

1527 "Like faithful Dioscuri." According to Homer's *Odyssey* (Book XI, ll. 298–304) and other ancient sources, the Dioscuri, Castor and Polydeuces (or Pollux), reflected the essence of brotherhood. Castor had a mortal for a father, Polydeuces had Zeus, so that when they were killed in battle, Castor's soul had to pass to the underworld, while Polydeuces rose to Olympus. Zeus acceded to their plea, however, allowing them to spend one day on Olympus, the next in Hades, but always together—like a constellation in the night sky. For Hölderlin these warrior brothers express the idea of Revolutionary *fraternité:* see the poem "To Eduard" and the later incomplete rewriting of this poem dedicated to his Jacobin friend Sinclair, "The Dioscuri."

1528 See the note to l. 1443 on "statues." Recall too that in Empedocles' request to Critias that he take his daughter to Delos or to Elis, the statues among the laurels of Olympia are to comfort her. See ll. 810–16, above.

1530 "Letting law tie confederate bonds." Hölderlin's word *Bund* translates the French *confédération*—July 14 is the *fête de la confédération,* which Hölderlin in a letter to his brother (July 1793) translates as *Bundesfest.* (On July 14, 1792, Hölderlin and his friends, among them Hegel and Schelling, had celebrated a *Bundesfest* around a "freedom tree" on a meadow near Tübingen; they sang the *Marseillaise,* which Schelling had translated into German.) In the following lines of the play, Empedocles encourages the Agrigentians to celebrate the θεοξένια, the festival of the Dioscuri (at Delphi it would have been a feast in honor of Apollo), at which gods and mortals, countrymen and foreigners, sit down at the same table. Hölderlin's great poem *Friedensfeier,* "Celebration of Peace," is dedicated to the idea of such a festival. In our time, Roberto Calasso, in *The Marriage of Cadmus and Harmony,* writes of such festivals with passion and insight.

1545–46 FHA (although not CHV) deletes the *Und* and closes up the space.

1561 FHA (although not CHV) interpolates the words *die Schlafenden,* so that ll. 1559–62 read as follows:

> . . . The breath of ether there
> Surrounds all-lovingly
> The sleepers; soaring with the eagles
> Their eye imbibes the morning light, etc.

1567–69 FHA (although not CHV) strikes these three lines. "Niobe fettered to her mountain." Niobe, the daughter of Tantalus, insults Leto, the mother of Apollo and Artemis, who in turn slaughter all her children. Niobe herself returns to her homeland, Lydia, where she mourns until she turns into stone. Sophocles' *Antigone* interprets her tears as the snowmelt of the mountain she has become. (In Hölderlin's translation of *Antigone,* see ll. 856–58 and the corresponding "Notes.") For a detailed discussion of Niobe, an important figure for Hölderlin, see the eighteen references listed in the index to TA, but especially the discussion at 349–51.

1561–87 FHA (although, again, not CHV) drops most of these lines and restructures Empedocles' monologue so that it speaks unequivocally of downgoing: instead of a "new day" one is left with "a falling star" and "farewell." In other words, whereas the other editions preserve the ambiguity of Empedocles' ideal deed by including all of Hölderlin's attempts here, Sattler sees Hölderlin working steadily toward the banishment of all illusion. As Sattler edits it, Empedocles' monologue concludes as follows:

> . . . and soaring with the eagles
> Their eye imbibes the morning light; yet there are
> No blessings for the dreamers, precious little of
> The nectar that the gods of nature offer every day
> Will go to nurture creatures caught in slumber,
> Until they tire of toil in coiling bonds,
> And life, remembering its origins,
> Seeks living beauty and happily
> Unfolds upon the presence of the pure,
> And then, with me, life's star is extinguished!
> Farewell! It was a mortal's word,
> And they tell true who never will recur.

See FHA 12:141–42 for the various drafts of Empedocles' peroration and 12:228 for Sattler's reconstituted—and drastically reduced—text. Finally, with regard to l. 1587, "And they tell true who never will recur," note the contradiction with the earlier proclamation of recurrence, which insists also on "my" recurrence. By now it seems to be clear to Empedocles, as it will be clear millennia later to Nietzsche and to Gabriel García Márquez, that no lineage is granted a second chance on the earth and that each human being has at his or her disposal no more than one hundred years of solitude.

1602–3 "And when the glorious days of Saturn come, / The new, more manly days." On Saturn and the Golden Age, see the earlier note to l. 1373. That Hölderlin calls these days "more manly" is strange. He may be thinking, as Schmidt avers (DKV 2:1161), of a Golden Age reflected now at a stage of higher consciousness, something that Schiller had written about in his treatise *On Naive and Sentimental Poetry.* Such enhanced consciousness would be reflected in the fact that whereas

Empedocles earlier on encouraged the citizens boldly to forget their ancient laws and customs, to deny the voices of their fathers, he here encourages them to embrace these things once again. Yet more than consciousness is involved. As Schmidt himself admits, such a rejuvenated Golden Age itself depends on a nearness to the earth and to nature, thus referring at least as much to the feminine and the maternal as to the paternal or "manly" sky god. In the end, the reference to "manly" speaks to the struggle between those two lines of inheritance in Empedocles, to wit, the fire of heaven and the magma of earth. That Etna can be (and *is*) apostrophized as both father and mother is both strange and revelatory. As for the new, "more manly" days to come, one should perhaps recall the trial of Leopold Bloom in Nighttown—Bloom, the new womanly man, woman's woe with wonder pondering. If Hölderlin is the poet of *Zärtlichkeit,* or tenderness, he may be closer to the new Bloomusalem than one might have supposed. During the time he was working on *The Death of Empedocles* Hölderlin expressed the view that in all the higher forms of Greek poetry—and this certainly includes tragedy—nothing other than "a certain tenderness," *Zartheit,* rescues poetry from generalities and abstractions (CHV 2:851). And if all this seems too blooming fanciful, one ought to recall that fragment of the ancient Empedocles (transmitted by Porphyry and contained in Stephanus) that explicitly states who ruled in the Golden Age: neither Cronos nor Zeus nor Ares nor Poseidon nor any other king held sway, ἀλλὰ Κύπρις βασίλεια, that is to say, "queenship was Aphrodite's" (DK B128; Stephanus 29). No blood of sacrificed bulls besmirched her altars during that age, Empedocles adds, but these were the times when paintings of animals, costly unguents, frankincense and myrrh, and red-golden honey were the sole acceptable offerings.

1612, 1614 FHA and CHV delete these two lines.

1633 "I've lived." Schmidt refers us to Horace, *Carmina* III, 29:41–43, as well as to Hölderlin's ode *Rousseau.* In the twenty-fifth line of the latter we find the exclamation *Du hast gelebt!* (Rousseau, one might say, is a modern incarnation of Empedocles—as Hölderlin understands them both.) In a letter to Neuffer, dated November 8, 1790, Hölderlin writes: "In the evening you may pronounce a brave 'vixi' [I have lived]." To his sister, in the autumn of 1800: ". . . then I shall go wherever I must, and surely in the end I will say: I have lived!"

1638–40 FHA and CHV excise these three lines.

1697 "Egypt." The Oriental becomes increasingly important as the three versions proceed. See the discussion of Manes in the following notes to version three.

1716–17 FHA and CHV delete the sentence, . . . *Es muss / Bei Zeiten weg, durch den der Geist geredet,* ". . . The one / Through whom the spirit speaks must part betimes."

1719–20 FHA and CHV strike the clause *so erkennt / Das vielversuchende Geschlecht sie wieder,* "and only thus does / Our ever-probing race come to know of her again." The marginal note that DKV and StA attach to this line, *stärker! stolzer! letzter höchster Aufflug,* "stronger! prouder! his last supreme flight," FHA and CHV attribute to Empedocles' entire speech.

1728 FHA and CHV strike the words *bei guter Zeit,* "upon / The fitting hour," and restructure the following lines.

1734–35 ". . . He was not to wane / By ticking off the days." On the theme of counting off the days of mortality, recall the important passage from *Hyperion* cited in the General Introduction (on p. 9, above), "And now tell me, is there any refuge left?" Recall also the Frankfurt Plan and Empedocles' discomfiture with the time of succession. In the ode, "The Blind Singer," we find these lines: "Now I sit silent and alone, from one / Hour to another. . . ." Hölderlin's poem "To the Germans" tells us that we "see and count off the number of our years." The poem "Elegy" invokes the "all-too-sober kingdom" of the dead, where the defunct count off the hours in a frozen, desiccated wilderness. Perhaps the most telling ticking-off of the hours and days is that which Danaë recounts to Zeus. In the fifth choral ode of *Antigone* we hear, in Hölderlin's translation (or deliberate mistranslation) of Sophocles: "She counted off for the father of time / The strokes of the hours, the golden." See the extended discussion in chapters 9–11 of TA.

1742 To this line FHA and CHV attach a marginal note that DKV and StA omit: *(Hauptstelle),* "(Principal passage)." "Divinity dropped the veil" is presumably that principal passage, expressing Hölderlin's hope that Empedocles' ideal deed, his voluntary death, will be a revelation.

1743–45 FHA and CHV condense these three lines to two, reading the text as follows:

> . . . für ihn . . .
> Den Licht und Erde liebten, und der Geist
> In dem sie sind, zu dem ich sterbend kehre.

> . . . for the man . . .
> Whom light and earth did love, and the spirit
> In which they reside, to which I in dying return.

1751 "Accompany your friend until the evening." Schmidt points out the many parallels between Empedocles' conversation with Pausanias and John's account of Jesus' departure from his disciples, emphasizing the importance of joy rather than mourning. Yet the spirit that dominates Empedocles' departure is a *world* spirit, and a spirit of *nature* (DKV 2:1163). Elsewhere (DKV 2:1167–68) Schmidt refers to the Stoic conception of a good death, which is one in which joy outweighs grief. This is not joy in the overcoming of death ("O death, where is thy sting?"), but a cheerful willingness to return to the whole of nature, to which one feels intrinsically and intimately related. Schmidt rightly cites *Dichtermut,* "A Poet's Courage," as exemplary of this attitude. Its second draft concludes with the following stanza:

> So then, pass away, when one day it is time
> And spirit nowhere relinquishes its rights,
> So let one day within the earnest sway of life
> Our joy die, but let it be a lovely death!

If one may look to the future, we can juxtapose to the spirit of Hölderlin's text that of Nietzsche's *Thus Spoke Zarathustra,* in which Zarathustra the godless insists that death be met with joy and celebrated as a festival. Fidelity to the earth demands nothing less of the overman. See the notes to ll. 1144–59, above, and 1859 and 1891–97, below.

1760 FHA and CHV delete this line.

1764 FHA and CHV excise this line, substituting these words: *Das Auge zu befrein vom Tagewerk,* "In order to liberate the eye from its daily chores." If one retains ll. 1764–65 in DKV, as I have done, reading "Go out into the sacred grove to bring / A feast to all the gods of nature," one is reminded once again of the theme of *theoxenia,* the hospitality mortals and immortals share—both in antiquity and in modernity. Schmidt cites M.-L. Biver, *Fêtes révolutionnaires à Paris* (Paris, 1979), which expounds on the Jacobin enthusiasm for new feasts and festivals, an enthusiasm that endured in the period of the Directorate, contemporaneous with the composition of Hölderlin's mourning-play. The very first of the *décades,* that is, the celebrations of every tenth day in the calendar, designed by Jacques-Louis David and celebrated in June 1794 by Robespierre himself, was the festival "of the Supreme Being and Nature." To celebrate divinity was to celebrate nature, since, to repeat, divinity is legitimated in nature—not the other way around. Harmony in and with nature is the fundamental aim of the Revolutionary festivals.

1768 FHA and CHV fill the blank space with the words *Wie Harfenlaut,* "Like the sound of harps."

1776–77 FHA and CHV delete these two lines.

1787–88 FHA and CHV delete these two lines.

1800 FHA and CHV transpose this line to the very end of Empedocles' speech.

1802 FHA and CHV read, *Den Fliehenden bei seiner treuen Rechte,* "The one who flees by his faithful right hand."

1816 "O son of Urania!" Compare version three, l. 317. The muse of astronomy, Urania is one of the most important symbols of cosmic harmony. Named after the sky, οὐρανός, she is literally "the heavenly one," Οὐρανία. In his *Gesang des Deutschen,* the poet exclaims, "You last and first of all the / Muses, Urania, receive my greetings!" Schelling's *Philosophy of Mythology* takes Urania to be the very first name for the later figures, Kybele and Demeter; she is that feminine principle which alone enables divinity to develop in the direction of love. Yet like Demeter, or Deo, Urania is also a figure of divine suffering, sorrow, and mourning, both because she seeks her daughter Persephone in vain and because she conceals Dionysos, who is the god to come, within herself. (For further discussion of Schelling's account of Urania, see TA 397–401.) Urania is also an important figure in *Hyperion,* for example, in Letter 21 of I, 2 (CHV 1:663): ". . . and in the midst of sobbing Chaos Urania appeared to me." In his early "Hymn to the Goddess of Harmony," Hölderlin cites Wilhelm Heinse's *Ardinghello,* which equates Urania with Artemis, Pallas Athena, and Aphrodite: "Urania, the radiant virgin, holds the universe together in ecstatic rapture by means of her girdle of enchantment." In short, in Hölderlin's view, Urania is much more than a muse; she is doubtless as august as Ouranos himself, and probably more so. She is the very Φιλία of Empedocles' teachings, the amity that holds the sphere in equilibrium—if anything can.

1817 FHA (although not CHV) strikes the word *Nein!* See FHA 12:159.

1824–26 FHA (although not CHV) condenses these three lines.

1848 FHA and CHV excise this line and close up the space.

1853–55 FHA (although not CHV) condenses these three lines.

1859 "More joyously than all the radiant joys of humankind." To add a final word to the earlier discussion of joy (see the note on l. 1751), Schmidt cites the famous late hymn, "Patmos," as follows: *Und es sahn ihn, wie er siegend blickte / Den* Freudigsten *die Freunde noch zuletzt.* "And it happened that at the very end the friends saw him, / Saw the way he gazed victorious, saw the *most joyous one.*"

1862–63 "But it's enduring, like the stream the frost / Has fettered." Compare Hölderlin's ode from 1800, *Der gefesselte Strom,* "The Fettered Stream." There the metaphor carries quite a different sense, however, one that would support Pausanias—not Empedocles—in the present context. Perhaps Empedocles' words to Pausanias here are but a sophism of love.

1869–70 FHA and CHV drop these two lines.

1871 After the apostrophe, *O Jupiter Befreier!* both StA and CHV, although neither DKV nor FHA, add a marginal note to the text: *stärkerer Ausruf!* "stronger exclamation!" However, Sattler's variorum text does include this note (FHA 12:163), and Schmidt's DKV too cites it, albeit only in his extensive notes (DKV 2:1166). Hölderlin repeats the apostrophe at l. 1880. The epithet ἐλευθήριος, "liberator," "emancipator," traditionally belongs to Zeus. Schmidt cites Pindar's Olympic Odes, 12:1; Hölderlin employs the epithet once again in "The Blind Singer."

1879 FHA (although not CHV) adds these lines to the reconstituted text of Pausanias's speech:

> Wie anders ists! zu wachen wähnt' ich,
> Zu leben sonst, und Schlummer war es nur.
> Und gross an Kraft und Freude wähnte sich
> Der Knab'. Fahr wohl! du Spiel! Hab' ich gelebt?
>
> How different now it is! I thought I was awake,
> And otherwise alive, but it was only slumber.
> And great in force and joy he thought he was,
> The boy. *Bon voyage!* mere whimsy! Have I lived?

1891–97 These seven lines are heavily emended and expanded in FHA and CHV, which read them as follows:

> Und jetzt erst bin ich—o das wars, das wars
> Dass mitten in der Wonne dich so oft,
> Du Müssiger! ein Sehnen überfiel—
> Reichst du doch nie stückweise deine Freuden
> Den Lieblingen, Natur! oft fehlte mirs,
> Nun find ich in der Einen Tat, der heilgen
> Euch Siegeswonnen all, wonach mein Herz
> Gedürstet. Sterben? nur ins Dunkel ists
> Ein Schritt, etc.
>
> And only now am I—oh, that was it, that was it
> That in the midst of your delight so often,
> You ineffectual man! a languor overcame you—

> You never do extend your joys piecemeal
> To those you love, O nature! Often I was lacking,
> Now I find in but one deed, the holy deed,
> All you delights of victory for which my heart
> Was thirsting. Dying? it's only into darkness,
> One step; etc.

"That you would find the joys of overcoming all / In one full deed and at the end?" reads ll. 1895–96 in DKV. Likewise here in the FHA and CHV texts, the joys or "delights of victory" that are extended by nature are said to be not offered piecemeal but in one holy deed—taking that step into the dark. The essay, "The Basis of Empedocles," discusses this "one full deed" in the following terms: ". . . the times demanded a *sacrifice* in which the whole human being becomes actual and visible, a sacrifice in which the destiny of his times appears to dissolve and the extremes appear to unite actually and visibly in one, although precisely on that account are united too intensely, and in which therefore the individual goes down in an idealized deed and has to do so. . . ." Yet the necessity must be a joyous one, so that once again comparing Empedocles' call for joy in the face of death to both the Gospel of John and Nietzsche's consistent message concerning death and dying is compelling. Zarathustra says, "That your dying be no blasphemy against human beings and the earth, my friends—that is my request to the honey of your souls" ("On Free Death," KSA 4:95). Max Kommerell comments, "Instead of the sense of penitence, another sense of death opens up, one that excludes penitence: that of a festival. Death is not penance, it is reconciliation, and something more—reunification of those that have been separated. In penitence one walks hunched over; to a festival one paces upright; death is a privilege, and so it cannot be a penance . . ." (MK 340). See once again Kommerell's remarks on *the earth* in the note to ll. 1144–59, above.

1902–3 "Shuddering / Exaction!" In the ode "Empedocles," cited in the General Introduction, Hölderlin uses this same expression, *Und du in schauderndem Verlangen / Wirfst dich hinab, in des Ätna Flammen.*

1905 "The terrifying chalice." *Der Schreckensbecher,* or "beaker of terror," refers to the *crater* of Mount Etna. The Greek κρατήρ is a wide, shallow chalice in which water and wine are mixed.

1910 "O Iris." Iris, a messenger of the gods, embodies the very *rainbow* by means of which she descends to earth. Empedocles mentions her in fragment B50. Plato's *Cratylus,* at 408b, derives her name from εἴρειν, to speak, which is what messengers do, and *Theaetetus,* at 155d, calls her the daughter of Thaumas—she is thus related to the θαυμάζειν, or wonder, that is the source of all philosophy.

1912/1913 Friedrich Beissner's StA alone of the four editions opens scene 7 with a speech by Delia. The textual basis for this speech, according to Sattler's variorum edition, lies on the final page of Hölderlin's first version: see FHA 12:177–78. Sattler tells us that after a gap of more than a page a final speech by Delia indeed appears in the holograph; yet Hölderlin gives no indication as to where it belongs. See Schmidt's note, which is critical of Beissner's solution, at DKV 2:1130–31, along with my note to ll. 2009a-g, below.

1913–18 FHA and CHV excise these six lines. The variorum basis for them appears at FHA 12:171–72.

1921 "More transitory are the ones you love." In his first fragment "On Achilles," Hölderlin calls Achilles "my favorite among the heroes, so strong and tender, the most successful and the most transitory blossom in the world of heroes—according to Homer, he was *born for such a brief time. . . .*"

1928–31 FHA and CHV restructure this dialogue and omit Hölderlin's marginal note to Delia's observation concerning the world's beauty: *Zu hart entgegengesetzt,* "too stark an opposition."

1941–44 FHA and CHV excise these four lines.

1953 FHA (although not CHV) deletes this line.

1977–81 FHA (although not CHV) drops these five lines.

1983 "Proudly self-sufficient." The Greek virtue of autarchy (αὐτάρκεια) was highly prized among the ancients. Plato's *Timaeus* describes the spherical universe as "an autarchic and altogether perfect god" (68e 3). In *Hyperion,* the hero-narrator describes Diotima in precisely these terms.

1997–98 "What / Remains of all this, tell me, what here still has life?" Delia is repeating with greater insistence the earlier question of Pausanias himself at l. 1861, "And all of this should pass away?" To Empedocles' reply that everything endures like the frozen stream, Delia poses the question of *life.* For the stream that appeals to the poet Hölderlin is the one that, at first fettered by winter's frost, breaks free in the thaw.

1998–2000 FHA and CHV restructure these lines as follows:

. . . Was soll
Es mirs gedenken, hat der Sterbliche
Der Welt sich aufgetan, der kindlichfremde, etc.

> . . . What am I
> To think, once the mortal has opened
> Himself to the world, so strange to the child, etc.

2000–5 All the editions vary in their reconstruction of these lines.

2009a-g These are the lines discussed briefly in the earlier note to ll. 1912/1913. Sattler locates Delia's speech at the very end of the final scene, making that speech the termination of the play. Both Schmidt (DKV) and Knaupp (CHV) drop Delia's speech altogether—although see Knaupp's commentary at CHV 3:344 and Schmidt's at DKV 2:1130–31. Because the speech is important for the central conflict of the play—that is, the conflict between the affirmative and negative motives behind Empedocles' "one full deed and at the end"—I am reluctant to drop it, but I am also reluctant to have the first version end with these words. I have therefore made my own conjecture, adding these lines to the end of Delia's final speech in DKV, ll. 1996–2009. In this way, both her words and Hölderlin's marginal note concerning them are preserved. Hölderlin's note originally read as follows: *(weil Empedokles es so leicht nimmt),* "(because Empedocles takes it so lightly)." Hölderlin then clarified the "it" by writing *weil Empedokles das Menschenleben so gering achtet,* "Because Empedocles has such low esteem for human life." Finally, he altered *Menschenleben* to *Zeitlichkeit,* "temporality": *(weil Empedokles die Zeitlichkeit so gering achtet),* "(because Empedocles has such low esteem for temporality)." The marginal note thus builds a bridge back to one of the earliest formulations (in the Frankfurt Plan) concerning Empedocles' contempt for, or restiveness while in the grip of, "the time of succession." The German text of Delia's speech as recorded by Beissner (Reclam, 74), Sattler (FHA 12:178, 240), and Knaupp (CHV 3:344), and placed by me at 2009a-g reads:

> Sie sagten mir: es denken anders Götter
> Denn Sterbliche. Was Ernst den Einen dünk',
> Es dünke Scherz den andern. Götterernst
> Sei Geist und Tugend, aber Spiel vor ihnen sei
> Die lange Zeit der vielgeschäftgen Menschen.
> Ach! mehr wie Götter, denn wie Sterbliche,
> Scheint euer Freund zu denken.

Notes to *The Death of Empedocles,* Second Version

1–145 In the rough draft of the second version, Hölderlin begins by writing the names "Panthea, Delia" at the top of the page, proceeding then to compose the *second* scene, involving the priest Hermocrates and the archon Mecades (formerly Critias), with a crowd of Agrigentians in the distance. Hölderlin apparently intended to preserve the first scene much as it was in the first version—although this is only a supposition. At all events, he dropped all references to the Panthea-Delia scene when preparing the neat copy of the second version, which explicitly calls the Hermocrates-Mecades scene the first. In general, just as the plot and incidents in this second version are tightened and compressed, so too the lines in version two are shortened to something closer to iambic trimeter. That said, the length of the lines is highly irregular, and meters other than iambic are involved on occasion, especially trochees and anapests. (The closing lines of this version are among the most striking lines in trochaic meter.) Because the translation tries above all to render the meaning of the lines, their length and sometimes even their meter cannot be respected—at least, not by this translator. Note that ll. 1–145 are taken from the neat copy, or *Reinschrift*; at that point, and after an adjustment of the line numbers, the translation reverts to the rough draft.

24 After this line, Hölderlin's neat copy excises two lines of the rough draft: *Und was sie ergriffen, es war / Wie leichte Beute den Kühnen,* "Whatever they would seize / Was easy prey to these bold ones."

34–37 "They thank him / For having robbed the sky of / The flame of life, / Betraying it to mortals." The reference to Prometheus the Titan, who rescues humankind from Zeus's intention to destroy it, is significant. Prometheus and the Titans in general play an important role in *Hyperion*. Likewise, the great river hymns, along with many other of Hölderlin's most famous odes and hymns, including "The Titans," take up the questions of the problematic relations of mortals, immortals, and demigods, the struggle between nature and destiny, and conflicts between birth and education—arguably all bound up with the Prometheus myth. That one of Hölderlin's favorite ancient texts is the *Prometheus Bound* of Aeschylus, or pseudo-Aeschylus, is no accident (see Hölderlin's letter to Neuffer of June 4, 1799). Prometheus, like Tantalus, is an erstwhile favorite of Zeus, but like all of Zeus's darlings he comes to suffer mightily. The rapid alternation of love and strife—or, still worse, the inability of strife to be neutralized even when Aphrodite rules at the center of the sphere—is at the heart of Hölderlin's mourning-play and perhaps of all tragedy.

41–42 "They say Apollo built / The city of the Trojans." Hölderlin had already translated that poem of Pindar, the eighth Olympian Ode (ll. 40–63), in which Apollo is said to have built the city of Ilion. Throughout the *Iliad,* we remember, Apollo's support of the Trojans causes Athena, Hera, and their favored Achaeans so many pains. In Hölderlin's drama, these lines spoken by the archon are not easy to interpret. Mecades seems to be juxtaposing—for purposes of irony—heroic Troy and pathetic Agrigent, inasmuch as the latter has an entirely utilitarian relation to its gods.

48 "Wandering star," *Irrgestirn.* The Greek word for the planets, πλάνητες ἀστέρες, literally means wandering or vagabond stars. See Plato's *Timaeus* (38c 5–6), which discusses the wandering stars (ἄστρα πλανητά) in terms of *time.* Intriguingly, Timaeus also calls woman's womb a wanderer, πλανώμενον (91c 5), the source of all hysteria. That would be a detail worthy only of an appendix, which is where Timaeus places it in his long speech, were it not for the fact that the major cosmological and ontological dilemma of the dialogue—how to get immutable being and mutable becoming together by means of some scarcely describable third, some impossible, inconceivable container, as it were—invokes all the language of mothers, midwives, nurses, "wandering causes," and womanly Necessity (ἀνάγκη). This is of course the famous problem of χώρα, to which even the very young Schelling had been drawn: his 1794 commentary on *Timaeus* ends on the threshold of choric "space" and "matter." Finally, we should note that one of the very first words for that necessary but impossible container, which we see only in our dreams and which we talk about only in illegitimate discourses, refers to a vessel in which the Demiurge mixes his compounds of cosmic soul, stirring them like water and wine. The word, of course, is κρατήρ. See *Timaeus,* 41d 4. Readers of *The Death of Empedocles* may pause to wonder whether the site of Empedocles' voluntary death is precisely the mixing bowl of the universe. In the third version, we will find Hölderlin using Plato's *Timaeus* and *Critias* in yet another way, so that such ontological and cosmological musings, speculations that however manly are forced to confront very womanly sorts of questions, are not simply caprices—at least not on this wandering star we call Earth.

63 Originally the line on "regret" read, in translation, ". . . he'll come to regret / His having regarded the mortals as mere fools." The contradiction between Empedocles' reputed misanthropy and philanthropy—his reputation as both tyrant and democrat—is something that Diogenes Laertius had reported. For Hölderlin himself, the struggle between contempt for and love of humankind was more than a theoretical issue; it touched on one of the deepest conflicts in his own troubled life.

83 The next two lines are added in the neat copy.

104–34 The archon's speech is expanded and emended in many details in the neat copy. The changes are not enumerated here, inasmuch as the substance of Mecades' accusation of Empedocles remains consistent.

138 Originally, in translation, "Who felt themselves at one with all the world."

139/140 The lettered lines result from material added in the neat copy. Hölderlin stopped working on that copy to write "Emily on the Eve of Her Wedding," a poem commissioned by his friend Neuffer. Hölderlin never returned to either the neat copy or the rough draft of version two, but he began to develop the thoughts that are reflected in the theoretical essays (see chapter 4). My own integration of the neat copy and rough draft follows that of Dietrich Sattler, even though the verb *entzündet,* "enflame," is a conjecture on his part. See FHA 13:304, 311.

152–53 Here again I follow Sattler's conjecture. See FHA 13:262, 311.

173 "Would speak what never should be spoken." This is the ἄρρητον, the *ineffabile,* or "unspeakable," which refers to the ideas, practices, and cult objects of the mystery religions, including those of the Pythagorean Brotherhood, influential throughout southern Italy and Sicily. Such cults almost always insist that their secrets not be betrayed—under penalty of death. The name of the god may not be pronounced or written, and the cult symbols may not be shown. Jochen Schmidt cites Hölderlin's *Germanien* in this regard: ". . . Describe it in a threefold way, / Yet also unpronounced . . . it must remain." A fragment of Empedocles that Hölderlin may or may not have known suggests that the ancient Empedocles was at least aware of the need to remain silent, "to safeguard within your mute heart" (DK B5) your key beliefs.

177 All editions other than DKV include the expression, *Bescheide dich!* "Restrain yourself!" as the opening words of this line. Schmidt does not accept them, but I have let them stand.

194–96 FHA and CHV condense these three lines into two.

211–14 "For at / The fitting hour his melancholy altered; / His proud and quietly indignant sense / Became his own worst enemy. . . ." Compare Empedocles' fragment DK B132, which Hölderlin knew: "Blessed is he who has inherited a treasury of divine thoughts; wretched is he in whom a shadowy delusion concerning the gods dwells [σκοτόεσσα θεῶν πέρι δόξα μέμηλεν]" (Stephanus 28).

213 To this line FHA and CHV append a marginal note by Hölderlin: *objectiv sinnliche Darstellung seiner Zurückgezogenheit,* "objective, sensuous presentation of his seclusion." The apparent meaning is that Hermocrates should offer a more compelling and intuitive account of Empedocles' seclusion, melancholia, and rage.

295–96 All other editions construe these two lines somewhat differently. Here I have followed DKV.

319 FHA and CHV strike the words "Condemned in his own soul." Note that from l. 313 onward in this second version Hölderlin revises Empedocles' soliloquy quite radically. Compare the first version from here to the end.

321 "The friend of gods?" In version one (see l. 329 and the notes to ll. 212–13, 329, 1567–69) Tantalus is explicitly named; here the theme is generalized to include all those who come into dangerous proximity with the divine.

354–57 ". . . you / Have drawn unto your master, ancient Saturn, / A new Jupiter, a novel yet / A weaker and more insolent one." In the poem "Nature and Art or Saturn and Jupiter," Saturn is identified with untamed nature, and Jupiter with the arts and crafts of culture. Cronos-Saturn is the more aorgic force, the Titanic force of nature, whereas Jupiter-Zeus is the orgic, the organizing force of culture. Saturn is invoked in both *Hyperion* and *The Death of Empedocles* as the shepherd of the Golden Age of humanity, Jupiter as the instauration of a new age, as liberator and father. Yet here the reference is clearly to the Hesiodic tale of Jupiter-Zeus's rebellion against Saturn-Cronos—the son raising his hand against the father, which is the cardinal crime cited in Empedocles' *Purifications.* The fact that Jupiter-Zeus can be named both father and parricide introduces the worst sort of trouble into what might otherwise appear to be a relationship where filial piety rules. The further fact that Jupiter-Zeus is simply acceding to a family tradition, inasmuch as Saturn-Cronos had rebelled against and emasculated his father Ouranos, offers little comfort to one who like Hölderlin loves the old stories. See Hesiod, *Theogony,* ll. 154–82. For a fascinating account of the transformation of Saturn-Cronos from the shepherd of humankind to a child-devouring ogre, see Jonathan F. Krell, *The Ogre's Progess: Images of the Ogre in Modern French Literature,* forthcoming, chapter 3.

397 "Like Endymion." Zeus preserves the youth and beauty of the shepherd Endymion by means of unending sleep. Precisely why Zeus does so is a bit of a mystery; some say it was because he feared that Hera might get a look at him. As it turns out, Selene, the moon, visits Endymion every night in his cave on Carian Mount Latmos; with his sleepy concurrence Selene produces fifty daughters. Hölderlin's use of the figure as one of rousing is therefore strange. See, of course, John Keats, *Endymion: A Poetic Romance.*

463 FHA and CHV excise this line.

465–66 These lines are construed differently in FHA and CHV.

495/496 Between these two lines FHA and CHV insert the line, *Liegt nicht vor dir der Menschen Schicksal offen,* "Does not the destiny of humankind lie open to you?"

499–514 "Correct! I know it all, can master all." This bizarre speech of Empedocles, which Pausanias will interpret as Empedocles' "mocking" himself, that is, as being entirely disingenuous, does seems to be utterly hubristic. Knowing how to hear it is difficult. Difficult also is the statement by Empedocles of Acragas that he no longer belongs among the "ephemera," that is, human beings, but wanders among mortals as θεὸς ἄμβροτος, a statement Diogenes Laertius reports and one that Hölderlin certainly knew (DK B112; Stephanus 23). He also knew the preceding fragment, the one that today concludes the series "On Nature" (DK B111; Stephanus 23), which reads as follows:

> And you will learn potent poisons or cures [φάρμακα], as many as there are as aids against sickness and old age, for I will fulfill all this for you alone. You will learn how to calm the violence of inexhaustible winds, which harass the earth and destroy the fields with their blasts; and, on the contrary, when you will, you shall be able to stir up those winds. You will be able to stop the dark rains and allow the earth to dry out at the propitious time for men, but you will also be able to end the droughts of summer by bringing on the cloudbursts that stream from the sky and nourish the trees. You will restore the defunct forces of men who have returned from Hades.

This seems to be precisely what Empedocles did for Panthea, yet is it not from beginning to end hubris? Is not the *claim* nefarious? Is it not black magic? That is most likely what the Latin scholar who used the Stephanus volume centuries ago thought when he wrote into the right margin the word *Magica.*

530–44 These lines are quite fragmentary, their syntax and sense difficult to make out; the scene thus comes to a halting and insecure close, perhaps because "shaping a world" has become its theme. For it is by no means clear that Empedocles, for all his gifts, has been able to form or reform Agrigent. Indeed, everything speaks against that.

530 FHA and CHV take the first two words, *Mit Ruhe,* to be a stage direction for Empedocles' speech: *"(calmly)."*

533 FHA and CHV delete these words.

547 FHA and CHV strike *Du Unbedeutendes!* "You utter insignificance!"

592–93 FHA (although not CHV) relocates these two lines, placing them after Pausanias's first speech in the next scene.

597–99 FHA (although not CHV) strikes these lines.

600–1 FHA (although not CHV) excises these lines.

606–20 FHA (although not CHV) deletes all these lines. But see FHA 13:291 for the variorum text in which they appear.

631–34 FHA and CHV delete the four lines *Es ist / Nicht eitel Überredung, glaub es mir, / Wenn er des Lebens sich / Bemächtiget,* "It is / No vain persuasion, do believe me, / When he empowers / His own life." These lines, no doubt, are difficult to decipher in the context of Pausanias's speech.

670 "All too gladly, Empedocles." Jochen Schmidt recognizes the importance of Delia's objection and rightly points to the dialogue with Manes in version three as the continuation of that objection. In general, one should note that Delia's objection is given far more amplitude in this second version than in the first—evidence against the view that Delia and Panthea are incidental or accidental characters whose roles diminish as the three drafts succeed on one another. Schmidt also refers us to the following lines of the third version of "Voice of the People": "For, oblivious of oneself, all-too-prepared / To fulfill the wish of the gods, that which is mortal / grabs hold too quickly / When one fine day with open eyes / It wanders its own path // Taking the shortest route back into the universe. . . ."

683 "He took it well," *Schön hat ers genommen.*" In balance with what was just now said about the danger of dying all too gladly, of being too prepared to take the shortest route back, is the ancient Stoic notion of dying beautifully, καλῶς θανεῖν. This is the ultimate goal of Stoic praxis, which accepts all that nature commands. In *Hyperion,* Hölderlin has Notara affirm in this way the beautiful death of Diotima; in the poem "A Poet's Courage," Hölderlin uses the identical language of "a beautiful death." One also cannot help but think of the letter from Sinclair, dated June 30, 1802, which was waiting for Hölderlin in Stuttgart on his return from Bordeaux, the letter that informed him of Susette Gontard's ("Diotima's") death: "She remained equal to herself up to the very end. Her death was like her life" (RA 46). Finally, recall the earlier note (to l. 1751 of version one) on Nietzsche's *Zarathustra,* which also affirms this ideal of a timely and beautiful death. The perplexing difficulty, of course, is to know whether such a free death can be utterly devoid of reactive, negative motivations and *ressentiments.*

685 FHA and CHV delete this line.

705–6 "For have not myriad heroes, / Like him, gone to the gods?" Perhaps Panthea is thinking of Heracles, who dies by fire. Yet as Schelling points out in his *Philosophy of Mythology,* Heracles mounts and ignites his own funeral pyre to purge all that is mortal from himself and to accede to the immortality that is already guaranteed him. Empedocles' leap into the crater therefore seems more like the fiery consummation of the mortal Semele, the mother of Dionysos, who dies by lightning bolt. Jochen Schmidt is right to warn that the *furor heroicus* often strikes Hölderlin as hubristic, as a desire to trespass beyond the boundaries that mortals must respect. Certainly, the tears that Hölderlin sheds in the late poem *Tränen* for "the wrathful heroes" are abashed. If, as "Mnemosyne" says, "And always / Into the unbounded a languorous longing goes," if many heroes have died because of this yearning to escape from mortal bonds and boundaries, and if such heroes have failed to "safeguard their souls" from this transgressive longing, then it may well be that our mourning them is out of place. In that case, *fehlet die Trauer*, mourning is mistaken and goes astray. Admittedly, nothing is more difficult to interpret than the late hymn, "Mnemosyne." Yet the poem surely would have given Panthea pause and Delia encouragement.

719 FHA and CHV excise this line.

Notes to the Essays toward a Theory of the Tragic

THE TRAGIC ODE

As though in proleptic agreement with Nietzsche, who argues that the Dionysian dithyramb and the "spirit of music" generally give birth to tragedy, Hölderlin begins his reflection on tragic *drama* with a thought about the tragic *ode*. His argument, reduced to a single phrase, is that the tragic ode begins with fiery enthusiasm, advances to meet its subject's nemesis, which imposes on the ode a strongly opposing mood, and ends by returning to its initial—although now more reflective—affirmative tone. The odes of Pindar, themselves based on the antiphonal structure of choral odes in Greek drama, regularly exhibit a set of triadic structures, consisting of strophe, antistrophe, and epode; the first is usually affirmative and celebratory in tone, the second confronts some difficulty or obstacle, and the third offers a resolution and a return to affirmation. The second set of three stanzas of the first Olympian Ode may serve as an example: the strophe sings the praises of Charis (grace, beauty, the charms of love) that we earlier saw Hölderlin sketching into the first version of *The Death of Empedocles* as a sort of motto; praise and celebration then pass over—still in the strophe—into a positive account of Pelops, son of Zeus-blessed Tantalus; the antistrophe, however, tells of Pelops's seduction by Poseidon, who carries Pelops off to Olympus, leaving his mother to mourn the boy; there is even the story, says Pindar, that Pelops is dismembered by his father and served up in a stew to the gods; the epode announces, however, that the gods dare not be considered cannibals and that all we can say of Pelops's father Tantalus is that he proved "unable to enjoy his great prosperity." Furthermore, even the formally irregular Romantic ode shows the same sort of advance from affirmation, through opposition, to some sort of reconciliation. True, we often forget those antistrophal clouds that take "a sober colouring" from man's mortality, although these clouds gather nowhere else than in Wordsworth's "Intimations of Immortality." And we are astonished when Philip Roth finds the exergue for his *Everyman,* which portrays unsparingly "the weariness, the fever, and the fret" of mortality, nowhere else than in Keats's "Ode to a Nightingale." In short, every song of celebration and praise, if it is to rise above a modest, "unassuming" state and achieve genuine seriousness, must go to confront something that opposes it in substance and in tone. If an ode, especially of the Pindaric sort, but also of the Romantic varieties, may be defined as an extended lyric poem of "passion and visionary boldness," written in an "elevated style," with an "elaborate" stanzaic structure, and involving tension or even conflict between or among its strophes and antistrophes, then Hölderlin's brief essay, no matter how impenetrable at first, actually conforms to a long tradition. See M. H. Abrams, *A Glossary of Literary Terms,* 5th ed. (Fort Worth, TX: Holt, Rinehart and Winston, 1988), 124.

THE GENERAL BASIS [OF TRAGIC DRAMA]

4 When Hölderlin refers here to "the tragic poem," he presumably means the tragic *dramatic* poem, which he is now contrasting with the tragic ode. Max Kommerell calls the tragic ode "a poem that borders on the tragic, but does not compel it to the point of decision" (MK 323). He continues, "In the tragic moment [*Augenblick*] of tragedy itself [that is, of the tragic dramatic poem] there appears quite clearly—in the midst of the rapid alternation of opposites—what tragedy actually means, and that moment is actual death" (ibid.).

12 "Inmost heart" here translates *das Gemüt,* perhaps the most notoriously untranslatable word in German philosophy from Kant through Heidegger. "Mind," "soul," "inner disposition," "temperament" (which was the word chosen to translate *Gemüt* in the first line of the Frankfurt Plan in chapter 1), and "heart" are all candidates, yet each of these is also used to translate other German words. I have been guided by the expression *etwas zu Gemüte führen,* "taking something to heart." Perhaps all we need to remember is that Empedocles of Acragas (or Agrigentum) was one of those Greeks who associated *thinking* with the flow of blood through and around the *heart.* "For the blood that surges in humankind around the heart [περικάρδιόν] is what empowers their thought [νόημα]" (DK B105). Perhaps all we need to note in addition is that the "inmost heart" is the site of excessive intensity.

17 "Denies its ultimate basis, and has to do so." In a much-discussed letter to his friend Neuffer, dated July 3, 1799, Hölderlin refers to his strategy in revising *The Death of Empedocles* as "the proud renunciation of everything accidental," "renunciation" being the word here translated as *denial,* namely, *Verläugnung* (CHV 2:781). Such denial or

renunciation therefore plays a key role in Hölderlin's ruminations concerning the essence of the tragic. For further discussion, see the General Introduction and the Analysis to this volume, along with LV chapter 1.

20 *Nefas,* literally, "the unspeakable," is what the Romans took to be that which is forbidden by the gods. By extension, or perhaps originally, *nefas* refers to religious mysteries that dare not be shared with the uninitiated. In Hölderlin's usage, *nefas* surely has to do with that excess of intensity, the "too much," that characterizes the tragic hero and all tragic unification. As Jochen Schmidt (DKV 2:1191) notes, *nefas* is approached each time a mortal moves toward the infinite, unbounded, or indeterminate, *das Unendliche,* in thought or action. One might add that the *nefas* is broached each time a mortal, waxing aorgic, tantalizes the gods—whether intentionally or inadvertently, whatever the reason and whomever we may wish to chastize.

27 "Likeness" here translates *Gleichnis,* more technically understood as *simile.*

31 "Displacement or foreign configuration." Here one should recall the well-known letter to Casimir von Böhlendorff dated December 4, 1801, which compares a people's native gifts to the talents of foreign peoples, and which, paradoxically, urges poets to explore the foreign precisely in order to secure their own native gifts. What the present essay adds to this is the notion that tragic dramatic tension—or intensity—can best be heightened by such egress and return.

59/60 Although missing pages make completing Hölderlin's sentence impossible for us, he clearly wishes to stress once again that the heterogeneity of the foreign material and its differentiation enhance dramatic intensity. As for those missing pages, a gap of at least one sheet, perhaps even a folded double-sheet, occurs at this point in the holograph. (In these closing lines prior to the gap, DKV 2:427, bottom line, inserts a second parenthesis into the long parenthetical remark; FHA 13:333 deletes the parenthesis, adding a comma after the preceding word, *annimmt.* I have eliminated both the open and close parentheses here, substituting commas.) Readers should also note that the material following the gap, which consists of a single sentence that is already under way, is extremely difficult to decipher and translate. Sattler (BA 8:40) is surely correct when he surmises that it has to do with Hölderlin's identifying a flaw in tragic drama when it seeks to have one of the ancillary characters undergo an experience on the hero's behalf. Heroic action is always autarchic, autonomous activity, *Selbsttätigkeit.*

The Basis of Empedocles

1–7 "Nature and art." The precise relation of art and nature, or, as Hölderlin will soon say, of the more organizational and the more aorgic, as reciprocal or even supplemental, is perhaps impossible to grasp, essentially "undecidable." Such a relation surely has to do with what Derrida, in *Of Grammatology*, has called "the logic of the supplement." See part two of that work, especially chapters 2 and 4. Sattler (BA 8:57) notes that the very opposition of organizational and aorgic challenges the inherently organizational discourse of dialectic; indeed, it seems as though Hölderlin's invocation of the aorgic necessitates a step beyond all dialectic. Yet that would set Hölderlin quite apart from what one calls German Idealism.

7 "More organizational" here translates *das Organischere.* One might be tempted to translate *organisch* by the cognate "organic." Yet whereas the Anglo-American "organic" suggests something close to nature, Hölderlin's use of the word goes back to the Greek sense of the ὄργανον as a tool, hence is more related to the world of culture and technology than to nature. Kant's third *Critique* tended to use *organisch* in this more Aristotelian sense of the "organized," and Hölderlin follows and radicalizes him here. Hölderlin contrasts the "more organizational" with the "more aorgic," the privative-a here suggesting those aspects of elemental nature that escape or at least resist the human organization of them. The more aorgic relates closely to that *intensity* and *excess* that everywhere fascinate Hölderlin, an intensity and excess that are bound up with the infinite (or indeterminate, unbounded—Anaximander's ἄπειρον), the universal, and the divine. We should note here that Hölderlin very often uses these terms in their comparative forms, the *more* organizational, the *more* aorgic, as though he is dealing with an element that is essentially continuous, a spectrum, a chord, a tension within the single Empedoclean sphere.

11–16 That the "knowable" is reached only by "separation" is a fundamental thesis of the early essay, *Urteil und Sein,* "Judgment and Being," in DKV 2:502–3, an English translation of which is contained in the Pfau volume (37–38). Note that "autonomous activity," *Selbsttätigkeit,* is the subject of the lines that follow the gap in "The Tragic Ode."

46 "Supreme enmity, supreme reconciliation." Hölderlin drew a number of small diagrams in his manuscript to clarify for himself the meaning of this convergence of enmity and reconciliation. Of the several drawings, the two reproduced overleaf seem most fully elaborated and most significant. The one on the left refers to the dispersion from the midpoint undergone by both art (the organizational) and nature (the more aor-

gic), a dispersion that occurs in the most radical enmity—perhaps the vortex that Empedocles of Acragas calls Νεῖκος, or Strife—while the one on the right tries to demonstrate some sort of higher unification or reconciliation of the two. That the reconciliation seems to come from the outside, as it were, merely being tacked onto the lines that are in waxing separation, suggests perhaps that we should stress the word *scheint,* "appears." Hölderlin soon will write that "the outcome will be that the unifying moment, like a mirage, will dissolve more and more" (BA 59–60).

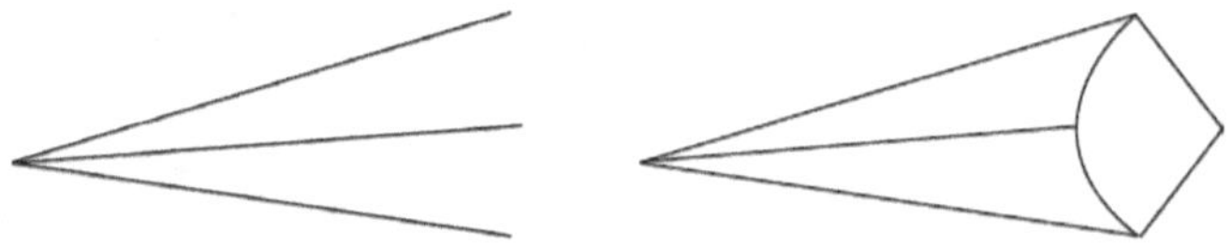

56 "Mirage" here translates *Trugbild,* the word that Manes, in the third version of the play, will fling in the face of Empedocles. Essential to Hölderlin's notion of the tragic is the equivocal nature of any particular or individual attempt to solve the riddle of destiny. The apparent reconciliation of which Hölderlin will soon speak is therefore quite remote from the reconciliation we usually attribute to German Idealist thought, especially in Hegel. *Das Trugbild* is closely related to *Betrug,* the "felicitous fraud" that the essay will also soon invoke. Hölderlinian hyperdialectic, if one may call it that, has less to with successful synthesis and victorious forward movement to a determinate third object than with recognizing the necessity of decline, demise, and death. As Hölderlin will soon say, all unification is *tragic* unification, bound for dissolution.

141 "Goes down in an idealized deed," *in einer idealischen Tat das Individuum deswegen untergeht.* Recall the lines in the first version of the play depicting Empedocles' suicide: "That you would find the joys of overcoming all / In one full deed and at the end?" (1895–96; see also the long note to ll. 1891–97, above). The word "proleptic" translates *vorzeitig* here. The suggestion is that Empedocles, who unites nature and art too singularly and too intensely, is somehow ahead of his time, somehow premature; if, as Hölderlin elsewhere says, nature abhors untimely growth, Empedocles' proleptic dissolution of the problem of destiny runs counter to the very nature that the hero so reveres.

150 The distinction proposed here between a material and formal solution to the problem of destiny is very difficult to follow. The apparent reconciliation that is at least suggested by "a more mature, true,

and purely universal intensity" may point to Hölderlin's tendency—as he turns toward the third version—to relocate the solution of the problem of destiny, taking it out of the hands of the heroic individual and finding it now in the general course of history. At all events, as far as the *living* individual is concerned, no such reconciliation is possible.

205–7 "To defend themselves against the too powerful, too profoundly approachable influence of the element, to preserve themselves from oblivion of self and from total alienation." The excessive approachability or amiability of the element, *gegen den . . . zu tiefen freundlichen Einfluß des Elements,* is difficult to understand. It may refer to that luxuriant landscape of Sicily or to the glorious sky and sea of Greece in general. Or it may mean to say that the Agrigentians were not wise to the less amiable, more aorgic power of nature, taking the elemental to be entirely subject to their organizational powers. Empedocles does not so much reject this stance toward nature, but rather takes it "one step farther." He yearns for the time of his youth when the gods and all of nature were friendly to him; he does so, however, not by yoking nature under "sheer serviceability," but, as we will soon hear, by an "excessive penetration" of its objects. In general, the notion of *das Element* in Hölderlin's thinking is one of the most difficult: for a discussion, see TA 54, 57, 235–39, 257–58, 299n. 15.

237–38 "In the spirit and in the mouth of this man." This odd locution may have been inspired by a fragment of Empedocles (B3) that Hölderlin certainly knew (Stephanus 20, bottom line): "Yet, O gods, the madness of men distracts everyone from my tongue; let the pure source flow from your holy mouth [ἐκ δ' ὁσίων στομάτων]!"

256–57 "His own freest determination." The last word in this phrase, used once again immediately after the semicolon to describe the determination of Empedocles' "circumstances," tries to translate *Stimmung,* a complex word that can also mean "attunement," "disposition," "mood." Readers of Heidegger's *Being and Time,* as well as his later works, will be familiar with this word. Hölderlin's poem "Stimme des Volks" (The People's Voice) might also be a place to go in order to reflect on *Stimmung. Bestimmung* would more straightforwardly be translated as "determination," which is admittedly too insipid and overused a word to render adequately *Stimmung.*

272–73 "A solitary who cultivates his gardens." Readers will no doubt recognize the allusion to Voltaire's *Candide,* the concluding lines of which remind us also of the solitary promenader, Rousseau—one of Hölderlin's heroes, as important to Hölderlin's idea of modernity as Empedocles is to his idea of antiquity.

314–37 The "opponent," *der Gegner,* is neither the cynical priest, Hermocrates, nor the political crony, Critias; he is more like Mecades in the second version or Strato in the third, that is, more like the hero of an epic. It would prove interesting to compare and contrast the figures of Strato and Manes in the third version with the "opponent" described here, namely, the man of intellect who loves definition and the "clear divide."

321 "He is destiny itself." In his novel *Hyperion* (1792–1798), Hölderlin had contrasted "the school of nature" with "the school of destiny." By the latter he meant all those forces of culture and education that stultify the individual who thrives on nature. One could argue that *The Death of Empedocles* and the theoretical essays surrounding it continue to develop this fundamental theme of Hölderlin's work and life—the conflict between the singer who is close to nature, nurtured by nature, and the surrounding sociopolitical and cultural world that opposes him. The school of destiny, to repeat, always seeks a "clear divide" for deciding matters. "Clear divide" tries to translate *Scheidepunkt,* a key term—as is the related *Mittelpunkt,* or point of equilibrium, for Empedocles' divine synthesis of nature and art—in Hölderlin's poetological reflections. (See "Once the Poet Has Become Equal to the Spirit" [CHV 2:87] and LV chapter 2.) The school of nature tends, by contrast, to devote itself to the more aorgic ways of the natural world. Hölderlin describes the character of such devotion in two contrasting ways: first, excessive penetration of the object, and second, a radical openness to all particulars by virtue of a highly refined sensibility and receptivity. Note that the subjective and objective realms exchange places in "the opponent" as well, except that in him endurance, steadfastness, security—and, as always, the "clear divide"—remain the prevailing qualities.

The Fatherland in Decline

20–21 The final phrase of this paragraph is difficult to decipher. If the word *sie* should actually be *die,* the phrase would read, ". . . so that by way of the infinite the finite effect comes to the fore." This seems to be consonant with the thought that the essay develops. However, Sattler and Knaupp (FHA 14:83, 96; CHV 2:72) surmise an *als* before *Unendlichkeit,* so that the phrase would read, ". . . so that by means of it [that is, the particular mode of relating], as infinity, the finite comes to the fore." My translation is based on this supposition of Sattler and Knaupp.

20–22 "Transition," "transitional period." Jochen Schmidt (DKV 2:1199) rightly notes the importance of the period of *transition,* the *Übergang* that follows or overlaps with the period of *Untergang,* or downgoing, and asserts the importance of the temporal dimension of *the present* for the transition. To be sure, in the period of transition an old world is dissolving and a new one is slowly, almost indiscernibly, taking shape. It is a time of uncertainty and anxiety, and Hölderlin appears to be searching for a therapy that will transform actual dissolution into ideal dissolution, "ideal" here again having the sense of the ideational, of that which has been subjected to reflection and meditation with a view to the universal, thus becoming both more lucid and more tranquil. Yet it cannot be, as Schmidt suggests, that Hölderlin is confident about some sort of "anticipation" of the inchoate new world because of a putative "cyclical view of history." True, the character Empedocles hints at an eternal recurrence of the same. Yet neither Empedocles nor Hölderlin draw much comfort from it, just as after them Nietzsche will regard that idea as a rigorous test, not a therapy. The problem is that (as Nietzsche would say) the ring of eternity closes in and as the moment of time, closes once and for all one more time (as Derrida would add). In the present case, that closing moment is the impending death of Empedocles and the ensuing political and religious crisis in Agrigent. No anticipation, and no therapy, can provide comfort. The unification of old and new in the period of transition—as Hölderlin will soon argue—is invariably *tragic* unification. Our disquiet in the present, at least during the reign of strife, can never be mollified by the thought that what goes around comes around. Hölderlinian tranquillity has little to do with complacency or safe prediction—of that we may be certain. Indeed, Max Kommerell focuses on the word "transition" to designate Hölderlin's essential character as a poet—he calls it *Aufgeschlossenheit zum Übergang*, "readiness for transition" (MK 318), and he means by it a readiness for the unexpected. Hölderlin is less disposed to shut himself off from the world (*abgrenzen*) and to assert himself (*sich behaupten*) than "to be for himself merely in transition and to let things be for him only in transition" (ibid.). Eternal recurrence, yes, but never of precisely the same—unless "the same" is ineluctable transition.

25–26 "For how could dissolution be apprehended without unification?" This may be an allusion to the transcendental unity of apperception in the Transcendental Deduction in the second edition of Kant's *Critique of Pure Reason*. "Thus the synthetic unity of apperception is the supreme point to which every use of the understanding and even all logic, and, with logic, transcendental philosophy, must cling; indeed, this faculty is the understanding itself" (B134).

71–72 "Run through infinitely in a single moment." Note the parallel with Descartes' principle of *enumeratio* in his *Rules for the Direction of the Human Mind.* No doubt, Hölderlin is thinking of a certain unity of life and of historical epochs, not of Cartesian principles and equations. For a discussion of *enumeratio,* see D. F. Krell, *Of Memory, Reminiscence, and Writing: On the Verge* (Bloomington: Indiana University Press, 1990), 56–58.

120 Epicureanism is a style of life that concentrates on the sensible and the present, endeavoring always to "seize the day." The quotation from Horace is from *Carmina* 3:29, ll. 29ff. (cited at DKV 2:1204), and in more extended form reads: *prudens futuri temporis exitum / caliginosa nocte premit deus, / ridetque si mortalis ultra / fas trepidat.* "Prudently the god swathes the outcome of future times in dark night, / and he laughs when mortals fret / beyond the proper measure." Note that the proper measure, *fas,* has to do with what can be *spoken,* that of which one is *permitted* to speak. *Ne-fas* negates *fas,* and is thereby the "unspeakable." See the earlier note to l. 20 of "The General Basis" for a discussion of *nefas.*

142–44 ". . . lyrical . . . in epic." Jochen Schmidt (DKV 2:1201) points out that the references to lyric and epic here do not mean the genres of lyric poetry and epic poetry as such; rather, they allude to lyrical and epic tendencies within the tragic dramatic poem itself: *lyric* refers to the playwright's expression of an intense feeling of unity with his or her subject, *epic* to the depiction of the particular heroic deeds that unite and found a nation—although perhaps also to reflections that contemplate the fate of a nation. In all these cases, Hölderlin insists that the unification is *tragic.*

170–72 These final lines are difficult to understand. Yet they may suggest something of the way in which Empedocles' "opposites" in version one, namely, the characters Critias and Hermocrates, have to move in the direction of reciprocity, as they seem to do in version two; finally, with the dialogue between Manes and Empedocles, in version three, we may see something of a tragic unification of opposites. In any case, I read the second *nach* in the first sentence (*nach dieser Gegensätze*) as having occurred prior to, and being on the way toward, the tragic unification of opposites.

Notes to the Plan of the Third Version of *The Death of Empedocles*

Jochen Schmidt notes that Hölderlin follows the plan up to scene 3 of the third version, although "follows" here does not mean a great deal, inasmuch as little more than the number of the scene and the list of personages appear in the plan. Note that in the plan, the archon (Critias in the first version, Mecades in the second) is now called "the king." The archon-king (he will be called *Strato* in the third version itself) is now said to be a *brother* and an *opponent* of Empedocles. Hermocrates the priest is now replaced by "the wise man" or "the old man." The change is important: the priest, at first the villain of the piece, gradually becomes something like an alterego of Empedocles himself, one who may attempt to mediate between the quarreling siblings—which now include Panthea, "the sister."

12 "The opponent." Compare the development of this concept in the final pages of "The Basis of Empedocles."

32 "Reflective, ideational," *reflekt. idealisch.* These terms, developed in the essay or schematic sketch, "Alternation of Tones," *Wechsel der Töne,* which is not included in the present volume, are exceedingly complex. Perhaps *idealisch* is the most difficult term. It does not mean "ideal" in some moral or aesthetic sense, but refers to *the idea* in drama, in the sense of a drama's central conflict and its proper theme. Perhaps Aristotle's notion of διάνοια in the *Poetics* is similar, inasmuch as "thought" or "reasoning" touches on every aspect of λόγος in tragedy, whether in the speeches of the characters or in the construction of the plot. *Ideational,* while an unforgivably awkward and archaic English word meaning "having to do with the formation of ideas," seems better suited to render *idealisch* than the word "ideal." Hölderlin's "Alternation of Tones" begins as follows: "Does not the ideational catastrophe dissolve whenever the natural initial tone turns into its opposite, the heroic? Does not the natural catastrophe dissolve whenever the heroic initial tone turns into its opposite, the ideational? Does not the heroic catastrophe dissolve whenever the ideational initial tone turns into its opposite, the natural?" (DKV 2:524). Claiming that the first phrase applies to the first version of *The Death of Empedocles* seems to make sense: its initial tone, with the speeches of Panthea, is natural; its final deed at the end ought to be expressed in the heroic mode—as the plan to the *third* version also intimates; yet that would mean that its catastrophe is ideational—precisely insofar as the idea of "one full deed and at the end" collapses and dissolves. That is no doubt too facile a reading, however, and is meant merely to initiate a discussion concerning the difficulty of *completing* the play—if only in our readerly imagination. The tragic poem is discussed in "Alternation" in terms of the following categories: (1) the ideational—perhaps, to repeat, in some of the various senses in which Aristotle talks about the importance of διάνοια in tragedy, especially in its plot and diction: for both Aristotle and Hölderlin, tragedy must above all be guided by thought and by ideas; (2) the heroic, in the sense of the actions and deeds of those who are somehow larger than life and "better" than the average citizen; and (3) the "naive," no doubt in Schiller's sense (clear and forthright delineation and depiction, as opposed to the expression of intense feeling in "sentimental" poetry). Hölderlin refers to these categories once again in his "Sketch toward the Continuation of the Third Version." For a good example of Hölderlin's use of *idealisch,* see his letter to Schelling (July 1799) at CHV 2:792.

36 "p. p." Hölderlin, following the usage of many eighteenth-century German writers, seems to be using these letters to indicate *et cetera.* The only two current uses I am aware of mean "by proxy," as when one signs

a legal document in someone else's name, *per procurationem,* or to indicate something "aforesaid," *praemissis praemittendis,* that is, presupposing everything that must be presupposed. This last may be the intended sense, yet it is odd, although apparently so common that none of the German editors comment on it.

42 "Enthusiasm of the son of destiny." Clearly a reference to Empedocles, who is said in the "Basis of Empedocles" to embody the problem of destiny for his age by means of his exceptional integration of nature and art. We also recall from that essay, however, that Empedocles only seems to resolve the problem of destiny, which no individual can resolve. Furthermore, one should note Hölderlin's attempt in version three of his play to make the king-archon a worthy "opponent" of Empedocles. That might make him too a "son of destiny," especially insofar as he is a brother.

57–58 "He intones the felicitous song of blessing." According to Jochen Schmidt, the *Glückseligkeitsgesang* to which Hölderlin refers derives from the Greek μακαρισμός, referred to by Aristotle in his *Rhetoric* (1:9, 1367b 33). Initially merely a song of praise, it becomes refined among the Greeks to a celebration of the happiness a human being has garnered in his or her life. Such a song—or the recognition of the need for such a song—has implications for Aristotle's ethics, which everywhere leaves space for good or bad fortune, hazard, and accident where happiness is concerned, much to the consternation of many medieval and modern ethicists. No doubt the biblical use of the term to praise the pious or blessed—*selig* means, above all, blessed—also has an influence on Hölderlin.

81 "The youthful sun." This odd locution, *Sonnenjüngling,* odd especially because of the reference to evening vespers, appears also in Hölderlin's ode "Sunset," likewise from 1799.

Notes to *The Death of Empedocles,* Third Version

The setting for the third version is a region of Mount Etna. All the events that took place in Agrigent are now in the reported past. In this third version, as in the second, Hölderlin drops the Panthea-Delia scene that opened the first version, although this time the scene is not even mentioned. Critias/Mecades is now called Strato, and he is now the brother of Empedocles. Panthea is now said to be their sister. Wife and children play no role; the family is now that of siblings. Although Diogenes Laertius mentions the ancient Empedocles' having had a brother and a sister, Hölderlin's decision can hardly rest on that source alone. One can only speculate. At all events, Hermocrates has been dropped from the play, and a very different sort of priest—Manes, the Egyptian—is introduced. (In the manuscript of version three, Manes is called simply "the old man"; however, I have followed DKV and CHV in using the name *Manes* proleptically.) The register of persons in the play now includes a chorus. From the "Plan toward the Continuation of the Third Version" one can see that Hölderlin planned to have the choral odes conclude rather than open the scenes—anticipating Hölderlin's translation of Sophocles' *Oedipus the Tyrant,* as opposed to *Antigone,* in which the odes *open* the scenes. The third version concludes with the sketch of a choral ode, "New world."

The meter is once again iambic pentameter, or blank verse, but it is more irregular than ever. Furthermore, the word choice and the modes of expression, along with the syntax of the sentences and the word order of the lines, are far more complex and surprising here than in the first two versions.

45–46 FHA and CHV delete these lines.

61–64 FHA and CHV structure these final lines of Empedocles' speech differently, dropping ll. 63–64 altogether.

65 All editions structure the opening of this scene differently.

67–68 FHA and CHV strike these two lines.

76 After this line, FHA (although not CHV) inserts a line spoken by Empedocles: *Hier oben ist ein neues Vaterland,* "Up here there is a new fatherland." See FHA 13:381, 423.

88 All other editions agree in construing the beginning of Empedocles' speech differently, and I have followed them here. DKV has simply, *Ihr heilgen Elemente!* "You holy elements!" proceeding then directly to l. 89. See FHA 13:381, 423.

124 FHA and CHV delete this line.

142–56 These fifteen lines of dialogue are structured differently in FHA, and differently yet again in CHV. See FHA 13:425, CHV 1:889. StA too reverses the order of some of the lines. See Reclam, 120.

190–93 FHA (although not CHV) structures these lines differently.

225 "Divine Heracles! even if you plummeted." Heracles, like Orpheus, Odysseus, and other heroes of mythology, descends into the underworld. His twelfth and final labor is the capture of Cerberus. Yet in the present instance the downgoing (κατάβασις) of the hero involves an even more foreboding labor: Pausanias envisages Empedocles plunging into the bottomless abyss to which Zeus has banished the Titans; of special relevance is the last Titan, Typhon, who is imprisoned nowhere else than beneath Mount Etna. Empedocles' task—as Pausanias envis-

ages it—is to reconcile the reigns of Cronos and Zeus, to settle the quarrel between the Titans and the Olympians. We recall pseudo-Aeschylus's Prometheus musing on the end of Zeus through heaven-storming Heracles. Hölderlin's allusion therefore has enormous theogonic, theodicean, or theocidic implications. Finally, recall that the dead Christ also "descends into hell." He is, as Hölderlin believes, in this respect too a brother of Dionysos and Heracles. See "Bread and Wine," which alludes to all three heroes and concludes with a reference to a pacified Cerberus.

243 When Hölderlin has Empedocles reply to Pausanias, "I am not who I am," we hear a remarkable reformulation of Yahweh's reply to Moses, who has demanded to know the name of God (Exodus, 3:13–14). Moreover, Hölderlin has thereby offered a clue to Empedocles' identity, which is essentially split. The dialogue with Manes will bring this split to light. One can imagine Matthew Arnold affirming that the phrase "I am *not* who I am," or "I am who I am *not*," is the identifying phrase of modernity, the age of depth psychology. One thinks of Jacques Lacan's twofold response to the Cartesian *cogito sum* ("I think, I am"): first, "I think there where I am not, or do not follow [*suis* means both to be and to pursue or follow]; thus I am there where I do not think," and, second, "I am not there where I am or pursue the shuttlecock of my thought; I think of what I am or what I pursue there where I do not even think of thinking" (*Écrits*, Paris: Seuil, 1966, 517). Something of this sort underlies Hölderlin's account, in "The Basis of Empedocles," of the reversal of the organizational and the aorgic qualities in Empedocles, who is most at home in himself when . . . he does not even think of thinking.

274–75 FHA and CHV excise these two lines.

293–97 FHA (although not CHV) restructures and condenses these five lines.

297 ". . . was mir die Zeit gehäuft." Compare Paul Celan's late collection of poems, *Zeitgehöft*.

303 "The Roman lands, so rich in deeds." An anachronism to the degree that Hölderlin's Empedocles is thinking of deeds from the ages of the Republic or the Empire; not an anachronism if he is thinking of Aeneas or of Numa Pompilius. For the last-named, see the note to ll. 1413–15 of version one.

306 "And you, Tarentum!" Tarentum was an important center of the Pythagorean Brotherhood in Magna Graecia, southeastern Italy (in the Puglia of today). Plato is said to have visited Tarentum. Pausanias is therefore being advised to pursue his education in the Greek philoso-

phy of the future and in the religious mysticism of the past and present once he has visited the (future?) praxis-oriented civilization of Rome. As we shall soon hear (l. 315), he is asked to complete his education in classical Athens and in ancient Egypt.

309 “My Plato.” Perhaps the most astonishing of the anachronisms. Plato had just been born when Empedocles died. They cannot have met. Yet Jochen Schmidt is right to suggest that Hölderlin is interested in establishing something like a brotherhood of thought—an *ideational* brotherhood, one might say—that would be parallel to the brotherhood of heroes. Plato learned much from the Pythagoreans, and the dialogue to which Hölderlin will soon refer (see the note to l. 315, below), *Timaeus*, is full of Pythagorean lore.

313 The Ilissus River flows through eastern Athens. Pausanias is therefore being told to visit Plato not only in Magna Graecia but also in his home city.

315 “Inquire of my brothers far away in Egypt.” One of those ancient brothers will soon come on the scene—the “old man,” or “wise man,” Manes. Egypt is to be the final stop on the path of Pausanias’s education. One recalls the importance of Egyptian Saïs to all the German Romantics and Idealists, for example, Herder, Novalis, Schelling, and even Hegel, insofar as they are all readers of Plato’s *Timaeus* (see 21e). See also the note on Manes, ll. 321ff., below.

317 On “Urania,” see the earlier note to l. 1816 of the first version.

317a-d FHA and CHV, although not StA, add these four lines. Because of the importance of the theme of *Zeichen,* “signs,” in this third version, as in Hölderlin’s late hymns, I have decided to include them. See FHA 13:401, 430, for the variorum and reconstructed texts.

319–20 “Go! fear nothing! everything recurs. And what / Is yet to happen already is accomplished.” Empedocles has alluded to the thought of eternal recurrence before: he speaks of the return of his youthful days in ll. 1169–84 of the first version. Yet there he asserts that “something greater” is yet to come—a strict recurrence of the same is therefore not invoked. One must wonder what sort of influence the talk of recurrence may have had on the young Nietzsche, who read *The Death of Empedocles* toward the end of his sixteenth year. More important, as Nietzsche’s extended and extremely ambivalent discussions in notebook M III 1 show, nothing is less certain in his philosophy than the meaning of the word *same* in the idea of the eternal recurrence of the same (KSA 9:441–575). It is crucial, however, to resist the notion—Schmidt here (DKV 2:1180) falls prey to it—that recurrence is inevitably a “fatalistic” thought, one that denies human freedom and agency altogether. That is clearly no more the case for Hölderlin than it is for Nietzsche. Precisely how recurrence is to be thought—as an affirmative thought, but a thought of tragic affirmation—is of course an intricate subject. Heidegger, for example, devotes himself to it in the most stimulating of his many lecture courses on Nietzsche, namely, the 1937 course on eternal recurrence of the same: see Martin Heidegger, *Nietzsche,* 4 vols. (San Francisco: HarperCollins, 1991), vol. 2, passim. For further discussion see D. F. Krell, *Infectious Nietzsche* (Bloomington: Indiana University Press, 1996), chapter 8, "Eternal Recurrence—of the Same? Reading Notebook M III 1"; on eternal recurrence in *The Death of Empedocles,* see LV vii, xv–xix, 5, 13–17, 30, and, on eternal recurrence in Gabriel García Márquez, 153–74.

321ff. Manes, in the plan to the third version called simply "the old man," is a remarkable character. He embodies some of the traits of Hermocrates, the priest of versions one and two, yet is closer to and even more intimate with Empedocles than Hermocrates could ever be. Even though Empedocles calls him his "evil spirit," one cannot deny that Manes puts essential questions to Empedocles—questions that trouble Empedocles' very identity and challenge the legitimacy of his claims and intentions. The origin of the name *Manes* in Hölderlin's project is uncertain. Manes is said to be a priest of the Egyptian war-goddess Neith, associated with the famous temple at Saïs. He is one of the brothers "far away in Egypt," to whom Empedocles has already referred. (A long tradition regards all the early Greek thinkers—including Empedocles of Acragas—as having visited Egypt and learned from the ancient Egyptian priests.) Manes is doubtless Empedocles' opponent, but he is an intrinsic opponent, an enemy on the inside. His name may be a pun on Empedocles' name, which has as its root the adjective ἔμπεδος, "steadfast," if *manes* can be heard as a form of *manēo,* "I remain." The Latin *manes, manium,* ambiguously masculine and feminine in gender, is apparently related to words meaning "the good," "the early," "the dawn." The *manes* are the souls of the departed, especially of one's own deceased ancestors, revered as divine. By metonymy, *manes* refers to the gods or powers of the dead and the underworld itself, and, albeit more rarely, the corpse; important in the present instance is that the word can mean the tutelary genius or δαίμων of a human being. An expression from Virgil's *Aeneid* reads: *quisquis suos patimus manes,* everyone must make amends "as their *manes* command." Before the name of the deceased on the tombstones of Roman graveyards often appear the letters DM: *Dis Manibus*—sacred to the gods (or the souls) of the dead. The assertion that *Manes* might have something to do with *manēo, manēre,* is therefore probably indefensible in strict philological terms, even if *bleiben,* "remaining," is assuredly a theme of Hölderlin's tragedy. Whether some relationship exists between *manes,* the Old Latin *manus,* meaning "good," and *manus* as "hand," especially in the sense of power, governance, or rule, is difficult to say. Hölderlin is clearly aware, however, of the multifaceted *manes*: early on in the first volume of *Hyperion* the narrator refers to himself and Adamas as "*manes* from times past," *wie Manen aus vergangner Zeit* (CHV 1:620). He is no doubt also aware that the Di Manes are δαιμόνες and that the realm of the tutelary spirits is τὸ δαιμόνιον. Hölderlin's late hymns, some of which are dedicated to the demigods who are river Titans, invoke the earth itself as τὸ δαιμόνιον. One may speculate that Hölderlin's early, inchoate plan to write a tragedy on *Socrates* surely would have involved Socrates' δαίμων. Finally, one should note that Schelling's *Philosophy of Mythology* proposes *Manes* as a variant spelling of the Mani, that is, the Persian Manichean sect; Schelling declares that their name means "the dividers," those who sunder life into two fundamentally opposed principles (*Sämmtliche Werke,* II/2:505). At all events, in version three of *The Death of Empedocles,* Manes rises as the alterego of Empedocles, a doppelgänger who emerges out of the Oriental past—and the early Greek present—to displace the so-called "steadfast" one.

323 "You mirage!" *Trugbild!* Compare *Schattenbild!* in version one (l. 326); there it is Empedocles' objection to himself. It is as though Manes becomes the externalized incorporation—the *fors intérieur,* as it were—of all the self-doubts of Empedocles and all the challenges to him from Pausanias and Delia. *Trugbild!* or, as Dietrich Sattler reads it, simply *Trug!* "Deception!" is the word Hölderlin also uses in his essay on the "Basis of Empedocles" (l. 49) when discussing the illusory nature of all the attempts of individuals to solve the problem of destiny. (Eternal recurrence and tragic affirmation neither banish freedom altogether nor nourish mortals' illusion of boundless power.) Manes accuses Empedocles of impersonating "the One," of being a mirage or *fata morgana* rather than the embodiment of destiny. The festival appropriate to Empedocles would not be "the days of Saturn," that is, not the commemoration of the Golden Age, but the Apaturia, the carnivalesque festival of Deception. See TA 61, 245, 365; see also the note to l. 336, below.

324–27 The editions vary in the presentation of Manes's speech. StA reads 324–25 as follows: *Der Armen / Einer auch / Von diesem Stamm, ein Sterblicher, wie du,* "One of the wretched also / Of this tribe, a mortal like you." CHV follows StA here. FHA has: *Der Wunderbaren, die / Wo sie der Stachel schmerzt, sich Träume spinnen / Zum Troste viel, vom Stamm der Armen einer, etc.,* "One of the marvelous, / Those who, when prick of thorn pains them, spin out dreams / That console them greatly, one of the tribe of the wretched, etc."

332 One of the few typographical errors in DKV: delete the commas before and after the word *reden.*

336 "Yes, a stranger here, and in the midst of children." Manes's avowal is almost a direct quotation from Plato's *Timaeus,* one of the dialogues that plays an important role in *The Death of Empedocles* generally—the very names *Critias* and *Hermocrates* probably come from its pages. Near the opening of *Timaeus* (at 21a-26e), Critias, upon a request from Hermocrates, tells a story recounted to him by his eponymous grandfather, a story originally told by Solon, the wisest of the Seven Sages of Greece, to Critias's great-grandfather. Critias says that the story is "altogether true," even though he hears it from his grandfather during the feast of the Apaturia, that is, the festival devoted to the sprites of deception, the Ἀπάτη. According to the story, Solon is told by an old Egyptian priest that neither Solon nor any Greek possesses a sense of history, inasmuch as the Greeks record no events by means of written signs: "O Solon, Solon," says the Egyptian, "you Hellenes are never anything but children, and there is not an old man among you" (22b). The priest elaborates: "When it comes to all the matters of the soul [τὰς ψὺχας πάντες], you are all neophytes; there is no old opinion handed down among you by ancient tradition, nor any body of learning [μάθημα] that is hoary with age" (ibid.). Hölderlin had already cited this passage from *Timaeus* in his *Fragment of Hyperion,* from the summer of 1794 (CHV 1:495, 3:303). Consistently in Hölderlin's works we find a tension between fidelity to ancient tradition (inculcated by the "school of destiny") and the need for a vital relation to that tradition (learned in the "school of nature"). All of Hölderlin's heroes seek to unite these two tendencies of nurture and nature, culture and the larger living world, even if the mark of their success is that they integrate them "too intensely, too uniquely." Perhaps the most interesting aspect of these Egyptian references is the fact that Hölderlin's "Orientalism" combines both tendencies. The Orient is both the seat of ancient wisdom and the often-feared and despised source of a more vital, more erotic relation to tradition and to nature than is common in the Western world. When in 1803 Hölderlin tries to make his translations of Sophocles "more lively," he does so precisely by seeking to revert to a more "Oriental" poetic language—even if, or precisely because, the Greeks themselves tended to suppress the memory of their debt to the East.

351 "The sacrificial beast," *das Opfertier.* Recall the discussion in "The Basis of Empedocles" of Empedocles as a sacrificial victim of his times.

358–88 "For one alone in our time is it fitting." Jochen Schmidt is right to emphasize here Manes's challenge to Empedocles' very identity and the legitimacy of his claims. Here the impact of the theoretical essays that intervene between the second and third versions is most keenly felt, but see also the late hymn, *Der Einzige,* "The Only One." Remarkably, the "one" in question is not only Christ but also all the sons and daughters of Zeus, especially Heracles and Dionysos. The poet yearns for the syncretic or ecumenical brotherhood and sisterhood of all gods, heroes, and heroines. As Hölderlin writes in "The Only One," "If I serve the one / I miss the others."

360–62 "For as the vine / Bears witness to the earth and sky when, saturated by / The lofty sun it rises from dark soil." The word for solar saturation, *getränkt,* reminds us of a fragment of the ancient Empedocles, which speaks of "immortal parts" that are "saturated [δεύεται] by the warmth and glistening rays" of sun and air (DK B21; cf. B73).

370–71 "What flames on high is inflammation, nothing more, and / What strives from down below is savage discord." *Doch was von oben flammt, entzündet nur / Und was von unten strebt, die wilde Zwietracht.* These remarkable lines from Manes could well be inserted into Empedocles' long final speech below, especially at ll. 425–44, on the parting god of one's nation. A close comparison of the two speeches reveals that, to repeat, Manes is not simply an "opponent" of Empedocles. Finally, compare Manes's lines to the concluding words of the "Rhine" hymn:

> . . . oder auch
> Bei Nacht, wenn alles gemischt
> Ist ordnungslos und wiederkehrt
> Uralte Verwirrung.

> . . . or also
> In the night, when all's a jumble
> Devoid of order, and what recurs is
> Primeval confusion.

The "primeval confusion" in question is described in Plato's myth of the ages of the world in *Statesman.* See 273d 1, where the Stranger speaks of τὸ τῆς παλαιᾶς ἀναρμοστίας πάθος, the ancient disharmonies that come to disrupt and bring to an end the prevailing age of the world—that is to say, the age of a humankind bereft of gods and left to its own devices. Such an age is surely dominated by strife, Empedoclean νεῖκος.

422–23 "When fathers failed / To recognize their sons." One of the most dramatic of the fragments from Empedocles' second book, Καθαρμοί, *Purifications,* is DK B137: "And the father, the wretched fool, lifts up his son, whose shape has changed, and slaughters him, muttering a prayer as he does so. . . . And in the same way, the son seizes his father and the children grapple with their mother, tear the life out of them, and engorge themselves on their own flesh." Here the allusion to Tantalus is enriched by the consequences of the doctrine of metempsychosis (transmigration of souls) and the prohibition of meat-eating among the Pythagoreans. For Empedocles of Acragas, the very heart of Νεῖκος and the source of the reign of strife in which humankind now exists is the homicide and cannibalism that have long been the human—if not the humane—practice. Empedocles is touching on nothing less than the problem described so provocatively by Jacques Derrida as "eating well." With respect to killing and eating, Derrida writes:

> In any case, it is a matter of discerning a place left open . . . for a noncriminal putting to death. Such are the executions of ingestion, incorporation, or introjection of the corpse. An operation as real as it is symbolic when the corpse is "animal" (and who can be made to believe that our cultures are carnivorous because animal proteins are irreplaceable?), a symbolic operation when the corpse is "human." . . .
>
> Discourses as original as those of Heidegger and Levinas disrupt, of course, a certain traditional humanism. In spite of the differences separating them, they nonetheless remain profound humanisms *to the extent that they do not sacrifice sacrifice*. . . . It would be a matter not only of recalling the concept of the subject as phallogocentric structure, at least according to its dominant structure: one day I hope to demonstrate that this *schema* implies carnivorous virility . . . : it suffices to take seriously the idealizing interiorization of the phallus and the necessity of its passage through the mouth, whether it's a matter of words or of things, of sentences, of daily bread or wine, of the tongue, the lips, or the breast of the other. . . . The subject does not want just to master and possess nature actively. In our cultures, he accepts sacrifice and eats flesh. . . . The moral question is thus not, nor has it ever been: should one eat or not eat, eat this and not that, the living or the nonliving, man or animal, but since *one must* eat in any case and since it is and tastes good to eat, and since there's no other definition of the good [*du bien*], *how* for goodness' sake should one *eat well* [*bien manger*]? And what does this imply? What is eating? How is this metonymy of introjection to be regulated?

See "'Il faut bien manger,' ou le calcul du sujet," *Confrontation,* Cahiers 20 (Winter 1989): 91–114; see esp. 108–14; now in Derrida, *Points de suspension: Entretiens,* ed. Elisabeth Weber (Paris: Galilée, 1992), 269–301; English translation by Peter Connor and Avital Ronell, in Derrida, *Points . . . : Interviews, 1974–1994,* ed. Elisabeth Weber (Stanford, CA: Stanford University Press, 1995), esp. 278–82. My thanks to Michael Naas for gathering these sources for me. For a presentation of Derrida's views on this subject, see D. F. Krell, "All You Can't Eat: Derrida's Lecture Course *Rhétorique du cannibalisme* (1990)," in the Derrida Memorial Issue of *Research in Phenomenology* 36 (2006), 130–80.

424–25 FHA (although not CHV) reads: *Und an der Flamme menschlichen Gesetz / Zerrann, fasst mich die Deutung schaudernd an,* "And in the flames human law / Melted, the meaning seized me and I trembled, etc." (FHA 13:414, 434).

436 FHA and CHV strike this line.

466 "Her arms of fire, stretching toward the ether." This is reminiscent of Empedocles' fragments B51–54: although fire characteristically "hurries" toward the sky, equally true is that "the ether, by contrast, dives down with its long roots into the earth." Indeed, "many fires burn below ground."

497 "New world." These words appear also at the beginning of "The Fatherland in Decline," which was composed immediately after the "Sketch toward the Continuation of the Third Version."

Notes to the Sketch toward the Continuation of the Third Version

The precise form of the "Sketch" varies in many important details in all the editions. I have followed DKV, but with important emendations from FHA, particularly in the long note on Manes. The sketch does not mention the three scenes that Hölderlin had actually composed; one may therefore presume, for strictly internal reasons, that the sketch postdates those three scenes.

17 "Lyric or epic." For a discussion of these genres, lyric, epic, heroic elegiac, heroic lyrical, and so on, see the essays "Alternation of Tones" (not in the present volume) and "The Fatherland in Decline." In the latter essay, Hölderlin isolates the lyrical and epic elements of tragedy, the lyrical referring to expressions of intense feeling, the epic to heroic actions of individual agents. The remaining designations, "heroic elegiac," "heroic lyrical," and "lyrical heroic," are discussed in Hölderlin's essay "Alternation of Tones."

25 "Empedocles is the one who has been called." Note that in the three scenes we have, however, nothing is less certain than the identity of Empedocles as "the one." It may not be too much to suggest that the sketch does not become a successful blueprint for a continuation of the play precisely because Manes's questions to Empedocles cannot be satisfactorily answered.

28–29 "His country's downgoing . . . its new life." This, we recall, is the central theme of the essay "The Fatherland in Decline."

35 "The festival of Saturn." The Roman Saturnalia were marked by a carnivalesque spirit in which the hierarchy of master and slave was reversed, or at least ignored, for the duration of the festival. In this respect the Saturnalia may not be that far removed from the Greek festival of Apaturia: see the remarks on ll. 323 and 336 in the notes to the third version of the play, above. For Hölderlin, Saturn or Cronos is the Titan who represents the more aorgic nature that underlies and nurtures—but also may counter and frustrate—all art and culture. He is also the shepherd of the Golden Age, in which humanity and nature live in harmony. Compare once again Plato's myth of the ages of Zeus and Cronos in *Statesman.* See also Hölderlin's important poem "Nature and Art, or Saturn and Jupiter" (DKV 1:297–98).

Analysis

IN THE AUTUMN of 1799 Hölderlin writes to Schiller:

> The valuable advice you gave me some time ago, and which your last letter repeats, I have not allowed to remain altogether unheeded; I am earnestly trying to cultivate in myself that tone which, without being capricious, seemed to lie closest to my natural, untrammeled way of thinking. I have now made it a maxim of mine to develop myself solidly in a single form of poetic creation and to attain character before I strive to be versatile. Versatility can only be the property of one who has *achieved* a secure standpoint. I believed I could execute most completely and most naturally the tone I wished to make peculiarly my own in the tragic form, and I have taken up the challenge of a mourning-play [*Trauerspiel*], *The Death of Empedocles*. . . . (CHV 2:819)

Searching for his proper tone and his own voice, so to speak, in an effort to identify his own character and the poetic form that is suitable to it, seeking something that he can declare his own (*Eigentum*) and occupy as a standpoint (*Standpunkt*), Hölderlin chooses the tragic tone that resounds in the legendary figure of ancient philosophy, Empedocles of Acragas. Why try to find one's own in what is antique and foreign? Why search for one's own voice in the throat of another, and why this particular other? Why are tragedy and philosophy conjoined in this way? Finally, why the past tense among those verbs dispatched to Schiller that tell of a project in which he is currently engaged? Is it simply because he has already begun? As we know very well by now, *The Death of Empedocles* is all about a failure, three times the failure to find—or at least to sustain—the voice, three truncations of the same *Trauerspiel*, three sets of ruins.

In this analysis it will not be a matter of subsuming the three versions of Hölderlin's *Der Tod des Empedokles* under any sort of philosophical program, whether of Hölderlin's time or our own, and whether that subsumption wants to close Hölderlin within or liberate him from the supposed confines of German Romanticism and Idealism.[1] To be sure, Hölderlin could readily have affirmed the entire "Oldest Program toward a System in German Idealism," that controversial document ascribed variously to Hölderlin, Schelling, and Hegel (see TA 22–26). Hölderlin's desire for a new relation to the natural sciences, for a "physics with wings," finds voice in Empedocles' *On Nature,* even if that is a generic title attributed to virtually all the thinkers of the Greek tragic age. Hölderlin is as susceptible to that voice as Hegel and Schelling are: like them, Hölderlin surely wishes to reverse the hierarchy of Kantian ethicotheology and physicotheology as developed in the *Critique of Pure Reason* (A620–43). Furthermore, the critique of the state and the church in the "Program" is one that Hölderlin subscribes to; indeed, his *Hyperion* has things to say in this regard that are as harsh as anything produced by his two roommates, Hegel and Schelling. As is universally affirmed, the final paragraphs of the "Oldest Program," on the all-unifying idea of beauty, the restoration of poetry as the instructress of humankind, and the call for a new mythology, have most to do with Hölderlin: when the "Program" insists that beauty is to be taken "in the higher, Platonic sense," we think of Hölderlin's proposed commentary on *Phaedrus,* envisaged in a letter to Neuffer in the autumn of 1794:

> Maybe I can send you an essay on *aesthetic ideas* . . . , which can be taken as a commentary on Plato's *Phaedrus,* since a passage from it serves as my explicit text. . . . Basically, it is to contain an analysis of the beautiful and the sublime, according to which the Kantian analysis can be both simplified and expanded, as Schiller has already shown in part in his treatise *On Charm and Dignity* [*Über Anmut und Würde*], even though Schiller fails to step far enough across the Kantian boundary, in my opinion at least. Wipe that smirk off your face! I may be wrong, but I've been studying the matter, studying it long and hard. (CHV 2:550–51)

Schiller's notion of "charm," *Anmut,* better translated by a combination of gracefulness, graciousness, and grace, is important to Hölderlin: we have seen and heard it in the mouth of Empedocles—this attractive, seductive, sublime, and even uncanny force of nature and rhetorical art—and we cannot

---

1. For an extensive discussion of Hölderlin's relation to Empedocles and a generous selection of documents, see JV 3:352–95. Jamme and Völkel emphasize the political aspects of that relation as well as the affinity of Hölderlin's mourning-play with Hegel's early political and theological essays.

suppress the memory that on one of Hölderlin's report cards a teacher wrote of him, *venusta, liebreizend,* "completely charming." Nevertheless, the unification achieved by beauty becomes, in the course of the three versions of *The Death of Empedocles,* an irrefragably *tragic* unification. This may mean that Hölderlin by this time is taking some distance from the buoyant optimism of the "Program," precisely in the way that his 1795 essay, "Judgment and Being," takes its distance from Fichte—a distance measured by Hölderlin's flight from Jena in May of that year (JV 2:1–51). Whereas Hölderlin may still affirm that the highest act of reason is an aesthetic act and that the philosopher must possess as much aesthetic force as the poet, inasmuch as all the sciences and arts are to be absorbed by *Dichtkunst,* it remains true that the three versions of Hölderlin's mourning-play take distance on all of this—uncanny distance.

As the General Introduction to this volume has already shown, if "Dame Philosophy" is a tyrant from whom Hölderlin is seeking release, it is nonetheless true that many of his extraordinary poetological and theoretical essays are written during the periods of such desired release. Even if Hölderlin is seeking release from the Fichtean absolute ego, and thus taking his departure from much of what we call German Idealism, he is never seeking release from *thinking.* When he listens for the voice that will be his own, he hears one of the greatest thinkers of antiquity. If this is a doubling of voices, it is no accident that the thinker who fascinates Hölderlin is the one who announces δίπλ' ἐρέω, "A twofold tale I shall tell" (DK B17), the thinker who may have confused himself with the gods, the thinker who tells of lovehate in the sphere, and the thinker who tells of an eon that, no matter how long lasting, is radically discontinuous.[2]

The so-called "Frankfurt Plan" of the tragedy, sketched in August 1797, precedes the work on the first draft by more than an entire year. Only in November or December 1798, in Homburg vor der Höhe, in the sanctuary arranged by Isaak von Sinclair, does work on the play itself commence. During that year of latency the Etna scene of *Hyperion* (volume two) and the lyric poem "Empedocles" are probably composed. Work on the *first* draft of the mourning-play stops probably in spring or early summer of 1799; work on the *second* version stops soon after that, in late June or July 1799. Some scholars have suggested that Hölderlin works on both the first and the second versions simultaneously, although the vast difference in versification argues against this. At all events, work on both is interrupted by Hölderlin's need to devote his time to a planned mensal review of poetry and criticism, *Iduna,* designed

2. See D. F. Krell, "Δίπλ' ἐρέω, 'A Double Tale I Shall Tell . . .': Empedocles and Hölderlin on Tragic Nature and Tragic Purification," *Epoché* 11:2 (Spring 2007), 287–304.

to reach a female audience, as well as the need to work on a commissioned narrative-epistolary poem titled "Emily on the Eve of Her Wedding." Hölderlin discusses the latter in a letter to Neuffer dated July 3, 1799, and we will examine it in a moment. Juxtaposing "Emily" with "Empedocles" is useful for insight into the difference between tragic and sentimental poetry, as Hölderlin practices them, inasmuch as the difference between *essence* and *accident* is expressed in that juxtaposition. Finally, completing the chronology, Hölderlin composes his theoretical text, "The Basis of Empedocles," in October or November 1799. He thereupon begins the *third* and final attempt in December—even if the September letter to Schiller, cited at the outset, uses those verbs in the past tense, as though the final failure has already been anticipated.

Luckily, several ideas expressed in the Frankfurt Plan are dropped in the execution of the play, such as the idea of having the central conflict revolve about a quarrel between Empedocles and his wife. Yet some aspects of the plan remain relevant, especially its famous opening paragraph:

> Empedocles, by temperament and through his philosophy long since destined to despise his culture, to scorn all neatly circumscribed affairs, every interest directed to sundry objects; an enemy to the death of all one-sided existence, and therefore also in actually beautiful relations unsatisfied, restive, suffering, simply because they are special relations, ones that fulfill him utterly only when they are felt in magnificent accord with all living things; simply because he cannot live in them and love them intimately, with omnipresent heart, like a god, and freely and expansively, like a god; simply because as soon as his heart and his thought embrace anything at hand he finds himself bound to the law of succession—[.] (DKV 2:421)

"Unsatisfied, restive, suffering." The secret of the affinity between Hölderlin and Empedocles, according to Max Kommerell, lies in the quality of this suffering. Kommerell puts it rather cryptically, yet the more time and effort one devotes to a study of *The Death of Empedocles* the more telling his analysis becomes. As though speaking of the two, Hölderlin and Empedocles together, Kommerell writes:

> Childhood did not speak out, but it did possess; manhood does speak out, but it is missing something. Such suffering assumes different forms—as we know from Hölderlin's own communications about himself at the various stages of his life. Such suffering is the mourning of one who loves. Whereas lovers reconcile between themselves all disconnectedness [*Geschiedenheit*], restoring the unity of the world in the personal life of a twosome, the lament of lovers is the most passionate experience of disconnectedness. It unfolds as three states, which determine the sequence

> of other themes in Hölderlin as well: as the shadowy state of missing someone, which is a Hades of the soul, as the state of memorializing the one who is missed, in which the all-surmising pangs of love open up the universe, and as the state of reconstitution, which mystically shifts the boundaries between our life in time and primeval life as such [*zwischen zeitlichem Leben und Urleben*]. (MK 320)

Kommerell summarizes his views on the shared suffering of Hölderlin and the ancient Empedocles in these words: "In the beginning was the suffering—missing all that is good in human interaction and in the actual world, the good that defined the poet's disposition from the very outset" (MK 336).

In the manuscript of the Frankfurt Plan, which is Hölderlin's first effort to outline his play, Sattler notes the name "Empedocles" and then eight empty lines, the next phrase being, "an enemy to the death of all one-sided existence" (FHA 12:20). Trapped within successive time, existence seems to be invariably one-sided, and omnipresence a mere dream. A more penetrating thinking through of temporal succession, of course, would require us to review Kant's "Transcendental Exposition of the Concept of Time" in the Transcendental Aesthetics of the *Critique of Pure Reason,* along with the Deduction in the second edition, where succession is treated as the result of a movement or action, in addition to the Schematism and the first two Analogies of Experience. We may assume that Hölderlin studied all these passages diligently during and immediately after his university years. Without going into detail, we may isolate a few Kantian propositions from these sections of the first *Critique.* First, only in successive time can two opposite and contradictory predicates be conjoined in one and the same object, that is, one after the other—indeed, this is a mere repetition of Aristotle's law of noncontradiction. Second, time is nothing other than the form of our inner sensibility, that is, our intuition of ourselves and of our interior condition. Third, this intuition has no form of its own, hence relies on the analogy of the line; the analogy is essentially faulty, however, inasmuch as the points of a line are contiguous and simultaneous, whereas the parts of time are always successive.

The relation of succession to one-sidedness is developed in a text Hölderlin wrote during the period of the Frankfurt Plan, a text Friedrich Beissner's and Jochen Schmidt's editions call "Reflections," Sattler's and Knaupp's editions "Seven Maxims" (DKV 2:519–22; FHA 14:43–45, 47–48). The penultimate aphorism tells us that because we come to know all relations only successively, we need to repeat them if an intuition is to become truly "lively" in us. Even so, when we merely grasp things repeatedly in the intellect, our knowledge is "one-sidedly askew." Hölderlin opposes such intellectual grappling to the recurrent revelations of love, which "is pleased to uncover tenderly" (*Da hingegen die Liebe gerne zart entdeckt*). Love, perhaps in all three states referred to earlier by Kommerell (lamentation, memorial, mystic reconstitution), intuits the whole nexus of relations "more intensely and more intimately" (*inniger*) than intellect can. Again we see the word *innig*, which appears in the Frankfurt Plan and in the essays on the tragic. Intensity is of the essence for Hölderlin, as it is for the Greeks: every "sudden heightening of intensity," according to Roberto Calasso, brings one "into a god's sphere of influence" (RC 95; cf. 283–84), a circumstance that, to be sure, may be a blessing or a curse. Often enough, the conflict between knowledge through the intellect and knowledge through love produces *Trauer*, the suffering and mournfulness that presumably get expressed in a mourning-play. In his "Seven Maxims" Hölderlin writes of "the profound feeling of mortality, of change, of life's temporal limits" (FHA 14:44, 48). A mournful sense of disconnectedness and loss thus always accompanies hopes for unification. Hölderlin's Empedocles, who spent his childhood in an amiable unification of nature and art, overindulged by the gods, undergoes this mourning process. His challenge is not to let chagrin or rancor destroy his life. "For he has attained much who can understand life without mourning," says the maxim (ibid.). Not to try to attain too much, not to hope for too intense a unity, not to seek to expunge the horizon of *Trauer*, not to try to escape the inevitable season of mourning with excessive hopes, yet also not to founder under the burden of an unending grief—that is perhaps Empedocles' double challenge, his balancing act on the crater's edge. The profound feeling of mortality may spur us to exercise all our forces, but it may also cause us to conjure up "some sort of phantom" and to "close our eyes" (ibid.). How, then, can we keep our eyes open to the unforgiving law of succession without losing heart? Is the hope for omnipresence a stimulant to our forces or a soporific phantom?

Two appearances of this omnipresence in the first draft of *The Death of Empedocles* may shed light on the problem. In act 2, scene 4, Empedocles tells Critias that it is not Empedocles himself that the people need. What should speak to them are "The flowers of the sky, the blossoms of the stars / And all those stars on earth, the myriad germinations; / Divinely present nature / Needs no speech" (ll. 1594–98). *Göttlichgegenwärtig* is Empedocles' word here for nature. Presence as such is the recurrence of the gods of nature. In the previous scene, immediately after his "transformation" into an essentially affirmative spirit, Empedocles tells Pausanias the same. They will climb the slopes of Etna to its summit, where the gods are more present still:

> Have you not seen? They are recurring
> The lovely times of my entire life again today
> And something greater still is yet to come;
> Then upward, son, upward to the very peak
> Of ancient holy Etna, that is where we'll go
> For gods have greater presence on the heights[.]
> (ll. 1169–74)

Yet for all the emphasis on presence and recurrence, the vanished past is what haunts Empedocles. His unity with the gods is, at present, only a memory. Whether that memory can be affirmed, that is, experienced affirmatively, or whether it must be suffered in bitterness and regret during the reign of dreary succession, or ticking off of the hours, is Empedocles' problem.

The question of memory may also be raised with regard to "Emily on the Eve of Her Wedding," the poem that interrupted work on both the first and second versions of *Empedocles* (DKV 2:579–600). The poem itself, a narrative-epistolary poem rather than a dramatic one, is full of contingencies and accidents, actually quite bizarre ones. Emily tells the tale in a series of letters to Clara. Emily recounts her brother Eduard's death in the Corsican wars and her encounter with Armenion—who is the exact double of her brother, a sort of fraternal doppelgänger. She tells of her father's initial opposition to their marriage and the eventual reconciliation. The duplex or duplicitous simulacrum of the brother-lover, Eduard-Armenion, remains disconcerting, however. In the forest with her father on the eve of her wedding, Emily sees—quite close by—her dead brother. Even though mentioning accidents of biography in a literary or philosophical context is indiscreet, worth noting perhaps is that Hölderlin himself was, for Susette Gontard, the exact image of her brother Henry—on whom she doted and after whom she named her only son. It is not a matter of incest, neither in life nor in the work, nor yet a reference forward or back to Antigone, who unites her brother and lover in death. Here it is simply a matter of the question of accidents—of the accidental and contingent. The final section of the Frankfurt Plan, which we have ignored until now, confronts the issue of contingency and accident when it outlines Empedocles' ripening resolve to unite himself with infinite nature and its gods by means of a voluntary death. The plan for act 5 reads:

> Empedocles prepares himself for his death. The accidental occasions [*zufälligen Veranlassungen*] of his resolve fall away altogether for him, and he now regards that resolve as a necessity proceeding from his inmost essence. In the brief scenes that he has here and there with the people who dwell in the region, he finds on all sides confirmation of his way of thinking, his resolve. His favorite arrives on Etna once again, having intimated the truth; yet the young man is so completely overwhelmed by his master's spirit and by the magnificent animatedness of the master's inmost heart that he blindly obeys his command and departs. Soon after that Empedocles casts himself into the searing flames of Etna. His favorite, wandering disconsolate and distracted through the region, soon finds an iron shoe, his master's shoe, which the volcano has catapulted from its abysses; he recognizes it, shows it to Empedocles' family and to

> his disciples among the populace; he gathers with these disciples at the volcano's edge in order to express their sorrow and to celebrate the great man's death. (DKV 2:424; FHA 12:24–25, 28)

The question, of course, is what these "accidental occasions" in the drama will have been and how they can be separated off from Empedocles' "inmost essence." One does not want the incidents leading to an "ideal deed and at the end" to turn up like bronzed shoes. Camus says somewhere that a person commits suicide because while he or she is in a phone booth making a call another person waiting to get into the booth scowls. A stranger's taciturn curse is enough. Even in ultimate situations, and especially there, knowing and portraying dramatically what is essence and what accident is difficult. Recall the marginal note at the beginning of act 2 of the first version, the note in which Hölderlin himself retreats from the notion of a voluntary death, that is, a death that would express Empedocles' inmost essence, and broaches instead all those unworthy accidents, banalities, and contingencies that propel the thinker in the direction of death: "Here the sufferings and humiliations to which he is exposed must be presented in such a way that it is impossible for him ever to return, so that his resolution to go to the gods appears to be more forced upon him than voluntarily chosen" (ll. 1066/67).

In his July 3, 1799 letter to Neuffer, about the time when work on the first two versions of his mourning-play ceases, we read that the material for "Emily" is not at all heroic, but sentimental. Yet the identical problem arises here as well, namely, how to avoid mere "submission to old forms," on the one hand, and sheer "rulelessness," on the other. If one tries to write a love story in the heroic style of the ancients, the lovers always sound as though they are quarreling. For a mourning-play, what seems fitting is a tone of grandeur, in which each scene follows on the last without any sort of embellishment, in "alternating harmony." One who writes a mourning-play must avoid the temptation of inserting something brilliant or tender (*Glänzendes oder Zärtliches*), and must practice a "proud renunciation of everything accidental" (CHV 2:781). A love story, by contrast, needs to affirm *"this tender awe in the face of the accidental* [zarte Scheue des Akzidentellen]" (ibid.). The problem with *The Death of Empedocles* is that Empedocles' heroism is a heroism of love—love of nature and the earth, love of the gods, but also love of Pausanias and Panthea. Or are these two characters mere accidents? And is love of the earth too a mere accident? Can the distinction between the heroic and the sentimental be maintained in dramatic practice?

If the doubts entertained by the two "favorites" of Empedocles eventually become the hero's own doubts, then regarding either these personages or their words as mere accidents or sentimentalities is impossible. It may well be that Delia, called Rhea early in the first draft, in the opening moments of the play asks the crucial question: *Wie lebt er mit andern?* "How does he live with others?" (l. 25). Panthea is the one who best recognizes Empedocles' suffering, his longing and languishing—*Sehnen* is her word. Even though she shies away from him ("A terrifying, all-transforming essence is in him" [l. 23]), she is nonetheless "a tender reflection" of his light: ". . . *und ich war der zarte / Widerschein von ihm*" (ll. 63–64). Both Delia and Panthea are tender awe personified; yet they are essential, and not accidental, to the central conflict of the play. Moreover, the second version ends with words spoken by Panthea yet taken from the very mouth of Empedocles' "inmost essence," perhaps the most famous of all the trochees of this second version:

> So will es der Geist
> Und die reifende Zeit
> Denn Einmal bedurften
> Wir Blinden des Wunders.
> (DKV 2:387)

> Thus wills the spirit,
> Time ripens and nears it,
> For, if only once,
> We blind ones required a miracle!
> (ll. 730–33)

In the third version, Panthea is to be no longer the woman who has been cured by Empedocles, no longer his "tender reflection," but his sister. To be sure, siblings too may be tender reflections, as "Emily" demonstrates and as Antigone will have proven. *Schwester naiv. idealisch,* say the plans. Are we to regard this as a reduction of Panthea's role? What speaks against such reduction is that her brother, Empedocles himself, is also designated as naive and idealizing, or "ideating": *Empedokles naiv. idealisch.* If the tender reflection is an accident, the hero is himself that accident: *zart* and *zärtlich,* "tender, tenderly," no matter how much our tradition wants us to relegate the words (and the things) to the sentimental and to melodrama, are among the most important words for both Hölderlin and Hölderlin's Empedocles.[3]

---

3. In the first chapter of *Lunar Voices,* I argued that the importance of the female characters of Hölderlin's drama *The Death of Empedocles* did not—whatever appeared to be the case—diminish but grew as the three versions of the play succeeded one another. Although Hölderlin's Empedocles is more than willing to soliloquize for himself, and out of his own mouth, so to speak, the poet needed the women Panthea and Delia (Rhea) to express his deepest insights. As Max Kommerell argues (MK 337), Panthea is the only one who understands Empedocles' suffering. She is the one who is

The question of Empedocles' blasphemy or sacrilege, his *nefas,* is doubtless also of the essence in the first two versions of the play. Hölderlin uses the word *nefas* in the "General Basis," and he continues to use it later in the 1803 "Notes on Oedipus" (DKV 2:851–52). Normally, one would translate *nefas* as blasphemy, sacrilege, or sin, related to the tragic flaw in a hero, Aristotle's ἁμαρτία. Yet Hölderlin never ceases to ask himself the questions, what *is* the hero and *who* may *become* a hero? Hovering somewhere between the celestial ones and the mortals, the hero approximates a demigod or a δαίμων in Plato's sense. How then can we, from our more lowly perspective, determine the hero's "flaw" or "sin"? If Tantalus is a paradigm of the hero, that paradigm is difficult to understand—even and precisely in the hero's most unspeakable deeds. The reference to Tantalus in act 1, scene 3 of the first draft arises in the context of Empedocles' accusation against himself in the antistrophe to his grand soliloquy, "Into my stillness you came":

---

determined by nature and by love to be, again in Kommerell's words, "the woman who interprets the world" and "the woman who interprets the interpreter" (ibid.). Panthea is therefore the new Diotima, until Panthea's place in turn is taken—if it ever can taken—by Manes in the third and final version of *Empedocles.* If the seer Manes *can* take Panthea's, Delia's, and Diotima's place at all, however, it is because Manes, like Tiresias, is somehow double-natured, of Orient and Occident, and is a woman-man. All these characters are remnants or remainders of Rhea, the daughter of Gaia; we will have to return to them in the course of the analysis. The questions I wish to pose here with regard to Hölderlin's *Der Tod des Empedokles* have not changed much since the first two chapters of *Lunar Voices.* Yet I would formulate them now in the following way. First, the question of time as decline, the downfall of an individual within a native land and an entire culture that are themselves in downgoing. Such individual and universal catastrophe appears in and as the eternal return of the tragic—the tragic absolute, if you will. Can one say *yes* to such an absolute? Second, the question of tragic unification (*die tragische Vereinigung*) as languor and languishment, and the relation of sensuality and sexuality—the remnants of Rhea, as it were—to tragedy. Third, the question of the omnipresence of Empedocles throughout the epochs of Western philosophical and poetic history, from the tragic age of the Greeks to Luce Irigaray's *The Forgetting of Air.* For further discussion, see the first two chapters in LV 3–51. Irigaray's *L'Oubli de l'air chez Martin Heidegger* (Paris: Minuit, 1983) appears in an English translation by Mary Beth Mader, *The Forgetting of Air in Martin Heidegger* (Austin: University of Texas Press, 1999). On the issue of tenderness, see D. F. Krell, "Tenderness: Aristotle, Hölderlin, Freud, Lacan, Irigaray," in *Mosaic* 39:1 (March 2006), 24–43. See, finally, Françoise Dastur's wonderful book, *Tragédie et modernité,* reissued under the title *Hölderlin: le retournement natal* (La Versanne, France: Encre marine, 1997), 25–96.

. . . you have
Yourself to blame, you wretched Tantalus
The sacred precincts you've besmirched,
With haughty pride revoked the covenant,
Pernicious one! (ll. 328–32)

The first letter to Böhlendorff (CHV 2:914) speaks of "old Tantalus, who became more of gods than he could digest" (*dem alten Tantalus, der mehr von Göttern ward, als er verdauen konnte*). We recall the myth: Tantalus served up his own son to the gods, who of course refused to partake—refused to be "tantalized." Perhaps Empedocles of Acragas is thinking precisely of Tantalus when in fragment B137 of the Καθαρμοί he portrays in such ghastly hues the father, the fool, sacrificing his son. Yet in Hölderlin's account, Tantalus does not offer something to the gods, but the gods offer something to Tantalus, something excessive, more than *he* can digest. Uncanny reversal! A key question for the very idea of the heroic would be, who tantalizes whom? Who is *capable* of tantalizing whom? When it comes to gods and heroes, where perfection and excess meet in an economy of sacrifice, the victim and the victimizer are never clearly separable. As for perfection, Calasso tells us that for the Greeks it "brings death upon itself, since one can't have fullness without spillage, and what spills out is the excess that sacrifice claims for itself" (RC 111).

With Empedocles, therefore, the question is how and why he tantalizes the gods, how he is capable of tantalizing them. Is it his destiny to tantalize them? In that case, they would be tantalizing him, as they once tantalized Tantalus and others—such as Oedipus. Four textual references, two on the side of *nefas*, implying Empedocles' guilt, and two on the side of fate or destiny, set this dilemma in sharp relief. In act 1, scene 2, of the first version, Hermocrates says that Empedocles "sits in the dark, soulless" ever since the day "the man, besotted, to be sure, in front of all / The people recklessly proclaimed himself a god" (l. 189–90). At this point Hölderlin enters a marginal note on the difference between modernity and antiquity with regard to this blasphemy. For us moderns, Empedocles' sin is a crime against the intellect. To proclaim oneself a god is a very stupid mistake. For the ancients, by contrast, it was not a nonsensical thing to do, but a crime, a crime they will not forgive, inasmuch as it offends their "delicate sense of freedom" (*ihr zarter Freiheitssinn*). Because they esteemed the genius more than we do, says Hölderlin, they were more profoundly afraid of his haughtiness and excessive pride (*Übermut*). In the same scene, Hermocrates (sometimes called the "old man," as Manes too will be in the third draft) says that the secret of Empedocles' crime is that he is "forgetful of the difference" between himself and the gods (l. 215). Here, now, are two textual references suggesting that tantalization is Empedocles' destiny, not the sign of his guilt or his flaw. In the very scene in which Hermocrates condemns Empedocles, he compares the thinker to those worshipers of Asia who carry a staff reminiscent of the thyrsus. Yet this puts Hermocrates in the position of Euripides' Pentheus and Empedocles in the position of the god Dionysos. *Übermütig*, the word that was applied to haughty Cleopatra in the lyric poem, is now used to depict both Empedocles and the Bacchants, the holy worshipers of Dionysos. (Pentheus too, however, will soon inevitably occupy the position of the god—as fragmented—when he becomes the surrogate victim, Dionysos Zagreus himself.) In scene 5, when Critias incites the people against Empedocles, Empedocles in effect compares himself to Pelops, the ill-fated son of Tantalus: "Come on! tear the flesh and share the prey / And let your priest beg blessings on your meal, / His family friends, all those avenger gods, he has invited!—" (ll. 725–27). This puts Empedocles in the position of the sacrificed son, not the foolish father. Indeed, as the "Basis" says, Empedocles is literally the son of his times, and he will be sacrificed as such. In short, determining whether Empedocles' words are those of an insane hubris or a measured knowledge of the lot that has fallen to him is virtually impossible. In act 2, scene 4 of the first version, Empedocles replies to Hermocrates, who has come (in bad faith) to invite Empedocles back into the city:

> Die
> Your vulgar death, it's only fitting, with
> The feelings of a soulless knave; to me
> Another lot has fallen; another path
> You gods once prophesied when I was born
> For you were present then—[.] (ll. 1319–24).

A marginal note by Hölderlin to act 1, scene 4 of version one (at line 466), states the paradox quite well. The context is Empedocles' admission to Pausanias that he has committed a grave sin, the "original" sin of insolent pride (*im frechen Stolz*). In the right margin of the manuscript Hölderlin jots the following note: "His sin is the original sin, and therefore is absolutely nothing abstract, just as little as supreme joy is something abstract; it is merely that this has to be presented in a genetically vital way" (FHA 12:60, 192). The *drama* requires that Empedocles' misdeed be brought forcefully onto the stage. Yet if there is something fateful or fated about that misdeed, how can one prevent its seeming to be generic and abstract? Pausanias's exclamation at the end of the first draft is infinitely abstract: "What can the son of gods do? / For infinitely all the infinite are struck" (ll. 2014–15). How is the playwright to portray on the stage the particularity of Empedocles' "insolent pride" if in fact the gods have elected him, if indeed he is "the One"?

The opposition between *nefas* and destiny is posed with even greater force in the second version of the play. Already the opposition seems to be beyond resolution, the conflict beyond remedy. This conflict may destroy the drama as such, inasmuch as it is fatally interwoven with the problem of Empedocles' melancholy and bitterness. For *ressentiment* might readily stir in one who since his birth is destined to become more of the gods than he can digest. The following lines from "The Rhine" show us how profoundly Hölderlin respected the fateful power of birth:

> For
> The way you began is the way you'll remain;
> Necessity too works many effects,
> And discipline; yet most
> Is achieved by birth
> And by the beam of light
> That goes to greet the newborn.
> (ll. 47–53; CHV 1:343)

Often enough, however, an obsession with birth arises from the spirit of vengeance: "For revenge goes backward," says a late fragment (CHV 1:424). Is Empedocles' ideal deed a forward leap or a slipping back into melancholy and anger? Does Empedocles contemplate the plunge into Mount Etna to embrace and affirm Mother Earth? Or does he mean to join forces with Typhon, Zeus's final enemy, who lies coiled in impotent rancor at the base of the volcano (pseudo-Aeschylus, *Prometheus Bound,* ll. 363–65)? We notice in the second draft a proliferation of explanations surrounding Empedocles' supposed *nefas,* the ostensible fault or sin of Empedocles. He is identified (in scene 1) as Prometheus the Titan, the one who stole fire from heaven and gave it to mortals. Hermocrates says that Empedocles is a spoiled child of the gods, one who was excessively happy in his youth, so that he is bound to be disappointed in later life. Finally, Hermocrates chides Empedocles for having loved mortals excessively—again, like Prometheus—and for having in the end been betrayed by the very ones he loved, in this case, by the citizens of Agrigent. Finally, Empedocles has betrayed a sworn secret—Hölderlin here picking up on Diogenes Laertius's report that the philosopher was accused of having exposed certain aspects of the Pythagorean mysteries. Mecades (formerly Critias) is reluctant to affirm these accusations and to join in Empedocles' persecution; his reluctance mirrors that of the spectator or reader who is aware that Empedocles has been destined or fated to his exceptional position. If the gods have spoiled him—well, then, the *gods* have spoiled him.

Perhaps the most philosophical facet of Empedocles' possible *nefas* appears in the magus's strange speech to Pausanias in scene three of version two. Pausanias feels that the speech is out of character and so takes it as mere sarcasm and self-mockery. Yet Empedocles seems to be speaking of his own past—which is actually the *future* of Kantian-Fichtean subjectivity in philosophy—in what follows:

> Correct! I know it all, can master all.
> I recognize it as my handiwork, I know it through
> And through; I steer it as I like, for I'm
> A lord of spirits, I am everything that is alive.
> The world is mine, and as servants are
> Subservient, so are all the forces now to me,
>
> she's become my handmaid
> This nature, she needs a lord. And if
> She still has honor, then it derives from me.
> For what would be the sky and sea
> And isle and star, and everything
> That lies before the eyes of man, what would
> It be, this mummery of thrumming strings, did I
> Not give it sound and speech and soul? what are
> The gods and what their spirit if I do not
> Proclaim them? now! say, who am I? (ll. 499–514)

Here *nefas* is the subjective idealism of Fichte run amok—the Faustian confidence in technique and mastery, or the reduction of nature and nature's gods to what the essays on the tragic call "sheer serviceability." Both the overweening confidence in subjectivity and the ruthless reduction of nature trouble every thoughtful mind down to our own times. Yet the question that troubles us most is whether Faust can be held accountable for the mess we are in, or whether something like a "destining of being" has brought us to this impasse. For it belongs to Faustian subjectivity that it deny fate any role, that it delude itself with thoughts of total control. "Now! say, who am I?" is not a mere taunt but a genuine question, perhaps equivalent to Kant's famous fourth question, *Was ist der Mensch?*

Some of the issues we have been discussing may be clarified when we analyze the *style* of the three drafts of *The Death of Empedocles,* that is, their versification, diction, and poetic form. Which issues? Without imposing a hierarchical order, we may list the following: the conflict between the supposition of a tragic flaw in Empedocles' character and the realization that in the case of Empedocles all is destiny; the problem of Empedocles' time as one of inevitable downgoing and decline, which raises the problem of any possible affirmation of a sacrifice made to that time; and the role of those characters in the play who may seem "accidental" but whose accident has to do with love—hence with Empedocles' inmost essence.

Certain formal aspects of the three drafts can be identified and stated succinctly. Hölderlin initially chose for his play the then current form of *Trauerspiel,* that is, a piece in five acts, with each act divided into multiple scenes, the whole presented in elevated diction and set in iambic pentameter, that is, five feet of one short and one long syllable each, or one each of unaccented and accented syllables—in a word, blank verse, what Charles Olson calls "iambic five" and the French, delightfully, *va-VOOM cinq.* What has to be said at the outset is that whereas Hölderlin strives to remain true to some formal strictures, such as the five-act requirement, he never adheres slavishly to any given meter, not in any of the drafts. Here we find little *va-VOOM.* The second version often cuts the line after three iambs (the antistrophe of "Into my stillness . . ." offers an apt example of this), and is otherwise full of metric variation. We noted earlier the particularly effective use of trochees *("So will es der Geist / Und die reifende Zeit").* The third version returns to blank verse, yet differs from the first in a way that is difficult to explain though easy to hear: it is the compressed, compact, trenchant, mature style—the inimitable style of the famous late hymns.

A comparison of the three initial soliloquies Empedocles speaks in the three versions may make the formal comparison more concrete. The second reprints the opening strophe of *In meine Stille* almost verbatim, which is quite surprising in view of the alteration of the length of the lines from the first to the second version. Yet the antistrophe is greatly altered: in the second version, the antistrophe is prolonged, its tone intensified, the change in mood from despair to defiance more brusque, as are the lines themselves:

> Weit will ichs um mich machen, tagen solls
> Von eigner Flamme mir! Du sollst
> Zufrieden werden, armer Geist,
> Gefangener! (DKV 2:373; FHA 13:273, 316)
>
> I want some space about me; dawn shall rise
> From my own flame! You should be
> At peace, you wretched spirit,
> You prisoner! (ll. 333–36)

The final strophe of the soliloquy in the second version achieves greater calm, as "The Tragic Ode" says it must. In keeping with the ultimate undecidability of *nefas* and destiny, it borrows and yet transforms some of the concluding lines from the soliloquy in the first version:

> Ist nirgend ein Rächer, und muß ich denn allein
> Den Hohn und Fluch in meine Seele sagen?

Muß einsam sein auch so?
(DKV 2: 374; FHA 13:274, 317; cf. 12:189)

Is there nowhere an avenger; must I then alone
Pronounce contempt and curse upon my soul?
Am I to be alone in this as well? (ll. 359–61)

The first soliloquy of Empedocles in the third version is markedly different. It opens the drama and therefore has to recount everything that the earlier versions dramatized. The tone of the soliloquy resists description—one is tempted to say simply that its tone and style are "sovereign." Note in this soliloquy the altered diction and word selection, the striking assonances and alliterations:

Euch ruf ich über das Gefild herein
Vom langsamen Gewölk, ihr heißen Strahlen
Des Mittags, ihr Gereiftesten, daß ich
An euch den neuen Lebenstag erkenne.
(DKV 2:398; FHA 13:374–75, 421)

To you I call across the fields that you
May come eluding sluggish clouds, hot rays
Of midday, you ripest rays, that I may know
Through you this new day of my life. (ll. 1–4)

The "sovereign" flow of the words is of course deceptive: in the manuscript, between the second and third lines, numerous tentative lines are sketched, then scratched out. Sattler's composite (variorum) text is nowhere as nightmarishly difficult as it is here. Yet in the end the words are gathered as parts of a composite whole, suggested by the three *Ge*-words that are themselves collective nouns: *Gefild, Gewölk, Gereiftesten.*

Earlier we looked at the lines in the first version that invoke Tantalus. In the second version the name *Tantalus* disappears, yet the diction and versification of the lines that invoke *nefas* and its consequences seem to intensify the affect that arises from tantalization. Empedocles is addressing nature, which he now says must despise and banish him because he is the one who has betrayed her:

Dein Geächteter!—weh! hab ich doch auch
Dein nicht geachtet, dein
Mich überhoben, hast du
Umfangend, doch mit den warmen Fittigen einst

Du Zärtliche! mich vom Schlafe gerettet?
(DKV 2:373; FHA 13:273, 317)

The one you banished!—woe! since I
Did not respect you, raised
Myself above you; did you not
Embrace me once with your warm plumage
You tender one! and rescue me from sleep? (ll. 344–48)

The initial three broken lines here, filled with monosyllabic words and hard consonants, are suddenly softened by the fourth and fifth lines, which introduce the memory of a more harmonious and tender relation with nature and her gods.

In the opening line of the first soliloquy (in versions one and two), *In meine Stille kamst du leise wandelnd,* one notes the liquidity of the *l*'s, the elegiac tone suited to the images of plant life, flowing streams, and light. In the antistrophe (in both versions, in spite of the many alterations to the lines) the tone is suddenly cold, even brittle; the lines are broken by rhetorical questions and cries of grief, all with a superabundance of harsh consonants:

—vertrocknet bin
Ich nun, und nimmer freun die Sterblichen
Sich meiner—bin ich ganz allein? und ist
Es Nacht hier oben auch am Tage? weh!
(DKV 2: 290; cf. 372; FHA 12:48, 188; cf. 13:316)

—desiccated now
Am I, no more do mortals take their joy
In me—am I all alone? and is it now night
Up here, the daylight notwithstanding? woe!
(ll. 302–5; cf., in version two, 300–2)

The final strophe of the soliloquy in the second version adds something new, however: a lamentation without any sign of aggression, rancor, or resentment—what Whitman, with reference to "Out of the Cradle Endlessly Rocking," calls a *threnody:*

Weh! einsam! einsam! einsam!
Und nimmer find ich
Euch, meine Götter,
Und nimmer kehr ich
Zu deinem Leben, Natur!
(DKV 2:373; FHA 13:273, 317)

Woe! lonely! lonely! lonely!
And never will I find
You, my gods,
And never more will I return
To your life, nature! (ll. 339–43)

Perhaps this threnodic style will help introduce one of the most important issues or themes of all three versions of *The Death of Empedocles,* a theme the analysis has ignored almost entirely. It may be no accident that only closer attention to the *language* of the poems enables us to descry this theme—which is *fidelity to the earth.* It is a theme expressed by the elemental thinker Empedocles, the thinker of all four "roots," whom one might otherwise easily take to be—in Hölderlin's version at least—excessively ethereal, solar, and celestial. Fidelity to the earth is expressed in act 1, scene 4, of the first draft when Empedocles speaks to Pausanias, inasmuch as Empedocles' love of Pausanias is sealed in their mutual devotion to nature and the earth:

So ward auch mir das Leben zum Gedicht.
Denn deine Seele war in mir, und offen gab
Mein Herz wie du der ernsten Erde sich
Der Leidenden und oft in heilger Nacht
Gelobt' ichs – ˘ ihr, bis in den Tod
Die Schicksalvolle furchtlos treu zu lieben
Und ihrer Rätsel keines zu verschmähn.
(DKV 2:293; FHA 12:54–55, 190)

For me as well this life became a poem.
Your soul was in me; openly my heart,
Like yours, gave itself unto the earnest earth
The suffering one and oft in holy night
I swore to – ˘ her, unto death
To love with fearless faith the fateful one
And not to scorn a single one of all her mysteries.
(ll. 383–89)

The allusions to the second choral ode of Sophocles' *Antigone* are surely no accident here: the long-suffering earth, earnest and fateful, scarred by the plows and machines of men, is the object of the hero's love. "All-patient nature!" exclaims the third version, and continues:

Du hast mich, und es dämmert zwischen dir
Und mir die alte Liebe wieder auf

Du rufst, du ziehst mich nah und näher an.
Vergessenheit—o wie ein glücklich Segel
Bin ich vom Ufer los,

Und wenn die Woge wächst, und ihren Arm
Die Mutter um mich breitet, o was möcht'
Ich auch, was möcht' ich fürchten. Andre mag
Es freilich schröken. Denn es ist ihr Tod.
(DKV 2:399; cf. FHA 13:377–79, 422)

You have me; between the two of us
The old love kindles once again
You call, you draw me close and closer to yourself.
Oblivion—oh, like a happy sailing ship
I've left the lee shore,

And when the wave would whelm me, then
My mother's arm embraces me; oh what have I
To fear, is there anything to fear. Others may
Be terrified of this. For it is the death of them. (ll. 43–50)

Here too the inimitable sovereign style—what Beda Allemann once called the hard rhythmic jointures—is not so easily won: between the first and second lines quoted here, the manuscript shows a full page of false starts, tenuous continuations, emendations, and restorations. Other lines seem to come quite readily, for example, those final lapidary phrases, almost an imitation of what is spoken in the streets: "Sure, others will be scared stiff by this. It's going to kill them." Preceding this direct language—which, incidentally, the late hymns always manage to insert when we are least expecting it—is an elegiac style that celebrates mother love and sexual love in the same embrace—the sweet assonances and alliterations of *wenn die Woge wächst,* the softness of the murmured *m*'s, *es dämmert . . . Mutter um mich . . . möcht' . . . möcht'.* The sweetness and softness are suddenly dispersed by the intrusion of the reality from which Empedocles has for the moment concealed himself: for the others, the mere mortals, the crater means death; for him, the embrace of the mother. The challenge for an ideating and thoughtful Empedocles is to not allow that embrace to obscure the mortal destiny, that is, his own impending death; to not allow the thought of eternal return to betray the earth with thoughts of a Typhon's revenge. For such a betrayal would mean the surrender of tragic intensity. Roberto Calasso affirms the importance of "the acceptance of a life without redemption, without salvation, without hope of repetition, circumscribed by the precarious wonder of its brief apparition. . . . It is only because life is irretrievable and unrepeatable that the glory of appearance can reach such intensity" (RC 117).

Other characters in the play, especially Panthea and Delia, often appropriate the voice of Empedocles, speaking from out of his "spirit and mouth," nowhere more so than when expressing fidelity to the earth. In the very first scene of the first version, Panthea says to Delia, ". . . here he feels like / A god within his element; his joy intones / A canticle of heaven" (ll. 85–87; FHA 12:35, 181). And again: "O eternal mystery, what we are / And what we seek, we cannot find; and what / We find, that we are not" (ll. 167–69; FHA 12:39, 183). When Delia (that is, Rhea) asks her how she knows so much about Empedocles, Panthea replies, "To be him, that is life, and / We others are the dream of life" (ll. 102–3; FHA 12:36, 182). Yet this invocation of Rhea reminds us of one more formal matter, which too may prove to be not entirely formal. It may be fully material and have to do with the mother's embrace and with fidelity to the earth.

The name *Rhea* disappears entirely from all three drafts of the Beissner text. In his manuscript, however, Hölderlin replaces it with the name *Delia* only in the final scene of the first version's first act, and he does so without comment (FHA 12:95, 208). A detail perhaps without importance, an accident. Yet when one looks at the first page of the manuscript of the first draft, what one sees are the names *Panthea. Rhea.* Panthea, a variant of the ancient Pantheia, means "all the goddesses," or "all divinity." Rhea, as we know, is the Titaness whose name means flow, flux, or flight. The two names together seem to play with the apocryphal Heraclitean phrase, ascribed to Heraclitus by Plato, πάντα ῥεῖ. "Everything flows." Or, more tragically, as Schelling understands it, "All divinity has flown."[4] All is evanescent, swept away by that river into which, as Nietzsche remarks, one cannot step even once. Rhea is the spouse of Cronos, the saturnine Titan who comes to be associated with time, Κρόνος = χρόνος. Rhea is the daughter of Gaia, the earth, and the mother of the Olympian brothers Zeus, Poseidon, and Hades. She is also the mother of Tantalus. Perhaps Rhea, coupled with Panthea, is to serve as a symbol of fidelity to the long-suffering, ever-changing yet always divine earth—the theme introduced only a moment ago.

One is tempted to say that if Rhea vanishes from Hölderlin's tragedy that is precisely what she is supposed to do, inasmuch as she is the flight of

4. Andrea Rehberg first pointed out to me many years ago at the University of Essex the way in which "Panthea Rhea" is reminiscent of this pseudo-Heraclitean doctrine, and I thank her again and again for it. For Schelling's analysis, see his *Philosophy of Mythology,* in F. W. J. Schelling, *Sämmtliche Werke,* ed. Karl Schelling (Stuttgart and Augsburg: J. G. Cotta'scher Verlag, 1859), Division II, 2:578; cf. 1:39. For further discussion, see TA 237–43.

the gods. Yet before she disappears, she speaks. She speaks perhaps for all the Titans, inasmuch as Rhea embodies the Titanic age as much as her consort Cronos does. The Titanic in general is something outside the binary opposition of immortals and mortals. It is therefore essentially closer to the heroic. By contrast—for example, in pseudo-Aeschylus's *Prometheus Bound*—the Titanic sometimes seems more divine than the Olympian gods themselves. For the Titanic is a theogonic and cosmogonic force, a force productive of sites, eons, events, and destinies, of space and time and fateful occurrences, of scenes in which gods and mortals come to play their roles. Sometimes that force seems to be nothing less than the force of fate—of the Μοῖραι, whom no god or mortal can touch. Is it the fate of the gods themselves that is disclosed "when divinity drops the veil"? Why, in what Hölderlin calls "the principal passage," does the veil drop "at the mortally propitious hour" (l. 1742)? "Mortally propitious" tries to translate the odd adjective, oddly capitalized, *Todesfroh:*

> In Todesfroher Stund am heilgen Tage
> Das Göttliche den Schleier abgeworfen—

A more literal translation would be something like this: "In the hour that is happy with death on that holy day / Divinity cast off the veil." The suggestion is that the veil of Saïs is finally lifted, or doffed altogether, at the instant of the hero's death. Would such a doffing or casting off leave divinity untouched? Or would this *deus nudus est* have to do with the trembling of the gods and the extinguishing of their fire? Would it have something to do with the final flight, flow, or flux of the gods?

Are there any remains of Rhea in *The Death of Empedocles*? If the name *Delia* signifies the isle that is sacred to Apollo, Delos—which is one of the places to which Panthea is to be sent for her protection, according to Empedocles' instruction to her father, Critias—is that to say that the grand Titaness is to be replaced by Olympian Apollo? Who *is* Delia? She is the incarnation of tenderness. Does she not seem to speak with the voice of Ismene, the sister of Antigone, whom Delia herself invokes? If Ismene is the voice of timidity in the face of the law, fear in the face of the king, is *Delia* a name for the docility of the little woman in the face of the big man? Is she, in other words, the sort of accident that experiences and expresses nothing of the tragic essence of an Empedocles? In the first version we see Empedocles in his garden, almost as one of the plants there, one of the sturdy oaks in his sacred grove. He is Empedocles-Pharmakeus in the apothecary's herbal garden. As a priest of nature, he is perforce faithful to the earth. The opening words of the play are Panthea's: "This is his garden." She adds that the plants seem to notice when he passes by and that the subterranean streams begin to flow wherever his staff touches the earth. Later she says that the plants "with all their forces" are open secrets to Empedocles. Yet this Empedocles who is so devoted to the plant life of the earth is also the self-proclaimed son of Ouranos, like Cronos himself. His most common apostrophe is *O Vater Aether!* If we pose the question of Empedocles' genealogy, we have to wonder whether a conflict or at least a tension exists between his maternal and paternal sides, between matriarchy and patriarchy in him. If Empedocles is elemental, "rooted," his genealogy is clearly both celestial and tellurian. One might also think of it in terms of the vertical and horizontal axes of sky and earth: if the horizontal axis is the earth and the vertical axis the sky, one might ask whether Empedocles—this son of the earth who nightly pledges an oath of loyalty to her—is not always craning his neck to scan the heavens. True, the heliotropic flowers and oaks do the same; the light is their life, and they look to it. However, does not Empedocles, like Oedipus, have an eye too many perhaps, a pineal eye located at the top of his skull? It might be not a Cyclopean or Titanic eye, nor the eye of Rhea, which looks to the horizon, but a Typhon's eye aimed in rancor at the sun. Empedocles' nostalgia for the gods who have flown—does it not seem an ascensional nostalgia, *aerienne,* as Gaston Bachelard would say?[5] Is not Empedocles—he who pledges himself to the mother—always anxious to quit the earth? The leap into the crater—is it an expression of profound fidelity to the earth or a chance to evaporate into the sky? Perhaps this is part of the *who* question that Manes incessantly puts to Empedocles.

We find in the second version of the play two passages that touch on the matter of the Titanic tension between earth and sky. First, in the dialogue between Pausanias and Empedocles, Pausanias insists on the powerful divinity of his master, whom he calls "heaven's favorite," *der Liebling des Himmels,* and whom grief is now "bending down to earth." Empedocles reaffirms his fidelity to the earth, but only after effusively praising the sun, and he finishes with a vision of *Aether.* In the second passage, Panthea and Delia come as close as they ever do to an argument, in which Delia (Rhea) takes the side of the earth, Panthea the side of heaven. The first version breaks off at the point where Delia complains that Empedocles thinks "more like the gods" than like a mortal—almost a reminiscence of Hermocrates' words concerning Empedocles' oblivion of the distinction between them. Hölderlin enters a marginal note into his manuscript at this point: "because Empedocles has such low esteem for temporality [*die Zeitlichkeit*]" (FHA 12:177, 240; see the note to ll. 2009a-g, above). In the second version the identical conflict appears. Why should the honor of mortals detain Empedocles, asks Panthea, "when / His

5. Gaston Bachelard, *L'Air et les songes: Essai sur l'imagination du mouvement* (Paris: José Corti, 1943), 17–18, passim.

father ether opens / His arms to him?" (ll. 573–74; FHA 13:289, 323). Delia replies, in perhaps "too stark an opposition," declaring the splendor and amiability of the earth (ll. 575–76). In the closing exchanges of the second draft, Panthea and Pausanias loyally uphold Empedocles' status as a hero, that is to say, one whose downgoing is holy, while Delia demurs: "All too gladly, Empedocles / Too happily you sacrifice yourself" (ll. 670–71; FHA 13:294, 326). Delia, one might argue, incorporates the remainder of Rhea in the play. And there is nothing "accidental" about the exchanges between these personages, who are themselves no "accidents." The theme of fidelity to the earth, and the question of the vanished Rhea, will not disappear from Hölderlin's third and final attempt, even if the seer should now be called a wise old man.

When we turn to the third and final version of *The Death of Empedocles,* we are struck by the differences between it and the earlier versions. We may well want to exclaim with Pausanias, "I no longer recognize you," and to reply with Empedocles, "I am not who I am." The difference may well derive from the theoretical texts that Hölderlin composes between the second and third versions. The essay that begins with the words *Das untergehende Vaterland . . . ,* is found in the margins of the final sketch for the continuation of the play. Undeniably, lucubrations of the sort represented in these essays have had an impact on this third version of the play. We need not enter into those essays here, except when the impact on the third version seems most clearly and powerfully felt. For the moment, we may set aside these rich texts, in order to read the third version of the play, begun in December 1799.

The issues of the Titanic, of Rhea, and of fidelity to the earth culminate in the vexing question of Empedocles' identity. Empedocles, despite his name, which has ἔμπεδος, "steadfast," as its root, proves to have little about him that is steadfast. He admires the trees of the grove, the oaks that are solid and well-grounded, precisely because that is what he lacks. He is not one of them. Even in the first two versions, one hears the question again and again, "Who are you?" Hermocrates goads the citizens, in act 1, scene 5 of the first version: "Yet you yourselves / Should ask him, who is he?" (ll. 542–43). In the same scene, Empedocles teases the citizens: "Am I not still that one? know you not the man / Of whom you said you could as beggars go / From land to land with him, if he elected you?" (ll. 683–85). In act 2, scene 4, the citizens challenge Empedocles in chorus: "Who are you, man?" (ll. 1419). In act 2, scene 3, Pausanias himself has already challenged his master: "May grief [*Gram*] thus bend to earth oppressively / The favorites of heaven? Are you not one / Of these?" (ll. 374–76). We have already heard the Empedocles of version three: "I am not who I am, Pausanias" (l. 243). Which may be Hölderlin's reluctant reply to Yahweh. Or, from another point of view, a bold recommendation.

Hölderlin now transforms the character Hermocrates into Manes, a priest from the temple at Saïs. Manes is one of those "brothers far away in

Egypt" to whom Empedocles has already referred. (See the long note on ll. 321ff. of the third version.) That Manes is not simply an opponent of Empedocles is indicated by the plan to continue the third version, literally the final page of the *Empedocles* materials. For the third scene of act 4, Hölderlin envisages the final exchange between Empedocles and the Egyptian priest. He characterizes Manes as follows: "Manes, who has experienced all, the seer, astounded by Empedocles' speeches and by his spirit, says that Empedocles is the one who has been called [*der Berufene*], the one who kills and who gives life, the one in and through whom a world dissolves and in the same instant renews itself" (FHA 13:419, 438). After Empedocles has committed his one final deed at the end, presumably in scene 4, the fifth and final scene gathers Manes and all the remaining personages of the play. Hölderlin's description of the action: "On the following day, at the festival of Saturn, he [Manes] wants to proclaim to all of them the ultimate will of Empedocles." (ibid.). The festival of Saturn is of course in honor of the "son of Ouranos," Empedocles himself. However, if this is Hölderlin's final plan for the play, the final pages that he actually sketched stray from it. In the manuscript of the play itself, Manes is called simply *Der Greis,* "the old man."[6] His exchanges with Empedocles have the effect of displacing Empedocles to an impossible remove and spoiling every ideal (or ideational) deed and every celebration. The entire third version is filled with displacements of time, day, and even epoch, displacements of scene and character. Pausanias is advised to go on an anachronistic voyage to Tarentum, and even on to Plato's Athens, where Empedocles says he himself has already been, but which lies a century and a half ahead; he is also instructed to travel to Rome, "the land of promises," which, apart from Numa Pompilius, lies either many hundreds of years in the past (with Aeneas) or half a millennium ahead (with the Caesars). Likewise, Empedocles himself is displaced from his very identity. The third version ends with Pausanias being sent off to Egypt as though both master and pupil were either Solon or Critias's great-grandfather in the story recounted at the outset of Plato's *Timaeus.* In the meantime, Empedocles and Pausanias are both displaced to the heights of Mount Etna, far from Agrigent.

The effect of these displacements is to dissolve the question of *nefas* versus destiny. Manes too will accuse Empedocles of a "dark sin" and will announce himself as one sent by god (here in the singular) to prevent Empedocles from taking himself to be "the one who is called." Yet because the identities of Empedocles and Manes slip into and out of each other, knowing who is sent by whom and for what is difficult. As for the remains of Rhea, and the

---

6. In this translation I have followed Beissner, Knaupp, and Schmidt in allowing the name *Manes* to appear in the third version as such.

all-important question of fidelity to the earth, this too slips into indeterminacy and even undecidability. The final lines that Hölderlin actually writes for the play are lines for a choral ode to be sung by a group of Agrigentian citizens—those citizens who have proved to be so ambivalent toward Empedocles in the first two drafts. The choral ode that closes the first—and only—act of version three is itself a sign of the end of all fidelity, even if it begins with the promise of a "future," a "new world," inasmuch as it accuses mother earth of mocking her children with false gifts, with "chaff." "Yet where is he?" asks the chorus of Agrigentians, who are in desperate search for "the one" who can save their city. Where is he? *Who* is he? Are you so sure of who you are and what you see? These are the questions that the third version leaves us with and without recourse.

The concluding lines of scene 2 (DKV 2:409, with added lines from FHA 13:401, 430), in which Empedocles is urging Pausanias to depart and undertake his educational journey, read as follows:

> And if the soul in you refuses rest, then go
> Inquire of my brothers far away in Egypt.
> You'll hear the earnest thrum of strings
> Urania plays and all their shifting tones.
> So many things await you that are luminous
> And grand; you'll learn that mortals standing
> Face to face are but images and signs
> Yet this will not disturb you, my dear friend!
> They'll open for you there the book of destiny.
> Go! fear nothing! everything recurs. And what
> Is yet to happen already is accomplished. (ll. 314–20)

"Mere signs and images," *nur Zeichen sind und Bilder.* Empedocles' main speech in response to Manes is also full of signs and images, images of the gods of nature, which the youthful Empedocles can address by name, signs of celestial lightning, cloudbursts, and earthly flames. The final sign is to be his own plunge into the crater. Empedocles asks Manes whether he would like to join him in producing this final sign. A bold sign, a strong sign. However, as Hölderlin observes in a brief and cryptic text composed during the time of his work on the Sophocles translations, the sign in tragedy = 0, which is to say that the hero is presented most originally and elementally on the stage when he or she appears not in strength but in mortal weakness and vulnerability (DKV 2:561). Hölderlin writes:

> The significance of the tragedies is most readily grasped on the basis of paradox. For, inasmuch as all abundance is justly and equally apportioned,

> no original appears as actual in its original strength; rather, it genuinely appears in its debility alone, so that quite properly the light of life and the appearance of debility pertain to every whole.[7] Now, in the tragic, the sign is meaningless in itself, without effect; yet the original comes directly to the fore. For the original can appear in a genuine way only in its debility. Yet insofar as the sign in itself is meaningless and thus = 0, the original too, the concealed ground of every nature, can present itself. If nature presents itself genuinely in its weakest gift, then the sign that is given when it presents itself in its strongest gift = 0. (DKV 2:561; CHV 2:114)

The type of *sign* or *image* Empedocles himself constitutes is now the capital question for Hölderlin. He has already written about this image in "The Basis of Empedocles" before beginning the third version of his play. What he says there has everything to do with the "book of destiny" and with the very meaning of tragic fate. We also recall the importance of written signs for the priests of Neith in Plato's *Timaeus*. The ancient Egyptian priests have to laugh at the Greeks, who are forever children because they are illiterate: they have no written histories, no alphabetic signs to record the deluges of the past, so that the cultures of Atlantis and ancient Athens are forever lost to them and they must always start from scratch. Manes, the doppelgänger of Empedocles, steps out of the pages of *Timaeus* into the third draft of *The Death of Empedocles*. As we will see, he offers Empedocles the strongest gift, the gift that equals zero.

The word *sign* appears several times in "The Fatherland in Decline." In the opening lines of that essay we read the words *eine neue Welt*, the very words that open the final chorus of act 1 in version three. In this essay, Hölderlin heralds the birth of a new world in the decline of a prior finite world, arguing that "such downgoing and commencement is something like the language expression sign depiction [*die Sprache Ausdruck Zeichen Darstellung*] of a living yet particular whole" (DKV 2:446). The word *image*, *Bild*, plays an important role in the essay written immediately prior to "The Fatherland in Decline," namely, the above-mentioned "Basis of Empedocles." In the third part of that essay, the remarkable word *Trugbild* appears—mirage, *fata morgana*, illusion. (In his reconstituted text, Sattler has merely the root *Trug*, which is very odd

7. The notion of *Lebenslicht*, "the light of life," is strange. Hölderlin employs the expression in several late poems as well as in a letter to Böhlendorff, where he identifies it with a "savage martial" and "masculine" character, in which the "feeling of death" is experienced in "virtuoso" form (CHV 2: 921). In short, the light of life is anything but debility in any usual sense, although it is shot through with a sense of mortality. See the additional references at CHV 3:402. See also Schmidt's helpful note at DKV 2:1253.

on its own—although Schelling uses the word.[8]) *Trugbild!* is the very word that Manes tosses in the face of Empedocles at the outset of their dialogue (FHA 13:405; cf. 401, 430). Manes's accusation is that Empedocles is simply deceived about his self-proclaimed status as elect, as the favorite of the gods. Or, if not simply deceived, that he is an imposter. Yet Manes is no carping, conniving Hermocrates, no priest of the usual manipulative, power-seeking sort. We sense this in the exchanges with Empedocles, in which the sage of Agrigent is wrathful and tempestuous, whereas Manes remains cool and distant, mildly ironic, taking the long historical perspective and urging caution. When we look back to "The Basis of Empedocles" we in fact discover that Hölderlin himself affirms Manes's principal point. There Hölderlin speaks of *Trug,* or *Trugbild,* and even of *der glückliche Betrug,* the "fortunate" or "felicitous" fraud. The word *fraud* or *betrayal* will also play an important role in the 1803 "Notes on Oedipus" (see chapter 9 of TA). For the moment, we can say that what Hölderlin has in mind is this: Empedocles appears to be the perfect resolution of the problem of his time, inasmuch as he combines the supremely developed qualities of both nature and art in his person. When he is least attentive to himself and most natural, he is a thinker, organizer, builder; when he is most meditative he is as wild as fire, entirely aorgic. Empedocles, born to be a bard, unites all the qualities a city could hope for—but he does so too intensely and too individually. His unification of these qualities is tragic, inasmuch as *no* individual can "dissolve the problem of destiny"—his, like all the others, can only be a "momentary unification" (DKV 2:233–34). Hölderlin does not state in so many words what "the problem of destiny" is, but he does insist that no individual can encompass an entire world; the *death* of Empedocles solves the problem more adequately than his life because only in passing away can an individual be the avatar of a passing world and the promise of a world to come. For all his exceptional qualities, then, Empedocles is bound to be a *Trug* and a *Trugbild,* his sign a null cipher, his ideal deed at the end *ein glücklicher Betrug,* a fortunate or felicitous fraud, a strength that = 0.

Two final passages from the third version, examined here also for their sovereign style, may help us to understand the nature of Empedocles' sign as

---

8. *Trug* and *Täuschung,* betrayal and deception, play an important role in Schelling's 1842 *Philosophy of Mythology.* There he notes that the ancient Greeks even had a number of goddesses, Titanesses, or sprites (perhaps modeled on the Furies) dedicated to betrayal and deception, namely, the Ἀπάτη. "How deeply these Ἀπάτη were felt by the Greeks can perhaps be concluded from the happenstance that they had their own festival, called the *Apaturia,* the festival of deception" (*Sämmtliche Werke,* II/2:148; cf. 623). See also Roberto Calasso's remarkable account of Ἀπάτη, the servant girl of Aphrodite, a story based on the effects of a woman's perfume and makeup—a story that would have delighted Baudelaire (RC 97, 201).

a null cipher—not in the sense that it is worth nothing, but in the sense that this sign reveals the elemental, the aorgic, and the original not in heroic strength but in tragic debility. First, Manes invokes Cronos—or perhaps Zeus himself—as "the lord of time," but a time that is now grinding to a halt:

> Der Herr der Zeit, um seine Herrschaft bang,
> Thront finster blickend über der Empörung.
> Sein Tag erlischt, und seine Blitze leuchten,
> Doch was von oben flammt, entzündet nur
> Und was von unten strebt, die wilde Zwietracht.
> (DKV 2:412; FHA 13:408–9, 432)

> The lord of time, grown apprehensive of his rule,
> Looms with glowering gaze above the consternation.
> His day extinguished, lightning bolts still flash, yet
> What flames on high is inflammation, nothing more;
> What strives from down below is savage discord. (ll. 367–71)

These lines, marked by simplicity of diction and complexity of thought, seem to flow from Hölderlin's pen; the manuscript shows very few alterations. Yet the thought transcends every notion of *nefas* and rises to the realm of divinity itself. "The one" who is called on by his time is given the task—at the hour that is happy with death, the mortally propitious hour—of righting something that is wrong with the heavens themselves. If the hero now does not storm the sky, he is not the one that is called for. The first line of this passage is fraught with the contrast between *Herr* and *bang,* "lord" and "apprehensive," two very simple monosyllabic sounds in German that we have considerable difficulty in hearing together. Lords rule, they do not fret. Yet the fire of the lord's days has gone out, even if his lightning still flashes. His lightning flashes, but *entzündet nur;* it seems to inflame rather than kindle. It merely mirrors the consternation on earth and does not steer it. Accordingly, all human striving in this time out of joint is *wilde Zwietracht,* "savage discord." These words point forward to the concluding words of the Rhine hymn, *uralte Verwirrung,* "primeval confusion," itself a recollection of Plato's *Statesman,* which speaks of τὸ τῆς παλαιᾶς ἀναρμοστίας πάθος, "the profound feeling of ancient disharmonies" (273d 1). Manes's tone is truly apocalyptic, as is that of Empedocles, who replies in this way:

> Wenn sich die Brüder flohn, und sich die Liebsten
> Vorübereilten, und der Vater nicht
> Den Sohn erkannt, und Menschenwort nicht mehr
> Verständlich war, und menschliches Gesetz

Da faßte mich die Deutung schaudernd an,
Es war der scheidende Gott meines Volks!
(DKV 2:413; FHA 13:414, 434)

When brother fled from brother, when lovers passed
Each other by in ignorance, when fathers failed
To recognize their sons, when human words no more
Were understood, nor human laws, that was when
The meaning of it all assailed me and I trembled:
It was my nation's parting god! (ll. 421–26)

Here too the language of brothers and lovers, fathers and sons, is simple, although the manuscript shows greater difficulty in finding and retaining the proper words. These lines uncannily resemble the fragments of Empedocles, especially those of the *Purifications*, and they match the power of those ancient prophetic words. In the final two lines, the words *scheidend* and *schaudernd* mirror one another: when the nation's god departs, all one can do is tremble, for this is not something that one can "grasp" conceptually, *fassen*, but something that seizes and assails one, *sich anfassen*. This, one might say, is a shuddering exaction.

Are you the One? Manes asks repeatedly. His long speech points or gives signs variously to Jesus Christ, Prometheus, Zeus, Dionysos, and Heracles—to all the gods, heroes, idols, and prophets one could imagine. His warning is that a certain *excess* is bound to cling to every claim of intimacy with the gods. Empedocles really is *too* much. Again one is tempted to speculate on the relation of the German *zu*, meaning "too," to the Greek ζα-, from δύο, meaning double, overmuch, excessive. If πύρος is fire, ζάπυρος is holocaust. Perhaps the prefix ζα- has to do with the δαι- of δαίμων, and even with what wants to be and yet does not want to be called by the name Ζεῦς.[9]

One of the most tentative suggestions one may make about the third version is that in it the voice of Empedocles becomes most fully Hölderlin's own voice. In "The Basis of Empedocles" Hölderlin says that nature appears "with all her melodies . . . in the spirit and in the mouth" of the ancient magus Empedocles, indeed, "so intensely and ardently and personally" that he was loved by the all the people and accepted by them (FHA 13:347–48, 365–66). How Hölderlin yearns for this kind of acceptance! Yet his own fate is

---

9. These philological musings between the Greek and the German are what lay behind the book *Daimon Life*—the title of that book itself a pleonasm. The point here, in any case, is that the *zu*, the "too much," marks the failure of Empedocles. Yet it is a failure that is as much of destiny as of the hero's own *nefas*.

described in words Empedocles uses in his opening speech, words that have not yet been placed in Empedocles' spirit and mouth in the first two versions. Empedocles is speaking of the people who have banished him; he says that he hears "The clamor of a hundred voices in my ear, / The chilling laughter, when the dreamer, / The jester, went weeping on his way" (ll. 29–31; FHA 13:376, 421). Hölderlin had written to Neuffer on November 12, 1798, of his having "to weep like a child." Several lines later in the play Empedocles accuses himself of a certain coldness, and the words Hölderlin uses are words his own mother had often hurled against a son she could never understand: "For much from my youth onward have I sinned / I never loved humanity in fitting human ways, / I served as fire and water blindly serve, / In turn my fellows never met me as a human being" (ll. 35–37; FHA 13:376, 422). In that same letter to Neuffer we read, ". . . I shy away much too much from the common and the ordinary in real life." Here *nefas* shifts from the grand Promethean blasphemy and sacrilege to the singer's alienation from his community, which in turn greets him with derision. If in "The General Basis" Hölderlin speaks of the necessity, in dramatic representation, of finding a bolder and more foreign simulacrum and exemplar than one's own subjectivity can be, especially when the *nefas* portrayed comes perilously close to *Innigkeit,* intimacy and intensity, the third version—undoubtedly the most historically conscious of the three drafts, on a grand scale and in the grand style—nonetheless gives us Hölderlin as well as Empedocles. This simply confirms what the "General Basis" says, namely, that the tragic drama too must arise from "the inmost heart and world of the poet" (FHA 13:331, 359). It might almost have said "from the spirit and mouth of the poet." And because all three versions are poems of tenderness, of languor and love, as also of a certain languishment, we recall those other words from the same letter to Neuffer, near the end: "I am nothing but a pedant, if you will. Yet, if I'm right, pedants are usually cold and loveless, whereas my heart is overanxious to be a brother to every person and every thing under the moon. I almost think I am pedantic for no other reason than love. . . ."

To be sure, most of the language of the theoretical essays surrounding *The Death of Empedocles* can be reduced to the sphere of German Idealism—presuming that entry into that sphere can be spoken of as a reduction. An exception perhaps is the word *Innigkeit,* unless it is mistranslated as "interiority" and so transformed into the very subjectivity and theoretical consciousness that Hölderlin is here struggling to overcome (LV chapter 2). The excess of intimacy and intensity in the figure of Empedocles is something quite new and startling. It is an excess that characterizes the rhetoric of the essays themselves—their oceanic sentences, their need to prolong the point, to locate the point everywhere on the line, and in the end to burn both point and line in celestial fire. The excess of intensity, *Übermaß der Innigkeit,* is that which shatters all unification, or lets unification appear only as an illusory resolution of the problem of fate. Every resolution, if it is tragic resolution, is *scheinbar,* an apparent, semblant, radiant simulacrum of resolution. The excesses of intensity and semblance ultimately prevent the absorption of Hölderlin into the philosophical systems of German Idealism, no matter how intensely he contributed to the "Oldest Program" toward such a system. By the time we have arrived at the third version, notes Max Kommerell, we are left with the lordship of *time* as *transition*:

> In the end lies dissolution, in which the human form can no longer sustain itself. Rather, it is swept away by infinite becoming, a dissolution in which the prophetic, to wit, that which must be said and which was sealed off in the poet, shatters him in order to reveal itself. The final phase of the *Empedocles* and the final stage of Hölderlin's life are conspicuously similar in this—that the god of time alone prevails in both. (MK 336)

Yet why does the ideal deed at the end, the speculative suicide of Empedocles, not avail? Why is Hölderlin unable to write it, unable to carry it out? The interpreter's *nefas* is to be too confident about a reply. Let us say that two things restrain the Empedocles of Hölderlin.

First, the need to leap into the crater not out of wrath or in the spirit of rancor but to rejoin earth and ether in gratitude and affirmation. Recall the marginal note that commands, "No curse! he has to love unto infinity; then he dies, in order not have to live without love and without his tutelary spirit. He has to *consume,* as it were, all the rest of that conciliatory force that perhaps could have restored to him his prior blessed felicitous life—had these things not transpired." "These things" are of course those accidents and contingencies that afflict the hero's inmost heart. Yet the command "No curse!" continues through all three versions. "I'll not go yet, old man! / From this green earth and her beneficence / My eye should not depart deprived of joy," cries Empedocles at the end of the third version (ll. 488–90; FHA 13:417, 435–36), having heard at long last what Rhea was telling him from the beginning. Act 2, scene 3 of the first draft ends with Empedocles' asserting that "In wrath as well I can proceed unto my gods" (l. 1267; FHA 12:123, 220). Yet it is not so. All the "accidents" of the play—Delia, Panthea, Pausanias—have been teaching Empedocles that essential lesson. Love will hold him back. Love? Let us say, that which reduces us to a certain tender awe in the face of the accidental, a certain desire, a certain languor and languishing, which is never aloof from the disconnectedness that assails us when we miss someone. These things may even lie at the secret heart of nature—in the crater of the volcano itself, which embraces in its magma the liquid fire of the sky and the fiery breath of the earth, but which nevertheless stretches out its arms to the sky, as though ardent for more fire.

Second, the undecidability of Empedocles' very identity holds both Empedocles and Hölderlin back. The questions, common to the two earlier versions, mount to a crescendo in the third: after Manes cries *Mirage!* and accuses the hero of a felicitous fraud, of deception and betrayal, Empedocles asks, "What! whence? Who are you, man?"—the very question that Pausanias put to Empedocles in an earlier draft. Manes, the wise "old man," asks Empedocles, "Are you that man? the very one? are you this?" And because Empedocles cannot answer, Manes asks again, "Oh, tell us who you are! and who am I?" And again, after Empedocles' long and magnificent swan song, Manes's simple yet caustic reply is, "How is it with us? are you quite sure of what you see?" (ll. 388, 391, 483; FHA 13:433–35).

These questions infuriate Empedocles before he can give himself over affirmatively to fire. They frustrate every possible ideal deed at the end. "Once you have a double on the scene," notes Roberto Calasso, "it's like entering a hall of mirrors; everything is elusive, stretching away into a perspective where nothing is ever final" (RC 229). Nothing is ever final, yet everything has already transpired. Empedocles' passing has already occurred before the leap. When the hero of Poe's "William Wilson" finally meets his doppelgänger, he knows that at least one of them is already dead.